Praise for *Randall Lolley: Thanks for the Memories*

Steve Pressley, through meticulous research and personal observation, has captured the essence of one of the great American pastors/statesmen/educators of the twentieth century. Randall Lolley's journey from LA (lower Alabama) to the pinnacle of power (and his "dream job") as president of his theological alma mater, is inspiring, dramatic, and, most of all, triumphant. To those who know him well, all you have to say is, "Randall." The name alone is synonymous with excellence, resilience, scholarship, leadership, and integrity. *Randall Lolley: Thanks for the Memories* is a real page-turner, probing the highs and lows of a man whose influence is writ large on tens of thousands of individuals who see him as a mentor, friend, exemplar, man of God.

—Michael C. Blackwell
President/CEO
Baptist Children's Homes of North Carolina

As the associate pastor who worked closely with Randall Lolley at First Baptist Greensboro, Steve Pressley is uniquely positioned to write the story of a man he came to admire and to love. His biography delves into the multiple facets of Lolley's illustrious career while contextualizing them into a chronology that takes the reader from Depression days in "Lower Alabama" to denominational leadership and, ultimately, to the beginnings of a new start for Baptist life. Through it all, Pressley shows how Lolley has alway been "out in the weather" with the people he led.

—Scott P. Culclasure
Author of In Every Good Work: A History of First Baptist Church, Greensboro, North Carolina

You cannot comprehend the last fifty years of Baptist life in America without understanding the story of Randall Lolley, and Steve Pressley provides a meticulously researched and creatively written biography of this pivotal figure. The book unveils the true person behind the public figure, and we discover they are the same man—a person of integrity who is honest and forthright. Randall is described first and foremost as a caring pastor, regardless of the various roles he filled during his career. His story will leave you laughing, crying, cheering, and amazed. For those who did not know Randall there could not be a better introduction; even for his close friends and colleagues, there is much to learn in these pages.

—*Tom Graves*
Former President, Baptist Theological Seminary at Richmond
Former Professor, Southeastern Baptist Seminary

Sometimes in a life, you have the privilege of coming alongside a person and observing as they navigate their days. Only as their story is gathered up do you truly appreciate how special they are. Steve Pressley gathers up the Randall Lolley story for us in a way that brings awe and wonder.

—*Charles Qualls*
Senior Pastor, Franklin Baptist Church
Franklin, Virginia

F. Buechner reminds us that we all need a room to remember:

> But there is a deeper need, I think, and that is the need—not all the time, surely, but from time to time—to enter that still room within us all where the past lives on as a part of the present, where the dead are alive again, where we are most alive ourselves to turnings and to where our journeys have brought us. The name of the room is Remember—the room where with patience, with charity, with quietness of heart, we remember consciously to remember the lives we have lived.

Steve Pressley has given us a special gift—a Lolley Room to remember. In that room, so lovingly created by Steve's words, are stored many storied treasures: a chronicle of an exemplary servant leader, Randall, with deep integrity, sheer giftedness, and focused discipline and an overwhelmingly singular vision of loving all people; the record of a loving marriage between Lou and Randall that honors both male and female; the tale of a denominational faction with a driving, destructive lust for power; the recital of the systemic misogyny that existed and continues to exist within Baptists of the South; and perhaps most importantly, a clear picture of courage—the kind that makes hard decisions, such as leaving, easy and powerful and the absolute right thing to do.

The memory of Baptist Theological Seminary at Richmond memory is also lodged in the Lolley Room, a literal room on the third floor of the Union Presbyterian Seminary in Richmond, Virginia. A portrait of Lou and Randall hangs on the wall, still influencing the work of theological education and the lives of Baptist students who will find welcome in the newly established Baptist House of Studies and Center for Faith, Justice, and Reconciliation there in the Lolley Room.

May the reading of these words create a Lolley Room in your heart, in your mind, in your soul. And may this room of remembrance bring fresh courage to meet the challenges of our day with joy, bucket lists, love of family, words, and travel, deep faith, lots of courage, and a caring heart for all people.

—Linda McKinnish Bridges
Former Founding Faculty Member and Closing President
Baptist Theological Seminary at Richmond (1991–2019)

Having only met Dr. Randall Lolley on one occasion in passing, I am grateful to have been able to meet this remarkable man and minister more fully through my friend Steve Pressley's biography of him. In reading Pressley's informative, impressive book, one will encounter laughter, loss, and love even as one will be reminded afresh of the influence and impact of a single life well lived. For those who would like a behind-the-scenes look at a fruitful ministry as well as a front-row seat to a now well-chronicled controversy, then pick up *Randall Lolley: Thanks for the Memories.* Once you do, you will likely not be able to put it down. There is much here to ponder, appreciate, and practice.

—Todd D. Still
Charles J. and Eleanor McLerran DeLancey Dean &
William M. Hinson Professor of Christian Scriptures
Baylor University, Truett Seminary

Smyth & Helwys Publishing, Inc.
6316 Peake Road
Macon, Georgia 31210-3960
1-800-747-3016

Library of Congress Cataloging-in-Publication Data on file

RANDALL LOLLEY

Thanks for the Memories

STEVE PRESSLEY

Warm regards!

Steve Pressley

9-29-21

To the First Baptist Church
Greensboro, North Carolina

Acknowledgments

Among the first questions a friend asked when I floated the idea of a Randall Lolley biography was, "Is Randall able to help?" In the early going, I did sit with Dr. Lolley at his memory care residence in Raleigh, interviewing him for an hour. He was himself in important ways, if not in all ways. He recalled his father's full name, his own birthdate and wedding anniversary, and the "L.A." (lower Alabama) location of his personal origin. To most questions, however, he supplied limited and general responses.

When his wife, Lou, arrived to escort us to lunch, she asked, "How did it go?" His response confirmed that he was indeed the Randall Lolley I remembered: "This fellow's got more questions than a cat's got fleas!"

Such family help as Randall himself was not able to provide, his wife and daughters did. Lou Lolley was constantly available to speak by telephone. She and Charlotte Murphy and Pam Frey spent the better part of an afternoon with me, recalling and reminiscing and filling in empty spaces in my research. Later the daughters responded to queries related primarily to their mother and to the personal and spiritual chemistry that she brought to the Randall Lolley story.

Several times Lou welcomed me into their home and into Randall's impressive upstairs study. Owing to his health, he had been unable to spend the time there that he had intended in 2012 when they arrived at The Cypress of Raleigh, their retirement venue. Nevertheless, the artifactual and documentary record that remained there proved invaluable.

Randall's nephew Tim Lolley, son of brother Tom and presently a pastor in Western North Carolina, lent a large notebook compiled during the denominational firestorm that engulfed Southeastern Seminary in 1987. Tim, who was completing his theological education there at the time, also provided a Lolley family genealogy that his late mother, Sydney, had researched.

A further invaluable documentary resource was the "W. Randall Lolley Papers," a collection Randall donated in late 1996 to the Special Collections and Archives department of the Z. Smith Reynolds Library at Wake Forest University. The donation comprises ninety boxes containing Randall's personal and professional files, beginning with his 1974–1987 presidency of Southeastern Baptist Theological Seminary and continuing through his subsequent pastorates in Raleigh and Greensboro, 1988–1996. Many thanks to Tanya Zanish-Belcher, director of Special Collections and Archives, for retrieving and cataloging the collection.

Several chapters in the present book are based primarily on interviews with people who knew and worked alongside Randall through the years of his seminary and church ministries. Particular appreciation goes to Dr. Mike Queen for contributing not only the foreword to this volume but also dozens of names and accompanying contact information for those who, like himself, studied at Southeastern during the days of the Lolley presidency.

Greatly helpful was the assistance of "Yellow Ribbon" group members Rita Vermillion and her husband, Dr. Tom Halbrooks, through their recollections and exhaustive research, which yielded the names and current locations of seminary professors, administrators, and ancillary personnel who served alongside President Lolley.[1] Only a minority are still living and accessible, but their contributions were insightful and entertaining.

Also insightful and enjoyable was the reminiscing of individuals fortunate to serve as church staff under Randall's leadership. From the still accessible few from the Winston-Salem and Raleigh pastorates to virtually the entire ministry staff contingent (my own colleagues) from the early mid-1990s in Greensboro, these people "counted it all joy" to recall their unforgettable "partner in the task."

Also from the Gate City days, First Baptist Church lay leaders added their own memories of the manner in which Randall Lolley

1. The "Yellow Ribbon" group consists of professors, administrators, and spouses who shared life with Lou and Randall Lolley in the years prior to his 1988 departure from Southeastern Seminary. As of this publication, their annual gatherings continue.

came to their congregation at an opportune moment, lending his personal sensitivity and pastoral acumen to a challenging congregational circumstance.

Chapter 14, "Mirrors on the Man," is entirely the contribution of four significant personalities from Randall's life journey, each of whom reflects on the impact he had on their lives personally, professionally, and pastorally. These are deserving of many thanks.

Very great appreciation is owed to people who read, commented on, and offered helpful suggestions with regard to this book. These include the aforementioned Mike Queen, who stands among the all-time leading fans of Randall Lolley, and especially Dr. Scott P. Culclasure—historian, author, academic, and fellow church member and friend.

Scott in particular came alongside early in the process of conceiving and researching the work. It was his introduction of the idea of a "topical biography" that prompted the organization of the book and suggested a workable approach to the research. Moreover, it was his thorough reading of the chapters that produced important refinements.

My gratitude to Rabbi Phil Cohen, published author and Scott Culclasure's colleague at Greensboro's American Hebrew Academy, who alerted me to the manner in which personal interviews may be helpfully interwoven into a biographical narrative.

Thanks also to current FBC Greensboro pastor Alan Sherouse, who offered his suggestion, as my ministry retirement approached, that I undertake a "legacy project" of my own choosing. And thanks to Keith Gammons of Smyth & Helwys for receiving and publishing what Keith, at its first mention, called "a necessary work."

Above all, thanks to Dr. W. Randall Lolley for his inspiration, mentorship, and friendship through the years of our pastor-associate pastor relationship and during all times since. And thanks to Catherine, my devoted and ever-encouraging wife, for her enduring love of the Lolleys and of me.

—*Steve Pressley*
Jamestown, North Carolina

Contents

Foreword

In the foreword to Cecil Sherman's biography, Randall Lolley quoted Bill Leonard as saying that "Being Baptist is messy." All three men could bear witness to the truth of those words. And while Randall's sojourn as a Baptist has, indeed, seen its share of messiness, he has remained a free and faithful Baptist through it all.

While many were affected, perhaps no one bore more scars of the Baptist battles than did W. Randall Lolley. Most of us knew him as a seminary president caught in the tangles of theological controversy. Every word he said or action he took was scrutinized by both sides. And while he, and the superb faculty he assembled at Southeastern Baptist Theological Seminary, set about building a school dedicated to gospel freedom, Jesus following, excellent teaching, and deep learning, there were those bent on disrupting all of that.

The public way in which his time at Southeastern came to an end garnered the headlines of both the Baptist press and the secular press. It is never easy to go through dark days with everyone else watching. None of us will ever know just how difficult that time was for him though Steve Pressley takes us inside the messiness and gives us a glimpse into some of what Randall endured. The pain, the hurt, and the lingering anguish are all there to be seen. But because Steve also knew Randall as a colleague and partner in ministry, he is able to take us to the places where Randall was at his very best, as a pastor to his people.

Just after he had left the seminary, I ran into Randall and his wife, Lou, at a football game. I asked him how it was going at the church he was serving. He laughed and said, "I forgot that when you are the preacher, Sunday comes every third day . . . and you have to have a new sermon."[1] Lou shook her head, and said, "That is not what he forgot. What he forgot was just how much pain there is in the life of a congregation."

This biography tells the public story of the seminary president, but more importantly, it tells the story of an extraordinary pastor. For all of us who know and love Randall, we all tend to believe we are one of his best friends. The amazing thing is that we are. At least he had the uncanny ability to make it seem so. For that, we are all grateful beyond words.

So his is but one life, but what a life it has been. He and Lou have influenced the lives of so many at the seminary and in the many churches they served. They raised two wonderful daughters, Charlotte and Pam. They have counseled so many of us in ministry, often as though we were the only one in need of help. Yet it seems like everyone has a Randall story to tell of his sage advice, his nudging challenge, or that time when he just listened. Thank you to Steve Pressley for letting us see the pastoral side, too.

Randall was a bit of a "neat freak." His desk was never cluttered. His inbox was never backed up. He was a sharp dresser. He planned everything meticulously. Yet he waded into the messiness of Baptist life in search of clarity and order, which, in some ways, finally came. Still, it was in touching so many of us in the mess of our lives that he was at his best. For a grateful Baptist family, we say "thank you, Randall" for what you have meant to all of us.

—Mike Queen
Wilmington, North Carolina

---

1. Traditionally, Baptist preachers were expected to preach twice on Sundays and a third time at a midweek service.

Introduction

Why write a biography of Randall Lolley?

As background, some years ago, Smyth & Helwys Publishing approached a Lolley contemporary, the late Dr. Cecil Sherman, to ask if he would be willing to pen his life story. What the editors and publishers were seeking, Sherman deduced, was a first-person account of the schism within the Southern Baptist Convention, a division that began in the late 1970s and essentially culminated by the early 1990s.

Sherman had earlier assumed principal leadership of a counter-insurgency, a "moderate movement" intended to resist a self-described "conservative resurgence" within the institutions and agencies of the convention. As such, he was uniquely qualified to write such an account.

And while he did contextualize it within the overall story of his life—from birth and education through service as a church pastor and 1994 retirement as the first coordinator of the Cooperative Baptist Fellowship—what Cecil Sherman provided was a story that centered on the breakup of the SBC and the subsequent birth of that new entity, the CBF.

In recognition of that purpose, it was Randall Lolley who wrote a foreword for Sherman's autobiography (*By My Own Reckoning*, 2008), where he described the latter as "arguably . . . the most important Baptist of his generation."

But if Sherman was in fact *that*, then Randall shared the prominence. What many observers of the era of the SBC fracture remember above all was that Southeastern Baptist Theological Seminary was the earliest target of those who sought to remake the denomination and its institutions and agencies. And Randall Lolley was the first institutional head to resign his position in protest.

In autumn 1987, Randall faced the reality that the majority of his seminary trustees represented the new conservative majority within the convention. What he regarded as an "alien vision" would henceforth be imposed upon himself, the faculty, the administration, and the students—in view of which he elected to quit the struggle and stand down from the post he had held since 1974.

However, Randall did not simultaneously quit the *ministry* that he launched while a student at Howard College (now Samford University) in the late 1940s. For in summer 1988 he returned to pastoring local church congregations, initially in Raleigh and soon thereafter in Greensboro. It was to pastoral ministry that he had first felt led by God, and it had been from the pastorate at First Baptist Church, Winston-Salem, that he was called to become Southeastern Seminary's third president.

Robert D. "Bob" Dale, who arrived at SEBTS from the SBC Sunday School Board early in Randall's presidency, recalled a conversation he and his future boss had prior to his own appointment. "What is it like to move from retail to wholesale?" Bob wondered—i.e., from pastoral ministry to a ministry of training pastors and others.

"Well, I consider myself," Randall matter-of-factly replied, "to be a pastor on loan to the denomination." Bob Dale construed the comment to mean that, regardless of his position as the chief administrator of a school of divinity, the president would continue to think of himself first, foremost, and always as a pastor.

So it was to be expected that the fifty-seven-year-old, upon leaving Old Wake Forest, home of Southeastern Seminary, would return to the leadership of local churches. Never settling comfortably at nearby Raleigh First, come Easter 1990 he answered the call of the First Baptist Church of Greensboro. As a fresh SEBTS graduate, the young Randall Lolley had served the Gate City congregation in the late 1950s as assistant pastor. He and Lou still had friends in the congregation, so it became an appropriate and happy place in which to continue and to conclude his active ministry.

I joined the Lolleys in Greensboro at the beginning of 1993, responding to the congregation's call for a general associate pastor. I had been told that Dr. Lolley was "working too hard," was not getting any younger, and might collapse under the load if he did not get able assistance. What I discovered, however, was a strong and energetic pastor who, though he was but a few years shy of a normal retirement age, was in no way showing signs of slowing down, or needing to.

Randall walked like a young man, with a visible spring in his step. He spoke in such ways as he needed to speak, depending on the occasion and the context. Were he in the pulpit, he was oratorically brilliant, drawing from an oversized vocabulary but speaking in short, neat sentences and phrases, many of which could easily have served as "sound bites" for broadcast news.

Were he in his office, or in his car, or in the conference room at church, Randall might revert to his native "Alabamese." Tobacco smokers might light up a *see'-gar*. Local law enforcement were called the *poh'-leese*. If summoned, they might arrive to the sound of a wailing *sy-reen'*.

Only a few words failed to slip gracefully from his tongue. The Montagnards—mountain dwellers who took America's side during the Vietnam War and thereafter repatriated to the US, some to Greensboro—Randall mispronounced as *Mon-tig-nards*. Similarly, the word *poignant* invariably came across as *poyg-nant*.

Some references were mysteries to the historically less informed, as when Randall would term groups of fledgling ministers "Young Turks" or speak of a potentially contentious committee meeting as a "set-to."

You knew he liked you should he ever label you "Peckerwood."[1]

When the Greensboro church staff sat together and underwent personality surveys such as Myers-Briggs, most were reminded that we were among that preponderance of church ministers who are natural introverts but who, of ministerial necessity, had cultivated a functional extroversion.

Our boss was different. On survey after survey, he tested in the upper ninety-eighth percentile for extroversion. It was noted that, while the rest of us must periodically withdraw in order to recharge

1. In the post-Civil War American South, the term may originally have functioned as an insult. Randall, however, invariably employed it affectionately.

our spiritual and relational batteries, Randall Lolley obtained energy through the sheer presence of other people.

Be that as it may, when evenings came around, or following major church events or receptions in the fellowship hall, Randall would retreat from buildings and people as quickly and gracefully as he could, avoiding notice. The highest compliment church people could pay their pastor, he once joked, was when they would look up and gaze around, punch glasses in hand, and wonder aloud, "Where'd he *go*?"

I once dropped by "the Lolley House," as he always called it, around eight o'clock on a Wednesday evening, following prayer meeting and Bible study. My boss was already in pajamas, robe, and slippers. By habit he retired early because by nature he would wake up early. He would bathe, dress, and head out in the pre-dawn darkness to drink McDonald's coffee and read over the daily newspaper or review his Sunday sermon.

Like others of its size and constituency, the particular church he and I and others served could place a heavy burden on a pastor. Half the congregation in 1993 were senior adults and retirees, and they were major consumers of pastoral care. They could, Randall suggested, be classified in one of three ways: (1) the go-gos, (2) the slow-gos, or (3) the no-gos. As associate pastor I was free to focus, he offered, on any one or two of the three as I wished.

Still, he never, in the nearly four years we worked together, surrendered his own focus on any segment of the congregation or on any aspect of its care and management. "You can't be their preacher till you've been their pastor," he insisted. So he pastored all of them—to the last woman, man, and child—in consistent, appropriate, timely, and equitable ways.

And likewise, I have been told, he did for every flock of every description that ever came under his oversight. As a seminary head he presided over a complex population of students, faculty, administrators, and ancillary personnel. Yet all appeared to regard him not primarily as president but more as pastor and friend.

Pastor and friend. Whether in the academy or the community or the denomination or the church, Randall Lolley was a pastor unlike any other that we ever knew.

This is the man whose story we now set out to tell.

The organization of this biography is primarily *topical.* This means that fourteen of the fifteen chapters (which include an epilogue) deal with various, specific topics of concern in the life and ministry of Randall Lolley.

The second chapter, titled "Unless You're Lead Dog," deals with the fact that Randall has shown himself, throughout his life, to be a uniquely gifted, multitalented individual—a league leader in various fields of human and spiritual endeavor. Few had greater awareness of this reality than the fellow church staff ministers who closely observed their boss over the course of his three post-graduate vocational pastorates.

Chapter 3 examines the pulpit proclamation that these ministers and their fellow church members heard between the decades of the sixties and the nineties. "No ordinary preacher" is the assessment hearers tended to apply.

Randall Lolley stood by a conviction, however, that he shared freely through the years: within the congregation, preaching is superseded by the necessity of pastoring. "Before You Can Preach" is the title of chapter 4, and lay leaders from one church will recall the way he applied the principle to the healing of their congregational woundedness.

Chapter 5, "Pastor on Loan," acknowledges the 1974 transition that Randall made from church leadership to the headship of one of his denomination's six seminaries. The chapter title recalls his self-designation when invited by a prospective faculty member to characterize his move. Faculty from the 1974–1988 Southeastern Seminary years describe the manner in which "a pastor's heart" guided their president's leadership.

Seminary students from the Lolley era look back in chapter 6, remembering how—in their various encounters with their president—he invariably made them feel like "The Most Important

Person in the Room." So close was their affinity with their pastor-president that, when the denominational firestorm beset them all, they stood by him virtually en masse.

Chapter 7, "Fight or Flight," details Randall's lifelong "rules of engagement" when dealing with adversaries of any kind in any setting. Drawing from a 1990 sermon titled "Conflict," the chapter illustrates how the preacher borrowed his principles from the life of Jesus and then applied them at congregational, seminary, and denominational levels.

Because the conflict that overtook the Southern Baptist Convention dealt primarily with attitudes and approaches regarding Christian Scripture, chapters 8 and 9—"Randall Lolley and the Bible" and "The Strength to Believe"—deal with Randall's understanding of the nature of Scripture and the manner in which the Old and New Testaments formed his theological perspectives.

Following his 1987 resignation as president of Southeastern Seminary, Randall turned his attention back to the pastoral leadership of congregations. Still, he kept an eye on developments within the denomination, particularly as they involved the formation of new "missions delivery systems." His participation particularly in the early growth of his state's Cooperative Baptist Fellowship of North Carolina is detailed in chapter 10, "And Quit the Fighting."

In an unusual compilation he labeled his "bucket list," Randall mentioned a total of fifteen trips he had conducted—as pastor, seminary leader, or retired pastor—to the biblical lands of Israel, Jordan, and Egypt.[2] A specific foray, which he led and recorded on his personal videocam in 2007, is the subject of chapter 11, "A Pilgrim Personality."

"Marrying and burying"—the performance of weddings and funerals—were in some ways the most pivotal functions of a church pastor, according to a view Randall shared with associates. His unique approach to each is explored in chapter 12, "Everybody Dies a Hero."

"Randall has always been very pro-woman," according to the woman he first encountered in a 1951 church revival service. But it was invariably Lou Lolley herself who topped his list. Chapter 13,

2. See Appendix C: Randall Lolley's Bucket List.

"Dearest Lou," provides an intimate portrait of their sixty-nine-year partnership.

"Mirrors on the Man," chapter 14, turns to a former church staff associate, a North Carolina Baptist institutional head, a physician who served as a deacon in one of the churches Randall led, and a Lolley family member to provide their own perspectives on an individual who impacted and blessed their lives in various ways.

The concluding chapter, an epilogue titled "The Oblong Blur," relies on Randall's own characterization of his personal experience with memory loss while relating the important ways his family and his residential community came to his side and sustained the quality of his living.

Meanwhile, the first of the chapters, "A Plain Vanilla Alabama Boy," is different from the others. In the manner of a conventional, chronological biography, it consists of a complete overview of Randall Lolley's life: from his birth through his formative years; from his college and seminary education through his first, post-doctoral pastorate; from his leadership of Southeastern Baptist Theological Seminary through his final two vocational pastorates.

Then following the main body of the book appear three appendices. The first, "Lolleyisms: A Glossary," features more than fifty familiar words, terms, and sayings from the mouth and pen of Randall Lolley, along with annotations, explanations, and illustrations.

The second appendix, "Rolesville Retrospective," features Randall's last known, formal narrative of the events that led up to his resignation as president of Southeastern Seminary.

The third appendix, titled "Randall's Bucket List," provides a bona fide world traveler's own accounting of the places he visited on all seven of the world's continents, including Antarctica.

Chapter 1

A Plain Vanilla Alabama Boy[1]

While the US census ranks it in the upper 4 percent of surnames, not many people actually know someone named *Lolley*. The state where one is most likely to encounter a Lolley is Alabama—yet only slightly more than 10 of every 100,000 Alabamians bear the name.[2]

It was in "L.A." (Lower Alabama), as he called it, that William Randall Lolley was born on Tuesday, June 2, 1931. The site of his birth was "the Tolbert Place," located in the Good Hope community just west of the Pike County college town of Troy. Randall's parents were Roscoe and Mary Sarah Nunnelee Lolley.

Roscoe's "Lolley" heritage has been traced for only four generations. The first person in his line known to bear the name was one William Lolley, a North Carolinian born in 1788.[3] William's family appeared thereafter to have migrated first to Georgia (where in 1816 his son William Jeremiah "Jerry" Lolley was born) and then to Coffee County, in southeast Alabama. Jerry's son Elijah Nathanael was born there in 1839, followed in 1870 by his grandson Lijah Mathanael (nicknamed "Pete") and in 1900 by great-grandson Roscoe Lee Lolley.

---

1. "I was a plain vanilla Alabama boy who made it half-way to the top of the country," so stated Randall Lolley in a handwritten note dated May 2010. ("Half-way to the top" referred to North Carolina, where he invested the greater part of his forty-five-year ministry.)

2. Determined using the search engine at mynamestats.com.

3. Family genealogical research was performed by Randall's sister-in-law Sydney Harrell (Mrs. Tom) Lolley. One website (houseofnames.com) suggests that the very first Lolley migrated to Maryland from Ireland in 1684.

Little else is noted about Roscoe's heritage except that his father, Pete, was a Methodist and his grandfather Elijah served with Company D of the 6th Alabama Regiment of the Confederate Army.

William Randall (whom Roscoe would call "Ran") was the middle of his father's three children. An older sister, Juanita, was born of Roscoe's first marriage, to his cousin Eva. Following the death of her mother, Juanita was raised by her maternal grandmother. Roscoe then married Mary Nunnelee, and their union brought forth first Randall and six years later his brother Tom.

Randall and Tom would walk similar paths in life, growing up in church together, attending the same college and the same seminary, pastoring local churches in North Carolina, and eventually serving their Southern Baptist denomination.

Early in their marriage, Roscoe and Mary Lolley moved to "the Tom Carroll Place," also in the Good Hope community.[4] By the time Randall entered first grade, the family occupied "the Lawrence Caffee Place" in nearby Goshen, about a dozen miles southwest of Troy. Like his father, Roscoe labored as a farmer, while his wife was a college-trained public school teacher.

Randall's hometown of Troy numbered only 7,000 residents, but his childhood community of Goshen was smaller by far, with fewer than 400. Goshen was a fifteen-minute drive, however, from Good Hope and the Baptist church that bore its name. Randall and little brother Tom would first attend Sunday school at that church, and two decades later Randall would return, as a college student, to serve as its pastor.

When Randall was nine years of age, his family departed Goshen and moved farther south, to Geneva County and the town of Samson, along the Florida state line. There his father co-owned and operated the Bowden-Lolley Feed Mill, while his mother taught at Samson Elementary School. The family of four—Roscoe, Mary, Randall, and Tom—transferred their church affiliation to Samson Baptist Church, where they worshiped and served regularly and faithfully. At twelve years of age Randall came to Christian faith and was baptized into the seventy-five-member congregation.

---

4. Rental properties were often identified by the names of their owners.

Meanwhile, Mary Lolley's brother Asa paid regular and occasionally lengthy visits to the Lolley household, where he occupied an extra bedroom. Particularly concerned that his religiously earnest nephew not be perceived as a "goody-goody," Uncle Asa frequently conducted young Randall on outings to a pool hall in nearby Troy.

From the moment he entered his mother's fourth-grade classroom, Randall showed himself a superior student.[5] He led his classmates all the way through elementary and high school, eventually to be named valedictorian of the Samson High School senior class. Perceived as appropriately "well-rounded"—given his involvements in church, school, community, and athletics—he recalled that he was recommended for a congressional appointment to the United States Military Academy at West Point.

While he always regarded himself as an American patriot, Randall turned that "signal honor" down. His prior obligation was a vocational Christian calling that he first sensed while still a public school student. Following his 1949 high school graduation, he joined himself to a "youth revival team." In a 2012 interview he explained:

> I was a product of the youth revival movement of the mid-late forties, just as WWII was ending. The whole country was caught up in the youth revival movement, which originated at Baylor University. Several teams of gifted and talented ministers would go out in the summers, all over the south, giving revivals directed to youth twelve to twenty years of age. When they came to my part of Alabama, a religious fervor like I have never seen swept the South.[6]

"I wasn't a preacher or singer," he clarified. "I was director of activities—I cut the watermelon!"

---

5. In a 2017 interview Randall was asked if his mother showed him favoritism. "No!" he protested. "She made it harder!"

6. Cynthia Dawne Savage-King, *Finding Somewhere Else to Go: The Effect of the Conservative Takeover of the Southern Baptist Convention on Ministers Who Would Not Conform to the New Leadership and Theology* (DMin thesis, Episcopal Divinity School [Cambridge, MA], 2012), 57.

Still Randall was awakening to a higher calling. "A call to preach," he believed, was "a call to prepare."[7] He opted to begin his preparation at Alabama's premier Baptist school, Howard College (now Samford University), in far north Birmingham.

Many young men sensing God's call, and seeking eventually to enroll in a seminary, would major in Bible or religion during their undergraduate years. But Randall, likely following the advice of someone at the seminary level, decided to equip himself first in secular disciplines—in his case, history and psychology. This would afford him a broader academic and cultural foundation on which later to build his training in divinity.

During his college days, a mid-century equivalent of "field work" took the form of pastoral ministry to small churches. Two of these were the Reese and Piney Grove congregations near Samson.

> During my freshman year two men in overalls approached me about becoming pastor of their church, Reese Baptist. It was a new church; they had bought a school house as a worship building. The men knew of me from my work in the youth revival teams, but they didn't know I was a watermelon cutter! It was a 200-mile drive one-way from Birmingham, 400 miles each trip.[8]

Later responding to the call of his childhood congregation, Randall found himself again driving south, in order to fill the pulpit of Good Hope Baptist Church in Goshen. Good Hope awarded him their entire weekly Sunday morning offering, a salary that supplemented the cost of his studies at Howard College.

Meanwhile the family's Samson Baptist Church initiated and accomplished the young pastor's ordination. The names of an ordaining council of forty people, including fourteen ministers,

---

7. In his letter of resignation from a two-year, post-seminary pastoral internship, Randall wrote, "Since being called into the ministry I have had a growing conviction that the call to preach is a call to prepare to preach" (*The First Baptist News*, Greensboro, NC, December 6, 1959). Having earned two degrees at Southeastern Seminary, further preparation would take him to Ft. Worth, Texas, where he would pursue and complete a ThD (Doctor of Theology).

8. Savage-King, *Finding Somewhere Else to Go*, 58.

appear on an ordination certificate verifying that William Randall Lolley had been examined "in regard to his Christian experience, call to the ministry, and views of Bible Doctrine." On Sunday morning, January 28, 1951, the congregation laid hands upon a man who was destined to become notable within the larger Southern Baptist family as a pastor, seminary president, and denominational statesman.

Randall returned to the area later that year to preach for a revival meeting at New Prospect Baptist Church midway between Samson and Geneva, and there he encountered Clara Jacobs, who was playing piano for the services. "Clara Lou," as she was then known, was a Geneva native. In the pattern of Randall's mother Mary, she was studying at Troy State College to become an elementary school teacher.

In spring 1952, Randall graduated Howard College *magna cum laude*. It was a stellar achievement, all the more because he finished in three years while starring on the college baseball team. Bearing the moniker "Lightnin' Lolley," he was recalled by classmate Jack U. Harwell: "Randall was a cracker-jack second baseman: he couldn't hit worth a hoot, but could cover second base like a pro."[9]

Following graduation, Randall made two commitments, one temporary and the other permanent. The latter constituted the vows he offered to Clara Lou Jacobs before God and her home congregation, Geneva's Westside Methodist Church, on August 28. The temporary obligation—which he undertook while waiting for his bride to complete her college education—was to Starke University School, a boys' military high school forty miles to the north in Montgomery. There, for two years, he taught English, science, and geography.[10]

During the first year of their marriage, the newly wedded Lolleys shared a rented room near the campus of Troy State. At Clara Lou's graduation they moved to Montgomery, where she taught fifth grade while Randall served the remaining year of his commitment to the military school. Meanwhile, a faculty member at his alma mater

---

9. "A Working Theologian," *Baptists Today*, c. April 1996.

10. To his psychology major and history minor Randall had added secondary education and a certification to teach.

Howard College made a recommendation that would set Randall Lolley's future direction in multiple ways.

A new seminary, to complement three other Southern Baptist seminaries in existence at that time, had been born at mid-century in North Carolina on the campus of Wake Forest College near Raleigh. Randall was told the new school was staffed with some of the finest minds in Baptist life. The host college—at that time the flagship school of the Baptist State Convention of North Carolina—would soon be moving to a new campus in Winston-Salem. All its buildings and amenities would come into the possession of the new Southeastern Baptist Theological Seminary.

"Old Wake Forest," as some termed the seminary campus and its adjoining small town, would be an ideal place for Randall and Clara Lou to live and to launch his divinity student career.

So the Rev. and Mrs. Lolley "packed up the Studebaker," as she later recalled, and drove the 600 miles of two-lane highway that lay between Montgomery and the SEBTS campus. Arriving at nearby Knightdale, where she had previously arranged a job interview with the local elementary school principal, Clara Lou was hired "on the spot." Knightdale Elementary became an erstwhile partner with the seminary as it provided its "teacherage" as housing for the Lolleys.

Over the course of four years of ministry training, from 1954 through 1958, two country churches would employ Randall as pastor. They were the Pine Ridge and Poplar Spring congregations, both located in the Franklin County community of Pilot. In 1955, the Lolleys moved from the Knightdale teacherage into a newly constructed parsonage "on the church field," where Randall continued to pastor while he completed two degrees at the seminary—bachelor of divinity (BD) and master of theology (ThM).

During Randall's Southeastern student days, Sydnor Stealey served as first president of the seminary, while Olin Binkley (later to serve as Stealey's successor) held the position of dean of faculty. "Not in my wildest dreams could I have believed that I would follow these two as the third president," Randall later mused. Nor, he added, did he imagine that he would achieve a perfect 4.0 grade point average in each of his degree programs, thereby graduating *summa cum laude.*[11]

But somebody besides the registrar was watching him. And that was Dr. Claud B. Bowen, chair of the seminary board of trustees and pastor of the First Baptist Church of Greensboro. Greensboro was then and continues to be the third-largest city in North Carolina. During the 1950s its premier Baptist congregation reached its zenith, with an impressive new church plant, 2,800 resident members, and an average Sunday school attendance that approached 1,800. Bowen was completing his initial decade as the church's senior minister, and he needed help. He and minister of education Dr. S. C. Ray had guided the congregation in remarkable growth, but the load was becoming heavy.

In the young Alabama native Bowen saw extraordinary leadership potential. In addition to pastoring rural churches, Randall Lolley had been a consistently outstanding student. By 1958, the young "theologue" was prepared to pursue his "terminal degree," a doctorate in theology. But in counsel with Dr. Bowen, the two decided Randall would do well to gain pastoral experience in a large congregation first.

The assistant pastorate to which First Baptist called Randall was similar to the pastoral residencies that some larger churches offer today. Yet, since he was already experienced in small congregations and firmly committed to a future pastoral vocation, Dr. Bowen regarded his new "assistant" as both a pastoral and a preaching associate.

The Lolleys settled into a rental house and later an apartment within their new church community. There they established a home base for ministry and set about rearing their two young daughters. Charlotte Lynn had been born during their final year of study at SEBTS; Pamela Jo arrived while they served the congregation in Greensboro.

Older members of the Gate City congregation—to which Randall would one day return to serve as pastor—remembered "the young

---

11. Thomas A. Bland, ed., *Servant Songs: Reflections on the History and Mission of Southeastern Baptist Theological Seminary* (Macon, GA: Smyth & Helwys, 1994), 32–33.

Randall Lolley" as a phenomenon: incredibly energetic, charismatic, and passionate about every endeavor. They recognized that keeping him and Clara Lou in Greensboro for many years would be unlikely.

Among the pillar-type church members who took note of his potential were Marion and Mary Eakes. Having enjoyed Randall's personality and contributions for a period of months, the Eakes made him an offer he could not refuse: go back to school, earn your doctor's degree, and *send us the bills.*

Simultaneously, Dr. Guy Moore, pastor of the storied Broadway Baptist Church of Fort Worth, Texas, answered Claud Bowen's invitation to lead a revival meeting in Greensboro. Impressed, like Dr. Bowen, with the church's pastoral assistant, Moore invited Randall to come to Texas, study at the Southwestern Baptist Seminary, and join his own staff as associate pastor.

Regarding future doctoral study, Randall's initial inclination had been to enroll at his denomination's oldest institution, The Southern Baptist Theological Seminary in Louisville, Kentucky. Southern, however, had recently been placed on probation by its accrediting agency following the resignation of thirteen professors in a dispute with their president.[12]

For several years, the Kentucky seminary was forbidden to accept new graduate students. So in late 1959, the young Lolley family said their goodbyes in Greensboro and set out for the Lone Star State. Randall worked hard and fast in Texas, completing all but his doctoral dissertation by autumn 1962.

In the meantime, word back in North Carolina had spread to Winston-Salem, indicating that the soon-to-be-minted "Dr. Lolley" would be a good bet for leadership of the Twin City's historic First Baptist Church. First Winston's pulpit committee chairman Jim Conrad journeyed to Fort Worth to extend Randall his congregation's invitation to become pastor. Shortly thereafter, on

---

12. The disagreement related to faculty influence in the recruitment of new professors.

November 11, 1962, the thirty-one-year-old Rev. W. Randall Lolley became the youngest person ever to assume that position.[13]

For the ensuing decade, until 1974, FBC Winston-Salem became what Randall and Lou Lolley would later term "our Camelot."[14] Membership, attendance, participation, and outreach multiplied rapidly. From the beginning, Randall expected success. In his first "Pastor to People" article in the weekly church newsletter *Together*, Randall wrote,

> The prospects of worshiping and working together with you are such as to demand our very best. We pledge to you and to our God to spare no effort to render the service and to guide in a ministry like which our city, our state, and Christians throughout the world have come to expect from this fine church. The future will be exactly what we all together, under God, make it. There is something both exciting and frightening in the prospect of holding so noble an undertaking in our collective hands.[15]

One month later, at a Sunday school class Christmas dinner, deacon chair Don Britt offered an early observation of the new pastor in a rephrasing of Clement Moore's famous holiday poem:

> The members were nestled all snug in their pews,
> While visions of a leader made no news.
> . . .
> When what to my wondering eyes should appear,
> But a chap so friendly and a family so dear, . . .
> . . .
> More rapid than eagles his words they came,
> And he smiled and preached and called them by name,
> "Now Baptists, now Unity, now Loyalty Day!
> On Deacons! On Committees! We'll never say nay,
> To the top in attendance, to the top, Y'all!

---

13. A close second is the current pastor, Rev. Emily Hull McGee, who arrived in 2015 at thirty-two years of age.

14. During the late 1980s, Randall dropped the "Clara" from "Clara Lou" in his letters.

15. November 15, 1962.

Now dash away, dash away, dash away all."
His eyes—how they twinkled! His dimples—how merry!
His cheeks were like roses, his head nice and hairy.
His droll witticisms were all aglow,
And the strength of his sermons would never go!

As if to underscore both the church's expectation and the pastoral emphasis Randall Lolley would apply to ministry endeavors of every nature in years to follow, Britt concluded his poem,

He spoke a few words, then went straight to his work,
Preaching and visiting, and turned with a jerk,
And laying his letters aside of his phone,
Giving a nod, a'visiting he had gone.

Nearly a year later, in the November 14, 1963, edition of *Together*, Britt reflected,

> Psychologists tell us that the first year of marriage is the most difficult. I think you (the congregation) will agree with me that the first year of our fellowship with Mr. Lolley has been free of significant rocks and shoals. This fact alone, I submit, would make this recognition of this first anniversary worthwhile. But beyond that, this day gives us a suitable and built-in opportunity to pay tribute to this dynamic man of God . . . .

Randall's doctoral dissertation, titled "The Christian Philosophy of John Baillie," was completed during his first year in Winston-Salem and defended before the Southwestern Seminary faculty during spring 1964. Seminary president Dr. Robert E. Naylor conferred the doctor of theology degree on July 17.[16] This, according to an article published the same day in the *Twin City Sentinel* newspaper, made

16. Bringing the commencement address was Dr. Homer G. Lindsay Sr., pastor of the First Baptist Church of Jacksonville, Florida. Lindsay's son Homer Jr. would figure prominently in the "conservative resurgence" that would divide the Southern Baptist Convention two decades later.

Randall Lolley "the only Baptist minister in Winston-Salem with a fulltime pastorate who has an earned doctorate degree."[17]

Going "straight to his work" implied more than ministry among the people of First Baptist, as two years following his arrival Randall was elected the first president of the Forsyth (County) Conference on Religion, Race, and Community Life. The conference was an ecumenical endeavor, comprising representatives of multiple Protestant denominations, plus a local Reform Jewish rabbi and a Catholic priest.

The major focus for the group was community racial relations in a time when desegregation efforts were intensifying across the South. The historic "sit-in" movement had recently been launched at a Woolworth's Department Store "white only" lunch counter in neighboring Greensboro.[18] In a Sunday morning sermon, Randall analyzed "our problem in the area of civil rights":

> [The problem] is rather with us naturally. It has come as a consequence of sociological, economic, political and spiritual factors in our times. The population of the races has increased. Intelligence, education and economic advantages have mushroomed. Desires of the races have been whetted through the media of modern communication such as radio and television.
>
> What's more, there is a thorn driving itself into our Christian conscience. It is the thorn of a growing conviction that those who want to abolish legally forced segregation are basically right, just as those who wanted to abolish enforced slavery were basically right; and for many of the same reasons, both are right.

Showing himself remarkably prescient, the preacher noted that a continuing revolution in love and law would "know no truce in our times."[19]

---

17. While a student at the Governor's School of North Carolina, meeting at Salem College during summer 1964, I recall worshiping at "First on Fifth" and hearing the church's popular preacher.

18. February 2, 1962.

19. Reported in "Church Notes," *Twin City Sentinel*, July 8, 1964.

Randall's personal and pastoral popularity crossed racial and ethnic barriers in his new home city. In 1966, he was invited to preach the baccalaureate sermon at Winston-Salem State College, a historically Black institution. Titling his sermon "Make It Your Own," he noted that the David and Goliath story in 1 Samuel 17 was usually characterized in terms of "the big guy versus the little guy." However, Randall expanded the interpretation:

> "It is really the description of a classic human situation. It is the account of youth bursting out of its small and unsatisfactory life—restless youth, explosive youth leaping out into the deep.
>
> "Graduates will have to develop something new to meet their Goliaths," he advised. He called on them to ignore the advice of the organization man which says, "Don't step out of line. Conform to life around you. Never question the system."[20]

In July and August 1967, Randall made local, statewide, and national news when he decided to devote his summer vacation to a preaching mission in Vietnam. The United States was midway through its decade-long participation in the twenty-year conflict, and First Baptist Church had multiple members who were involved, among them Marine chaplain Lt. Frank Jordan.

Landing in Chu Lai on July 25, Randall joined ranks with the First Marine Air Wing, preaching in various field chapels and counseling servicemen at the front lines and in bunkers on the perimeter of the giant American installation at Da Nang. With Chaplain Jordan he rode by helicopter into Viet Cong territory to encourage the establishment of a school for refugee children and also to visit with Montagnard (Fr. "mountaineer") tribesmen in Dalat.[21]

In local news coverage Randall—who at that time supported the war's officially stated purpose of granting the South Vietnamese an opportunity to form their own government—praised his

---

20. Luiz Overbea, "W-S State Graduates Told of Tests Ahead," *Journal and Sentinel*, May 30, 1966.

21. Years later, while pastoring in Greensboro, Randall would assist refugee Montagnards in the construction of a Vietnamese church on property owned by the Piedmont Baptist Association.

Winston-Salem congregation for their blessing and financial support of his mission. "The only permission to go to Vietnam which was difficult to obtain," he joked, "was my wife's!"[22]

Just as the new pastor had been well received by church and community, so also the local Pilot Mountain Association, the Southern Baptist Convention, and the Baptist State Convention of North Carolina paid tribute. During his dozen-year Twin City pastorate, Randall served the state convention by presiding over its Pastors Conference, holding trusteeship at Campbell University, and chairing a significant study committee on state-level Baptist education. At the national level, he held membership on the SBC's Executive Committee and served as speaker at the two denominational summer assemblies, Ridgecrest (NC) and Glorieta (NM).

A steadily growing church membership meant that some people within First Baptist did not know each other (or even their pastor and his family) well. Lou would recall sitting in the balcony one Sunday with young daughters Charlotte and Pam to either side and later hearing that a woman seated on the main floor had looked up and lamented, "That poor woman—she has to bring her children to church without their father!"

In 1974, trustees at Randall's alma mater, Southeastern Seminary, approached him about coming as the institution's third president. Dr. Claud B. Bowen, who had led Greensboro's First Baptist Church when Randall came as assistant pastor in 1958, served as trustee chairman and chair of the presidential search committee. For Randall, who at that moment was happily pastoring hundreds of local church parishioners, Bowen's inquiry suggested an opportunity to pastor hundreds of future pastors. It became an irresistible invitation.

Randall later noted "three elements" that influenced his decision to accept the seminary presidency: (1) at twenty-five years of age, the seminary was ready to accept the leadership of an alumnus who "sincerely loved" it; (2) with a dozen years' experience as pastor of the Winston-Salem congregation, he had been assured by many that "a pastoral-type president was needed to lead" at that juncture in the

22. Eugene Baker, "Winston Pastor to Spend Vacation in Vietnam," *Biblical Recorder*, June 1967.

history of Southeastern Seminary; and (3) "Southeastern's presidency offered me the best possible opportunity to multiply the impact of my own ministry through the training of other men and women for their ministries."[23]

During summer 1974, Randall and Clara Lou said their sorrowful goodbyes to the Twin City and set out for the village of Old Wake Forest, where they would settle into the stately president's mansion of SEBTS. Subsequent history proved that the following fourteen years, while greatly rewarding in important ways, would also become the most turbulent chapter in Randall's ministerial career. The Southern Baptist Convention was dividing over issues both political and theological, and Southeastern's increasingly conservative board of trustees grew steadily less supportive of the seminary's theologically moderate leadership.[24]

In 1988, Randall resigned his presidency and accepted the pastorate of the First Baptist Church of Raleigh. The city of Raleigh was to prove, however, too close to what he regarded as "the scene of the crime." He learned, as he would explain to the congregation, of "a genuine connection between proximity and pain."

"I went to Raleigh planning to stay," he insisted, "but it just didn't work out. It was like going to the graveyard every day, emotionally."[25] Many current and former SEBTS faculty and administrators held FBC Raleigh memberships, and every hallway conversation tended to devolve into the nursing of wounds. Much as he longed to respond to his former colleagues compassionately and pastorally, Randall also felt the need to "forget those things which were behind, and reach forth unto those things that lay ahead."[26]

Two years later, in 1990, his original First Baptist Church—in the nearby Gate City of Greensboro—struggled to identify new leadership following the termination of the previous pastorate. Because

23. Bland, ed., *Servant Songs*, 33.

24. This significant chapter in Randall's life and ministry will be covered later.

25. Scott P. Culclasure, *In Every Good Work: A History of First Baptist Church, Greensboro, North Carolina* (Atlanta: Baptist History and Heritage Society, 2009), 216.

26. Philippians 3:13.

of the church's high regard for the reputation and well-connectedness of its onetime assistant pastor, Randall was summoned to journey to Greensboro, consult with the search committee, and make recommendations.

Search committee member Margaret Wilson later recalled that, in the course of their discussions, someone asked offhandedly: "Randall, would there be any chance *you* would be interested in returning to Greensboro?" Randall was uncharacteristically taken off guard. Then, raising his eyebrows and smiling, he promised he would think about it, pray about it, and talk with Lou about it.[27]

As winter turned to spring, Randall and Lou relented and permitted the search committee to offer his name to the congregation he had served three decades earlier. On the Sunday morning of the decisive vote, February 11, 1990, the Lolleys drove from Raleigh to Greensboro for a 7:30 a.m. congregational reception. The reason for the early hour was to make it possible for Randall to return to his capital city pulpit to preach at the eleven o'clock morning service.

As her husband concluded his sermon to the Raleigh congregation, Lou sat by the phone in the pastor's study. During the singing of the invitation hymn, she stole back into the sanctuary and handed her husband a small slip of paper. On it she had written four words: "No negative votes counted."

Randall read his letter of resignation that same morning. Soon thereafter, on Easter Sunday, April 15, 1990, FBC Greensboro welcomed Dr. W. Randall Lolley back to the pulpit as only its fourth pastor since 1910. Thirteen hundred people—more than the church had counted since the heyday of the 1950s—heard their new pastor preach a sermon titled "Wanted: An Open Tomb on Sunday." Two weeks later, on April 29, Dr. Lolley, soon to be fifty-nine years of age, was officially installed and prepared to launch what would become a six-and-a-half-year pastorate, the climax of his forty-five-year ministerial career. As Lou—recalling that the Gate City was where they

---

27. Margaret Wilson described the sudden, unanticipated, and slightly awkward "courtship" that developed between Randall and the search committee as "the dance of the gooney birds."

had begun their ministry post-seminary—would later summarize, it had been "a long trip *from* Greensboro *to* Greensboro."

The term "unintentional interim," employed by church growth expert Lyle Schaller in a classic book, *Survival Tactics in the Parish*, may describe what actually transpired during Randall's half dozen years of ministry to his final First Baptist Church. The word "interim" related to a period of time sandwiched between larger and longer pastorates, featuring an element of preparation and waiting for the next chapter. The qualifier "unintentional," meanwhile, implied that a pastor had not foreseen what became an actuality during his time of leadership.

Scott P. Culclasure, author of the impressive 2009 publication *In Every Good Work: A History of First Baptist Church, Greensboro, North Carolina*, served as a member of the pastor search committee that returned Randall to Greensboro. Dr. Culclasure noted, "Although older and more experienced than his predecessors had been in their first days in Greensboro, Lolley brought an exuberance that did not fail to excite."[28] If Randall was aware that his capstone ministry would become a bridge between those of his predecessor and his successor, it was never apparent to the members of First Baptist, or even at first to his closest staff colleagues.

When I arrived in Greensboro as general associate pastor in January 1993, Randall Lolley was nearly halfway through his ministry there. Alert observers must have been aware that he had reached his early sixties, but none harbored—or at least stated—the assumption that he would be finishing up within the next few years. His "exuberance," joined to their "excitement," seemed to have forestalled any such thinking.

There had been possible hints. Writing on June 27, 1991, his weekly "pastorgraph" in *First Baptist News*, Randall stated, "I have a dream that every member of our First Baptist family become[s] a 'hands-on' missionary somewhere/somehow within the next five years."

Another indicator may have been the introduction, by late 1992, of a comprehensive long-range planning document titled the *Five-Year Plan: 1993–98*. At some point during his first year, the new

28. Culclasure, *In Every Good Work*, 217.

pastor had secured the services of Dr. Dennis Blackmon, director of missions for the local Piedmont Baptist Association and a certified consultant in long-range church planning. Blackmon would lead the congregation in laying out a ministry strategy for a period of time that would barely eclipse Randall's ministry.

A third indication lay in his approach to what he considered to be a boilerplate Baptist pastor obligation, that being the leadership of the Wednesday evening prayer meeting and Bible study. Following the traditional family-style meal and the making of announcements with the midweek congregation gathered in the downstairs fellowship hall, Randall would direct adults upstairs to the church chapel. There he would rehearse his expansive knowledge of the nature of the pastoral concerns that were denoted by church members' names on a printed prayer list, after which he would lead a prayer or call on someone else in the room to pray.

Then for most of the hour he would open his "parallel" New Testament (featuring four popular translations set side by side for comparison) and lead the assembled Bible students in a study of the four Gospels. Guiding the study was a document left from his days as president of Southeastern Seminary titled "The Life of Christ, Matthew, Mark, Luke, John: Analytical Outline of the Harmony." The study aid had been prepared by New Testament professor Malcolm Tolbert. It consisted of seven legal-sized pages of 199 themes, texts, and chronologies, set in such order as a teacher might seize upon one a week for several years in succession. In Randall's case, more than six years were required to complete the cycle.[29]

This enumeration of possible hints and indications does not require the conclusion that the new pastor understood—or came to understand early in his ministry—that his own term of leadership would be relatively brief in a church that historically had enjoyed much longer pastorates. But confidential conversation with close colleagues added substantial confirmation.

---

29. I spent several months following Randall's departure in late September 1996, finishing up the "Outline of the Harmony" teaching project at Wednesday evening Bible studies.

A favorite congregational memory of Randall's earliest days, beginning in spring 1990, was a lengthy series of "breakfast meetings" with deacons and other key leaders and personalities throughout the church. The stated purpose of these gatherings was to ask "a simple question that quickly became his mantra: 'What is job one?'"[30] This was the same question that he once scribbled on a small scrap of paper and presented to the members of the pastor search committee. Later it became a conversation starter as he gathered with various members of the congregation.

What he sought to accomplish was a familiar function of pastoral care known as "active listening." What he heard from members were not so much suggestions about future directions for the church as the airing of painful recollections of the congregation's recent troubled history.

Pastoral terminations typically divide churches. Some people who had supported the previous pastor departed the membership for other local congregations. But a substantial number remained, and among these were strong, supportive, high-profile lay leaders. Their presence simultaneously reassured and discomfited those who had labored on the other side of the disagreement.

Randall quickly became aware that "job one" for himself as the new pastor was the reconciliation of the formerly opposing and still unsettled parties, along with the reestablishment of a sense of brotherhood and common purpose. Pastoral conversation became pastoral counseling, and most members responded by growing in their awareness that a brighter future under positive leadership awaited them.

FBC historian Scott Culclasure identified three areas of pastoral focus that Randall may have plotted along the half dozen years that loomed between him and coming retirement. Two have already been mentioned: the structuring of a five-year plan to guide the church's near-term life and ministry and the transition of the congregation

---

30. Culclasure, *In Every Good Work*, 218. (At the time, Ford Motor Company advertised its slogan, "Where Quality is Job 1." Randall characteristically seized upon slogans and sayings from popular culture and used them to make a point.)

from what its pastor termed "checkbook missions" to "hands-on missions."

The third emphasis, which was navigating the congregation away from its historic identity as a Southern Baptist church, would in time come more clearly into focus. But first came the important matter of defining Christian mission and the individual church member's responsibility for carrying it out.

If not every member signed on for some form of missionary involvement, their pastor certainly did. Every summer witnessed an impressive corps of FBC members and friends styling themselves as "Builders for Christ," as they identified fellow Southern Baptist Convention congregations that were attempting with limited resources to construct new church facilities. Groups as large as forty or fifty people would travel northward or southward and spend a week or more assisting members of the targeted church in putting their "hands on" hammers, nails, lumber, and other building materials. New classrooms, fellowship halls, and even worship sanctuaries were the result.

Suspending his typical weekly ministry and joining the "Builders" was invariably their pastor. He was easy to identify in his trademark light blue jumpsuit and camouflage hunting cap as he set his own hands to the task and plied remarkable skills he had honed through many years of multifaceted mission and ministry involvement.

Other mission involvement combined hands-on and checkbook approaches, particularly those projects that drew participants abroad. Church members grew increasingly wary of contributing money through traditional denominational channels, such as the Cooperative Program of the Southern Baptist Convention, or the seasonal Lottie Moon or Annie Armstrong missions offerings. But supporting fellow members as they traveled southward to Chile to assist in church building, orphanage repair, or medical-dental clinics for indigenous Mapuche people; or eastward to refurbish buildings for a newly relocated International Baptist Seminary in the Czech Republic seemed a logical and acceptable alternative approach.

Meanwhile, departing the city of Raleigh and moving farther afield from memories and personalities associated with Southeastern

Seminary did not bring relief from denominational struggle, however much it might have been desired. By June following the Lolleys' Easter return to Greensboro, the moderate cause in the SBC was essentially lost. Standard-bearer and presidential candidate Daniel Vestal suffered a decisive defeat at the 1990 annual meeting in New Orleans, and the moderate wing began moving in earnest toward separating from the convention and structuring a new denomination-style missions delivery organization.

When it came to identifying those who would inspire the new quest, Randall Lolley—even though he had assumed a different profile as pastor of a local church—was impossible to overlook. Traveling with church members and three hundred other North Carolina Baptists to Atlanta in August, he sat among eleven members of a steering committee that established a Baptist Cooperative Missions Program, a precursor of the later Cooperative Baptist Fellowship (CBF).

And so came about the third emphasis of Randall's years in Greensboro. Back home he encouraged his own church's Denominational Relations Committee as it sought to lead the congregation in navigating the complicated path from cooperating Southern Baptist church to membership in the new denomination-like entity known as the Fellowship. This would entail withdrawal of money and messengers from the SBC, scrutiny and response to changes occurring within the Baptist State Convention of North Carolina, and ultimately the suspension of any form of participation in the local Piedmont Baptist Association.

All such transition was not to occur during Randall's six-year FBC Greensboro pastorate, but trajectories were set in place. First Baptist Church opened its doors to the first North Carolina meeting of CBF in March 1993, and the congregation dispatched representatives the following year to nearby Winston-Salem for the formation of CBFNC—the Cooperative Baptist Fellowship of North Carolina.[31]

---

31. Following his retirement from FBC Greensboro, Randall served the CBFNC as its fifth elected moderator (1998–1999), during which time he recommended the employment of the first full-time coordinator, Bob Patterson.

The three emphases—denominational transition, mission redefinition, and systematic congregational planning—seemed to call for strong, authoritative pastoral leadership of a type that Randall did not necessarily endorse. In a 1995 interview with *Verbatim*, a publication of the Pastoral Care Department of North Carolina Baptist Hospital, Randall observed that a wise pastor should learn the distinctive story of the congregation that he served: "In learning that story, among the things you seek out is the profile of the way the church makes decisions and the way the church shares power. . . . Lay-led congregations, in my judgment, are always stronger. I just don't buy into pastoral authority. I don't think it's right. The last time Jesus was seen, he was a shepherd of sheep, not a cowboy rounding up cattle."

However, in conversation with me, Randall spoke of an important difference between the final two congregations he served as pastor. Raleigh First was indeed a "lay-led congregation," he remembered. "All I had to do there was preach, teach, and visit the membership." Church laity worked through their committee structure to accomplish the tasks of administration, planning, and visioning.

Meanwhile, Greensboro was a "pastor-led" congregation, historically, he believed. With only four pastors since the first decade of the century, its people had anticipated—and mostly yielded to—the direction of the people it had elected as its primary leaders. While this was not the most comfortable model for its latest leader (while at Southeastern Seminary, Randall had committed himself to a "participatory" administrative style), he submitted to what he saw as a long-standing congregational expectation.[32]

This required the application of administrative skill reminiscent of Randall's erstwhile seminary presidency. With the support of a qualified and committed administrative assistant, he produced ream upon ream of documents, directives, letters, and memos to members, committees, and leaders throughout the congregation. Amazingly,

32. Once, when challenged to name "the most powerful and influential member" of the Greensboro congregation, Randall asked for a day or two to reflect. Returning to the inquiry, he named a gentle, quiet "prayer warrior" who had for years taught her elderly women's Sunday school class.

none of this detracted from an overarching devotion to preach, teach, and form a consistent pastoral presence throughout the congregation.

Despite the enthusiastic crowds with which it had greeted its new pastor in 1990, First Baptist Greensboro had been and remained a "plateaued" church throughout Randall's six-year tenure. Sunday school and worship attendance showed signs of slow but steady decline by 1996, and the pastor shared openly with the Sunday evening service his disappointment.

On the occasion of his announcement of his impending retirement at age sixty-five, Randall mentioned in a letter to the congregation their need for a new pastor with "fresh legs." Privately he spoke of his own need for rest and refreshment. "I'm not going out with the intention to keep right on preaching," he insisted privately. "I've got a lot of other things I want to do. Besides, I've had my say; others should have theirs."

At his September 1996 FBC Greensboro departure, deacon chair Lois Edinger mused, "Deep down, we feel like we haven't had him long enough. But I think you listen to God's call, and God's call comes at various times and in various ways. I'm sure that God has other things that he will call Randall to do."

Dr. Edinger proved prophetic. Rare became the Sunday when the retired Randall Lolley did not fill somebody's pulpit, somewhere. From North Carolina, ranging west and east, northward to Washington, DC, and southward to Florida, he went on to conduct a grand total of a dozen interim pastorates.

Chapter 2

Unless You're Lead Dog

Late in his concluding, vocational pastorate (Greensboro, 1990–1996), Randall grew fond of the expression, "Unless you're the lead dog, the scenery never changes." The expression was not original. Humorist Robert Benchley used the line in the 1946 Bob Hope/Bing Crosby film *The Road to Utopia*: "Did you ever stop to think of one of those dog sled teams? The lead dog is the only one that ever gets a change of scenery."

It was the Southern humorist Lewis Grizzard, however, who popularized the saying. The expression became a favorite not only of Randall but also of NFL head coach Buddy Ryan and President Ronald Reagan. What it meant was "If you're not in first position, you're looking at the *behind* of the person who *is* in first."[1] As it happened, Randall Lolley knew few times during his early years and later ministry when he was not in "first position." When in 1925 the widowed Roscoe Lolley married Mary Nunnelee, William Randall arrived as their first son. Six years later, with the birth of second son Tom, Randall functioned both as "big brother" and exemplar. In many ways Tom would look up to his older sibling and follow in his footsteps.

Still, Randall would be the family pacesetter. Throughout grade school and high school in his hometown of Samson, Alabama, he finished every year at the head of his class. It was as a stand-out performer for the Samson High School baseball team that he first earned his nickname "Lightnin' Lolley." Thereafter, at Howard College (later Samford University) he excelled in every subject, graduating with high honors.

---

1. Barry Popik, "If you're not the lead dog, the view never changes," *The Big Apple*, December 4, 2010, www.barrypopik.com/index.php/new_york_city/entry/if_youre_not_the_lead_dog_the_view_never_changes.

In the mid-1950s, in pursuit of his first two graduate degrees (BD and ThM) at the fledgling Southeastern Seminary, Randall achieved a perfect 4.0 grade point average. Only temporarily did he "look at the behind" of anyone who was his superior, as for two years following seminary graduation he served Dr. Claud B. Bowen in Greensboro as a pastoral assistant.

During autumn 1962, and in conjunction with his completion of his doctoral degree, Randall was invited to lead Winston-Salem's First Baptist Church.[2] This would be the initial of three North Carolina "tall steeple" First Baptist churches that he pastored during the following thirty-four years, punctuated near the midpoint by his fourteen-year presidency of his alma mater Southeastern.

Following his eventual 1996 retirement from the Greensboro congregation, Randall went on to serve a dozen congregations short-term, as senior pastor *ad interim.* Only in one of the churches did he confess to feeling outshone—by a charismatic music minister and composer who, he observed, was virtually idolized by the congregation.

This left Randall unfulfilled, for (after all), "Unless you're the lead dog, the scenery never changes." However coarse, the cliché seemed to befit his unique sense of calling. Richly and uniquely gifted from birth, he never regarded his accustomed first-place position in life and ministry as a status he had merited, but rather as a stewardship granted to him by the grace of God.

In the familiar parable of the five talents (Matt 25:14-30, NRSV), Jesus characterizes an unnamed man who sets out on a journey of uncertain duration and who commits his resources into the hands of three servants, presumably anticipating their faithful stewardship during his absence. The man's apportionment of the resources is curious, for to one servant he presents five talents, to a second he grants only two, and to a third servant he gives merely a single talent.

---

2. His Winston-Salem music minister Fred Kelly recalled that some people back at Greensboro had anticipated that their popular assistant pastor would return, following completion of doctoral studies, to succeed a retiring Claud Bowen as senior pastor. The latter, however, frustrated the scenario by remaining at his post for another decade.

The first two servants reward their master's trust by deploying his resources in some unspecified "trade," and in the process they double his investment. The third servant, meanwhile, fearful of failure and resentful of an overlord who seems invariably to enjoy undeserved profit, hides the single talent away as he awaits his master's homecoming.

After "a long time," the man returns from his trip and sets about settling accounts with his servants. The first two, having invested wisely, return the proceeds to their master. He in turn promises them—irrespective of the amount of the original investment and the subsequent return—positions of greater responsibility, along with concomitant "joy." From the hapless third servant, who makes lame excuses for his poor stewardship, the master snatches away the single, uninvested talent and awards it to the first servant—who at that point oversees a grand total of eleven talents.

The third servant's faithlessness aside, there is much in the parable that connotes unfairness from a conventional, human point of view. Luke's telling of a similar story (the parable of the ten pounds in Luke 19:11-27, NRSV) hints at that very opinion from a group of "bystanders." The bystanders observe the action of a nobleman who journeys to a distant country to receive "royal power" and then returns home to judge the faithfulness of ten of his servants during his absence.

From one of the servants, a faithless slave who confesses that he secreted away his pound in a piece of cloth, the nobleman removes the pound and awards the money to a servant who already has in his possession ten pounds—more than any other servant in the parable. At this the bystanders vehemently protest: "Sir, he already has ten!" (v. 25, NIV).

The nobleman in Luke's parable makes no apologies: "I tell you, to all those who have, more will be given; but from those who have nothing, even what they have will be taken away" (v. 26, NRSV). The returning nobleman, in the opinion of commentators, represents Jesus at his Second Coming; and the point of the parable is not an admission of unfairness in the assignment of resources and the presentation of rewards but rather an affirmation of the Lord's sovereign prerogative in gifting his people and in responding to their faithfulness or lack thereof.

Throughout Randall Lolley's life and ministry career, he unquestionably displayed the unique giftedness of a "ten-talented servant" of his Lord. From birth, he was (to use an incongruous metaphor that he applied to others) "bright as a briar."[3] Through his formative years and chapters of education, he was a league leader academically, athletically, and socially.

Across his ministry career, he had countless friends and few known enemies (at least until denominational strife engulfed Southeastern Seminary). Randall's personality was engaging, welcoming, inviting, encouraging, affirming, and memorably warm. He rarely forgot names or personal information. (Even if he didn't remember certain details, he had a gift for making people assume he did.)

Throughout his career in church and academia, Randall acquitted himself as both pastor-scholar and denominational statesman. His preaching, teaching, counseling, and administrative skills became legendary with his observers. The epitome of a "Renaissance man," he could do everything, it seemed, except *sing* (his brother Tom was the singer). Apart from that, he was, in the view of many, "the complete package"—prophet, priest, and wise administrator. Regarding personal, professional, and ministerial achievement, his record throughout his productive life was practically unmatched. A contributing factor, aside from his natural and spiritual giftedness, was an undeniable measure of "luck." Tom Lolley said it well, as he often quipped, "Randall could fall into a cesspool and come out smelling like a rose!"

One example of what might be termed "good luck" would be the circumstances surrounding Randall's move from his happy and fruitful twelve-year local church pastorate in Winston-Salem to the presidency of one of his denomination's half-dozen seminaries. In *Servant Songs: Reflections on the History and Mission of Southeastern Baptist Theological Seminary, 1950–1988*, he recalled how the transition took place:

---

3. See Appendix A: Lolleyisms: A Glossary.

> The presidential search committee worked for months before they contacted me in mid-March 1974. Claud Bowen, chairman of the trustees and chairman of the search committee, called to request a very preliminary meeting with me. In early April they invited me to meet again. Lou and I attended despite the fact that we were leaving almost immediately to lead a tour to Europe and the Holy Land.

Describing a sequence of meetings (faculty, administration, students) that he ultimately advised prior to the issuance and acceptance of any formal invitation to become the new SEBTS president, Randall referenced a letter from "the newly elected chairman of trustees Carl Hudson," which reached him while he and Mrs. Lolley were in Jerusalem:

> I opened that letter while standing at a spot near our hotel, where the Kidron Valley borders a grove of old olive trees that marks the Garden of Gethsemane. As I read the chairman's letter outlining the substance of the three meetings I had suggested, something inside me made a Gethsemane commitment: "Thy will be done."[4]

Not to be overlooked is the fact that the chairman of the presidential search committee and the (first-named) chairman of seminary trustees were the same person: Claud B. Bowen. It was the same Dr. Bowen who had in 1958 invited the newly degreed Randall Lolley to join his church staff. Their friendship continued through the ensuing years, and Bowen's admiration of Randall Lolley was apparent.[5]

Fourteen years later, Randall would—in his words—step aside from his seminary presidency "with no place to go." However, when he and Lou departed "Old Wake Forest" and vacated the presidential

---

4. Bland, ed., *Servant Songs*, ch. 2, "Years of Pleasure and Pain: 1974–1988," 32.

5. Neither Randall nor I would conclude that this concurrence of people and circumstances was merely a matter of luck. The "will" that Randall had invited God to perform as part of a "Gethsemane commitment" is summed up in the William Cowper (1731–1800) lyric: "God moves in a mysterious way His wonders to perform."

residence on July 31, 1988, the pastorate of nearby Raleigh's First Baptist Church awaited him the very next day. And when, after a year and a half, he concluded that he had made a precipitous and uncomfortable move to a church community with too many wounded former colleagues in its membership, Dr. Bowen's old church back in Greensboro was delighted to receive him.[6]

Returning to church pastorates after a decade and a half of leading an institution of higher education reminded Randall of similarities and differences between the two forms of leadership. Functioning as "lead dog" in a seminary setting called, in his thinking, for an egalitarian collegiality not typical in most multi-staff local churches:

> I came to the presidency committed to a participatory administrative style. We inaugurated a tailored form of Peter Drucker's "management by objectives." Happily, my concepts of shared governance fit very well with the standards of Southeastern's accrediting agencies. In our administration trustees, administration, faculty, students, and alumni all had clear roles . . . .
>
> I knew when it came to administration the buck stopped with the president. Yet I sought throughout to keep a pastoral perspective in my presidency . . . .[7]

On the other hand, Randall discovered that authentic "shared governance" as a model for church pastoral leadership worked better in some settings than in others. Returning in early 1990 to the Greensboro church, which he described as a "pastor-led" as opposed to a "lay-led" congregation, he encountered a community that, following the termination of its previous pastor, required compassionate but direct and intentional guidance from one who was comfortable with the role of "lead dog."

Through the years, observing him most closely and understanding him most clearly may have been the members of his several

6. This transition is detailed in chapter 1 above.

7. Bland, ed., *Servant Songs*, ch. 2, "Years of Pleasure and Pain: 1974–1988," 33–34.

pastoral staffs. At Greensboro's First Baptist there awaited a ministerial staff component with several vacancies, which the congregation had anticipated its next senior minister would fill. Church music and Christian education continued to be led by long-tenured staff, but the church needed new leadership in the vital areas of youth, children's ministry, recreation, and administration. Randall encouraged the congregation to elect search committees, but he also responded to the perceived need of the flock to honor their shepherd's sense of where to look and whom to call. As a consequence, new staff choices were made and were typically his own, even as they were happily endorsed by committees and congregants who trusted his instincts.

Basically, Randall evinced a flexibility in leadership style, asserting himself and his expertise as much as necessary, all the while accommodating the opinions and sensibilities of valued staff colleagues and other church members to the fullest practical extent.

Members of the Greensboro staff who greeted him in 1990 or joined him soon thereafter reflected on what distinguished Randall Lolley's leadership. Regardless of the circumstances under which they were called, they agreed that he sought to relate less as a boss or a chief executive officer and more as a friend and ministry collaborator. Inter-office memos were generally headed "Dear colleagues," and usually they were signed, "Thanks for your partnership in the task."

Church staff appreciated the liberty he gave them to conceptualize and carry out their separate ministries according to their own studied judgment. Recalled Ben Vogler, a youth minister whom Randall had first observed in Raleigh and subsequently lured to Greensboro, "Randall was comfortable in his own skin and believed in his convictions. [But] he allowed his staff to be leaders as well, and was not threatened by differing opinions. This empowered his staff and endeared us to him."

Did Randall ever censure or correct staff members or their performance? Memories of the Greensboro contingent varied, but some pointed to his gift for simultaneously cajoling and comforting. "He could call you out and pat you on the back at the same time," remembered Joye Brannon, a music minister who was in place before he arrived. On the other hand, recreation minister Harry Thetford, a layperson who had come reluctantly out of retirement from a managerial position, said, "He treated staff members as equals and solicited our advice; he never criticized." Nevertheless, countered Ben Vogler,

> You did not want to be on the receiving end of his disappointment. There is no one who could "chew you out" better than Randall Lolley. He would say things like, "Sloppy for Jesus is still sloppy!" The difference in his correction is that it was just that—correction. He was not demeaning you, but rather pointing you in the right direction so that you might be successful and better.

Perhaps the single characteristic of Randall Lolley's leadership most frequently cited by his Greensboro staff was a classic pastoral virtue: listening. He was attentive, empathetic, and focused on people in his presence. His pastoral administrative assistant Jo Covert, whom he named to her post from a general church secretarial position, observed, "Often, due to tight schedules, some ministers would not take the time to listen to other people." By contrast, "Dr. Lolley was a good listener" who could discern people's thoughts even as he carefully heard and weighed their words.

In the early 1990s, Greensboro's personnel committee charged the church's pastor with conducting annual staff evaluations. Randall accepted the responsibility with maximum seriousness, but he sought to reduce any anxiety that the exercise might arouse in individual staff ministers. His practice involved an invitation to lunch, followed by a car ride to a quiet setting (e.g., a city park) and then a guided conversation about past experiences and achievements, plus future plans and dreams.

"He always scored me higher than I did myself," remembered one staffer, who referred to the personnel committee evaluation form. The comment acknowledged the pastor's penchant for encouraging healthy self-criticism in the context of non-threatening supervision.

I came to the position of general associate pastor midway through Randall's six-year Greensboro pastorate and was struck by the reality of a busy and productive senior pastor who nevertheless found time to invest in the orientation, development, and direction of a new staff member. Every ride in the boss's gray Chevrolet Caprice (or later, a pre-owned gray Volvo) became an occasion for friendly conversation, ministry planning and evaluation, and mentoring with regard to the nature and importance of pastoral ministry.

Randall Lolley was a materially well-to-do church minister. Sound financial advice, which came to him initially and particularly during his Winston-Salem days, had produced investment strategies yielding a measure of wealth, over which he proved a consistently good and faithful steward. Among his stewardships were several residential properties, one of which was a wilderness cabin in rural Valle Crucis ("Vale of the Cross") in northwestern North Carolina.

In fit weather, Randall and Lou made the old log house available not only to themselves but also to former seminary colleagues for "Yellow Ribbon" reunions and to church staff for weekend getaways and individual retreats. As summer gave way to autumn, or winter to spring, there was always the necessity of "winterizing" or "de-winterizing" the cabin.

On one memorable occasion, I accompanied Randall from Greensboro eastward to "Old Wake Forest," to the home of Dr. Morris Ashcraft, to fetch a platform rocking chair on loan to the retired seminary dean; and then westward to Valle Crucis to deliver the chair and "de-winterize" the cabin. Completing the chore, Randall invited me to join him in relaxing on the front porch. There we sat and enjoyed the comparative silence of surrounding nature, while I spoke of my happiness in coming to the Greensboro position following an unhappy conclusion to a previous church ministry.

Randall listened attentively and then reflected on his own pain in parting from his "dream job" as head of a theological seminary, coupled with his embrace of the renewed challenge of leading local church congregations. I recall that it was a "forgetting those things which are past, and reaching forth unto those things which lie ahead" (Phil 3:13-14) moment, which Randall utilized to counsel the reality that God doesn't always call his servants to move "up." Occasionally he calls people "apart" or even "down" from positions they once had prized. Whatever direction it might take, the authentic calling of God is ever what the Apostle Paul described: "the prize of the heavenly call of God in Christ Jesus" (v. 14, NRSV).

Held in close tension with his self-understanding as "lead dog" was a pronounced egalitarianism in his relationships with church staff. Recalling that Randall had led the Personnel Committee in Greensboro to change staff-level job titles from the traditional "minister of education, minister of music" to "associate pastor with education, associate pastor with music, etc.," former youth minister Ben Vogler explained, "It was because he considered us all to be colleagues."

Ben expanded, "Youth ministers are often considered ministers in the making. Randall elevated my title to associate pastor with youth. This gave me a seat at the table. This opened the door for me to perform sacred rituals (baptism, communion), which was not the norm for youth ministers. He allowed my ministry to grow because he viewed me as a minister."

Three decades earlier, Randall had been instrumental in building "from scratch" a staff in Winston-Salem, whose First Baptist Church in 1962 had experienced the departure of most of its paid leadership. An early recruit was minister of activities Marshall Price, a former FBC member who had moved to Texas to study at Southwestern Seminary, and who there had encountered Randall Lolley when both were serving staff positions at Fort Worth's Broadway Baptist Church. Marshall and his wife babysat Pam and Charlotte Lolley, so the two families became friends.

While few knew it by that name, "networking" existed in the 1960s. During summer conferences at the North Carolina Baptist State Convention's "Assembly by the Sea" at Ft. Caswell, Marshall encountered Fred Kelly, a church musician serving in Virginia. As the Winston-Salem congregation was at that moment searching for a minister of music, Marshall recommended Fred to Randall.

Marshall and Fred agreed that they never knew a pastor who was as "people-forward" or "person-centered" as Randall Lolley. Echoing the opinion of his later church staffs, Marshall pointed to Randall's reputation as a good listener. "He could talk to anyone. And when he was talking with *you*, you were the only one present in the conversation."

Rather than invite Fred to Winston-Salem for an exploratory conversation, Randall drove to Virginia to meet his prospective musician at that state's summer assembly, Eagle Eyrie. There they shared a dorm room, where Randall occupied the top level of a tri-level bunk bed opposite that of Fred. "We talked until late in the evening of his dream for music ministry in Winston-Salem," Fred said. "Then he reached across the way, took me by the hand, and prayed for God's will."

The result was a music ministry that eventually eclipsed Randall's own tenure, as Fred continued in the Winston-Salem post until 1975. During the intervening years, he and Marshall Price witnessed the coalescence of a staff that Lou Lolley said her husband came to regard as his finest achievement while pastoring their "Camelot" congregation.

"It took three or four years to pull us all together," Fred remembered, but once the task was complete, "together" became the distinguishing word. "Randall wanted us to be friends. He wanted us to have a sense of our own calling. He wanted collegiality. He wanted for us to reach decisions together. He wanted us to spend time together."

Fred continued, "Above all, he wanted us—all together—to be ministers to the whole church, regardless of our areas of specialization." To that end, Randall recommended to the congregation that every minister on staff, from Christian education to music, from recreation to children's ministry, be ordained, set apart, and formally recognized as church ministers from within their own areas of concentration.

It was one-third of the way through Randall's Winston-Salem pastorate when a joint service was celebrated, with Fred's preacher-father Fred L. Kelly Sr. bringing the ordination sermon. The product of the evening was more than a stack of certificates attaching the label "Reverend" to the names of half a dozen church staff members. Much more than that, it was their sense—in the recollection of Marshall Price—that they were henceforth to be regarded as ministers in their own right, "free to do our thing," but in covenant with one another to work together for the good of the congregation and the advancement of the kingdom of God. It all worked so well, Marshall observed, that nearby congregations and their ministers began to notice and to invite Randall and the staff to visit their neighboring churches and describe the secret of their own success.

Greensboro's associate pastor with children Sandra Canipe, speaking for the staff that greeted Randall in 1990, observed, "We didn't know how to play until Randall Lolley came." If a deacons versus staff basketball game was announced, Randall—although he might be the shortest player—would show up in trademark striped shorts and serve as captain of the team. When staff entertained church volunteers at their annual appreciation banquet, their pastor would illustrate leadership by dressing as Captain Kirk and guiding the balance of his Star Trek crew along a bumpy ride through an intergalactic meteorite shower.

"Of course he wanted to be front and center," allowed recreation minister Harry Thetford, "but he'd grab everybody else and pull them in." Moreover, "He'd put up with anything. If you needed him in the dunking booth, he'd suit up and take it like a champ."

There were predictable payoffs for a pastor with such predilections and sensibilities. Winston-Salem's Marshall Price opined, "Everybody liked him. Most pastors get criticized, but not Randall. He wasn't pretentious—what you saw was what you got." Greensboro's Ben Vogler agreed: "He was the same Randall in every setting, the real deal. He was as comfortable and effective in dealing with maintenance staff as with the rest of us."

I observed that in Greensboro nobody lamented Randall's 1996 retirement and departure more than the church's African American custodians. For years thereafter they would recall his tendency to pause in the hallways and inquire of their well-being, visit with them in their break room, or provide opportunities and encouragement. For some he offered supplementary employment in the form of odd jobs around "the Lolley house." For one, who needed an affordable car, he located a suitable "deal" and assisted in the ensuing transaction.

A central distinguishing feature of Randall's leadership, in the memory of every staff member who served with him, was a profound and palpable *pastor's heart.* "I don't necessarily think he was the best preacher I ever heard," said Marshall Price, "but he was certainly the best imaginable pastor. If anybody in the congregation was in a crisis, he would go to their side immediately."

John Setchfield, who served with Randall in Greensboro as associate pastor with Christian education, remarked that he was in the beginning "surprised that a [former] seminary president had such a passion for pastoral care. I recall at a staff meeting, after we had been bantering on about something for a while, that Randall seemed frustrated and spoke of people in the congregation who had real needs. My interpretation was that we should stop wasting time and get through with our planning time so he could see people."

When babies were arriving at the local hospital, Marshall Price recalled that his pastor might actually arrive in advance of the expectant fathers.[8] There were even photographs of a smiling Randall Lolley, sporting a surgical mask, cradling in his arms a newborn, "fresh from God" (in his familiar terminology).

Dr. Billy Summers, who served as organist and music assistant throughout Randall's time in Greensboro, recalled the Saturday evening when his son was born in a local hospital. Dutifully, the organist arrived at First Baptist the following morning to rehearse the choirs and accompany the congregational singing. But his pastor intercepted him in a back hallway, congratulated him on the arrival of a firstborn son, then "told me to leave and get back to the hospital to be with Elaine and Bradley!"

Even more intense, purposeful, and personable was the level of care the pastor provided during times of tragedy and heartbreak. Winston-Salem's Fred Kelly remembered an incident where a family of five were involved in a head-on automobile collision. The mother, father, and one of the three children perished, leaving a boy and a girl as sole survivors.

"Randall was so good with them," Fred observed. "The way he sat with them and held their hands, got them to talk about their shock and grief, while reminding them what wonderful persons they

8. In Greensboro, Randall would often rise from his seat in the hospital waiting area and greet members of his flock as they arrived before dawn to check in for surgery.

were and how important to God. He had a way of making people feel some comfort, no matter how dire their situation."

Did anything about their pastor, team leader, fellow minister, and friend ever produce discomfort, frustration, or displeasure in those who worked most closely with him? "He never irritated me," replied Jo Covert, his administrative assistant in Greensboro. "He was a blessing in my life. I do not recall any frustrations or faults," although "at times, he gave so much of himself [to the congregation] that I became concerned about his health and well-being."

Jo's colleague Ben Vogler offered this observation: "I was endeared to the man, but intimidated by the legend. The deep respect I had for Dr. Lolley often caused me to walk a step or two behind." Ben added that this may have hindered his own communication with his pastor: "I didn't always give him my best, relationally."

Paul Smith, longtime minister of music at First Baptist in Raleigh, confessed, "My only frustration with Randall came about when I was in need of some very necessary information quickly, and not being able to grab hold of his very busy coattail."

Joye Brannon, Randall's "chief musician" in Greensboro, recalled her exasperation during the final eighteen months of his six-year pastorate. "He was determined to preach through the Bible, and I found it hard to plan appropriate music for some of the sermons. 'Just do the best you can,' is all he would say." She added, "I'm not sure it was a weakness or a fault, but he wanted to shy away from administrative or personnel matters, if possible."

Her colleague Harry Thetford, a retired layman who was called to the church's recreation department early in Randall's ministry, provided an illustration. Randall "seemingly absolved himself of my selection process, based upon [a fellow staff member's] recommendation." Harry recalled that, following the staff member's casual mention of the possibility of Harry's employment, Harry and his wife departed for a trip out of state.

Upon their return to Greensboro and FBC, Harry found himself "showered with a smorgasbord of surprised congratulations and bewildered wonderment" from friends. "Rank and file church members peppered [me] with ministry questions and planning ideas. The pastor's secretary asked when might the church recreation calendar be ready!"

Unknown to Harry, his extended trip had afforded his recommender and soon-to-be fellow staffer the opportunity to shepherd his proposal through the personnel committee, the deacons, and the church. Throughout the process, Randall had apparently stood back and provided simple acquiescence. Still there emerged a happy result, as "Dr. Lolley's subtle and effective leadership gave me confidence that I could—and should—serve as director of church recreation and activities. Beyond that, he convinced other staff members and church parishioners that the job was in good hands."

Randall's earlier recreation minister, Winston-Salem's Marshall Price, noted that his boss, who "knew everything that was going on" and got around to every part of the church building, didn't like Marshall's craft room. "He half-heartedly joked that it was the worst-looking room he'd ever seen! We disagreed on the point of his personal fastidiousness. For his part, he kept a neat office, and didn't seem to appreciate my 'creative clutter'!"

Marshall pointed to an otherwise positive attribute that could become a "negative" in his pastor's case. In any two-way conversation, Randall was strongly focused on the other person. "You were the only person in the room," Marshall said. But here was a quality that made his pastor a bad driver. "He was always turning around and looking in the back seat in order to focus on some person he was talking to."

Arriving in Winston-Salem in 1962, Randall encountered a congregation with an inordinate number of corporate, business, and community professionals in positions of church lay leadership. The chairman of R. J. Reynolds was a deacon and chair of the finance committee, while others represented companies such as Hanes Hosiery, Integon, and Atlas Supply. Their pastor, still a young man with enormous vision and concrete plans for the future of First Baptist, had to balance his dreams and ideals alongside the professed practicalities that were urged by highly influential advisers.

Sometimes Randall found himself in an awkward position. When in the late 1960s Milwaukee's Miller Brewing Company located a manufacturing plant in Winston-Salem, the company's local "city manager," a Christian and a Baptist, brought his family and joined First Baptist Church. His son and daughter became members of Fred Kelly's youth choir.

Meanwhile, Miller's general manager, an Episcopalian, purchased a house on Greenbrier Road, next door to the Lolleys. He and Randall became friendly neighbors and eventually confidantes, as the "G.M." would occasionally turn to his pastor-neighbor for advice.

When construction of the new brewery was complete and a dedication ceremony was planned, the city manager extended his boss's invitation to Randall to bring a prayer of invocation. Fred Kelly recalled that Randall—a traditional Baptist teetotaler—agreed but limited the substance of his prayer to a petition for the welfare of those who would make their living from the new employment opportunity.

Fred said the episode generated little or no conversation within First Baptist Church. But when he and Randall later boarded the "Convention Plane"[9] to attend the 1970 Southern Baptist Convention in Denver, Colorado, another pastor (critical of Randall) distributed the prayer to fellow passengers traveling to the meeting. The "brewery prayer" and the controversy that followed became "the stuff of legend" among those who would discuss Randall Lolley in years to come.[10]

Randall did not, however, always accede. I recall, when serving with Randall in Greensboro, the occasion when local pastors and pastoral care ministers were summoned to a breakfast meeting at the City Club. The invitation was issued by the head of a local funeral home, a man who had been prominent in area politics and civic affairs and who was a longtime member and lay leader at First Baptist Church. Nobody understood the agenda for the gathering, but what

9. An aircraft was chartered each June by Marse Grant, editor of the *Biblical Recorder*, the official newspaper of North Carolina Baptists.

10. I recall relating the "brewery prayer" controversy at a weekly breakfast gathering of Greensboro ministers who labeled themselves "The Downtown Six" (Baptist, Methodist, Lutheran, Presbyterian, Episcopalian, and Catholic). All seemed perplexed.

transpired was an offer to begin including honoraria for presiding ministers in the cost to a bereft family of a total funeral "package."

To the dismay of many (myself included), Randall was first on his feet during the ensuing question-and-answer time, protesting that he had never accepted pay from grieving families and did not intend to begin the practice! The stunned funeral director listened politely, nodded, and summarily dismissed the meeting without further discussion.

Along the way of his three career pastorates, Randall Lolley brought his staffs and congregations not only the occasional unorthodox gesture but also competent leadership, compassionate pastoral care, quality preaching and teaching, and (for want of a better term) *fun.* Marshall Price recalled a "great seamstress" in Winston-Salem who fashioned for her pastor the signature striped shorts that he would thereafter don for a variety of church recreational activities. On the first Sunday following his receipt of the gift, he acknowledged the donor by wearing the shorts over his trousers as he mounted the platform to preach.

In the early 1990s, the ponytail joined the earlier crew cut, the Ivy League, and the Afro as optional male hair fashion. One Wednesday evening in Greensboro, Randall entered the fellowship hall and mounted a portable dais to update the important announcements and pray thanksgiving for the midweek meal. Perched atop his head was a baseball cap, to the back of which was attached a bushy ponytail. The accessory perfectly matched the pastor's actual salt-and-pepper gray hair, causing some to think he had joined the latest fad.

Much of his humor was self-deprecatory. His Greensboro organist Billy Summers recalled that, on the occasion of his first baptism as pastor of the congregation, he entered the water only to discover a leak in his rubber "waders." Appearing nonplussed as the waders filled with water, he proceeded with the solemn rite but then had to be lifted from the baptistery by an attending deacon. There was still a sermon to be preached, so "Randall came to the pulpit smiling but soaking wet," Billy said.

Churches and pastors respected sacred spaces, but Billy's colleague Ben Vogler remembered a time when Randall purchased watermelons for a deacon gathering and cooled them by carrying them into the baptistery and covering them with ice.

On one occasion, Randall telephoned Ben and invited him to lunch at "a special place." The invitee, who had dressed in coat and tie in anticipation, was surprised when his pastor came to fetch him, attired in sports shirt and khakis. Their destination, as it happened, was the basement of Greensboro's Worldwide House of Prayer for All People, where "soul food" (chitterlings and Randall's favorite fried Spam included) was on the menu.

Raleigh FBC's Paul Smith described the single most humorous thing that Randall did during his brief pastorate there. In an image reminiscent of the pastor's willingness to fulfill the role of pastor/team player, Paul recalled, "During the 'Midwinter Banquet' in our church, the Social Committee asked all the male church staff to honor the banquet theme of 'Beach Retreat' and dress in a grass skirt and sing the Beach Boys song 'Kokomo' with appropriate gyrations. Randall was a hit!"

Randall shared funny stories about himself and also about his brother Tom. As an "area missionary" sharing communication between state Baptist headquarters in Raleigh and far-western North Carolina associations and churches, Tom Lolley would occasionally overnight with Randall and Lou in Greensboro. "He'd set up in our guest bedroom," Randall said, "with his own portable, battery-powered TV and a big bag of pork skins." On one occasion Tom brought along a half-eaten order of chicken gizzards, which had become almost too tough to chew. "As I sat there and watched him bite down and jerk back and forth—first I'd bet on Tom, and then I'd bet on the gizzard!"

Marshall Price and Fred Kelly both related the Sunday in Winston-Salem when a family of five, surnamed Peters, presented themselves for church membership. After introducing the husband and father and noting his occupation, Randall turned to the mother and observed she had the most important work of all, "staying home and raising three little Pe— . . . ." The pastor caught himself just in time, but Fred found it nearly impossible to keep a straight face before the congregation. "From that day on, I came off the platform after the anthem and sat on the front row."

Jo Covert, the pastor's administrative assistant whom Randall consistently and appreciatively acknowledged in introductions to bound copies of sermons, noted a humorous aspect of the service she rendered to her boss in Greensboro. "Every morning he would go get a sausage biscuit and coffee. On a napkin or placemat, he would jot down notes of things he wanted me to do that day. When I arrived at 9 a.m., he would already be in his office and would have the greasy napkin or placemat on my desk, instructing me of my first assignments for that day."

Fred Kelly said he "never knew of a smarter person, but you'd think he was just another guy from up the street." That, in many ways, seemed to be the persona that Randall Lolley wanted to present.

Fred mentioned a badly worn pair of work boots, which Randall later displayed in the president's office at Southeastern Seminary and after that in the pastor's office at the First Baptist Church of Greensboro. The backstory, as Fred related it, involved a homeless man who appeared at Randall's office at FBC in Winston-Salem. Randall listened to the man's story, felt unusual compassion for him, and drove him to a local shoe store.

Having fitted him in new footwear and paid the price of the shoes, he asked his homeless friend if he might keep the worn-out boots. The man consented, and Randall returned the shoes to his office, where he displayed them atop a bookshelf, with nothing to identify them or describe their significance. If questioned, however, he would explain that the old boots were there to remind him—and never let him forget—that not everybody was as fortunate as he knew himself to be.

Class of One

"That ain't no ordinary preacher."[1]

This assessment, offered by a Methodist minister upon hearing Randall Lolley for the first time, may not have been shared by Randall himself. In the introduction to a retrospective prepared near the conclusion of six decades of preaching ministry, Randall observed, "Every preacher/pastor perhaps at times has thought about their preaching over the years. I certainly have. In some ways, I think I might have been my own worst critic."[2]

Describing his first sermon as an "attempt," delivered a year after his high school graduation in Samson, Alabama, Randall went on to outline three distinct phases or transitions that had marked his subsequent career as a proclaimer. While all had connections to lessons learned as a seminary student, they nevertheless were precipitated by actual pulpit experience along the way.

> I had good teachers of homiletics but learned early on that one cannot preach by attending lectures and classes or by reading books. Preaching is an art and a science that requires "on the job training." One has to do it in order to learn how to do it. Of course, others can help us improve, enrich, and expand our preaching experiences, but nothing is more important than having opportunities to preach week after week in a local church and draw from the many "coaches" in the congregation.

Randall added that during his "early years" his focus was on what would homiletically be described as "topical preaching." Utilizing an

---

1. Quoted by Michael Blackwell (see chapter 14 below, Mirrors on the Man).

2. Randall Lolley, "If I Had My Preaching Ministry to Do Over," undated essay prepared for an uncertain occasion.

approach associated with theologian Karl Barth—who was said to have recommended preaching "with the Bible in one hand and the daily newspaper in the other"—Randall said he "carefully absorbed current events, the big stories in the media, and almost always got around to addressing them in my sermons, hopefully, in some interesting and practical ways." While "calling to task the high and mighty as well as the people in the pews," he also insisted that he was "never partisan."

For an unspecified "period" of years to follow, Randall shifted his approach. He became a "lectionary preacher." Cognizant of the advantages typically associated with the method, he appreciated its tendency to "expand the scope of preaching, utilizing less of a canon within the canon to include the entire biblical preaching landscape from Genesis to Revelation."

However, a downside to lectionary preaching occurred to him late in his career, and that was "the advent of the internet and the vast resources of the [worldwide] web." Identifying a temptation that could induce young preachers to prepare their sermons "on the cheap," he noted,

> With a few strikes of a key one can manufacture a sermon off the research and labor of others. This leads to many a "Saturday night special" which is more a product of the hand than the heart. I have found that one must actually work on preparing a sermon in order to possess that sermon and more importantly, to have the sermon possess her or him.

Whether and when such a possibility prompted Randall to transition to a third preaching model isn't known. But he wrote, "More recently, I have become more and more an 'expository' preacher. By this, I mean instead of trying to deal with topics out of the news, I read and study more the Scriptures in order to find the good news there and expound that message while applying that 'good news' to life."[3]

---

3. Ironically, in his use of the term "expository," Randall associated his practice more with that of conservative evangelicalism than the "moderating

Randall added that through all of his years of ministry he had been aided by the challenge of preparing and delivering preaching in a series of messages, which he termed "sequential sermons." While sometimes such a sequence would entail "two or three or more" sermons, he recalled that "[o]n one occasion, in a two-year period, I sought to preach/teach a sermon from each of the sixty-six books of the Bible."

Earlier, near the midpoint of his climactic career pastorate in Greensboro, he had crafted and delivered a sixteen-part series based on the multiple affirmations of the traditional Apostles' Creed. As with other "sequential sermons" that he delivered from that venerable pulpit, the Apostles' Creed series was printed and bound in-house and then made available to members of the congregation.[4]

Randall's later, fifty-eight-part through-the-Bible series was likewise first printed and distributed in-house and eventually issued in published book form.[5] In his preface to the book he noted, "The sermons have been printed as they were preached over a period of one and a half years. I acknowledge a large debt to Jo Covert, my able administrative assistant, for her help in producing the manuscripts from my handwritten notes."

Upstairs in his home at The Cypress, a retirement community in north Raleigh, remains the impressive personal library of W. Randall Lolley. The room is laden with valuable books retained from his years of ministry, hundreds of souvenirs and artifacts from his world travels, photographs of himself and Lou with people significant to their lifelong journey, plus scores of plaques, framed documents, earned and honorary degrees, and awards and other recognitions.

To one side of the room is a low, sagging bookshelf, weighed down by thirty-six black, ring-bound volumes of sermons. There is no obvious order to the collection, except that "sequential sermons" are placed together in the first two volumes, while individual messages

---

conservative" posture he ultimately applied to himself. See Appendix B: Rolesville Retrospective.

4. This publication was titled "Building on Bedrock: *Beliefs to Withstand Every Wind of Doctrine.*"

5. *Journey with Me* (Macon, GA: Nurturing Faith, Inc., 2015).

appear more or less chronologically, left to right, volume 3 to volume 36, from Randall's earlier preaching in Winston-Salem to his later preaching in Greensboro.

Immediately apparent is that virtually all of the sermons exist as his original handwritten notes. More than a set of notes, however, each sermon comprises lengthy sequences of sentences, separated one from the other by simple hash marks. While most of the sentences could have served as sound bites—each bearing its own concise message—they do not seem to be discrete talking points for the preacher to expound upon extemporaneously. Rather the sentences flow smoothly and logically, one to the next, from the sermon's introduction to its conclusion, usually suggesting a discernible outline in the mind of the preacher. Rarely do the individual sentences in Randall's handwritten notes form larger paragraphs. Paragraphs do appear in later, printed and bound collections, but these are the work of an editing process.[6]

An interesting exception appears in the *Building on Bedrock* collection.[7] All of the sermons there appear to have been edited—many of them featuring long paragraphs of up to a dozen sentences—except for one. That single sermon was titled "I Believe in the Forgiveness of Sins," and it is a credible example of the expository precision, rhetorical uniqueness, and creative use of imagination with which Randall approached the pulpit task during the concluding years of his formal, vocational pastoral ministry.

During the early 1990s, Sunday mornings at FBC Greensboro would usually find the church's pastor in his office, sitting on one of two opposing love seats before the fireplace. He would be engaged in conversation with a church leader, staff minister, or other member of the congregation. On his desk nearby would be his New International Version (NIV) preaching Bible, with the 5-by-8-inch separate leaves of his handwritten sermon neatly tucked within.

---

6. Randall worked with his administrative assistant Jo Covert to edit the printed series in Greensboro, while the *Journey with Me* sermons were edited by Tony Cartledge.

7. Preached in Greensboro between January and June 1994.

Randall would have completed the sermon earlier in the week, either in his handsome study in the furnished attic of his West Market Street home or occasionally at the simple writing desk in the loft of his rustic cabin at Valle Crucis, near Boone. Come Sunday morning he would have risen before daylight to "ponder" the finished product over coffee at a local fast-food restaurant.

Later, arriving at the church building on West Friendly Avenue, Randall was at the complete pastoral disposal of whoever wished to confer with him, whether by appointment or by casual drop-in to his study. His focus was always on the person in his purview. The morning sermon firmly committed to his head and his heart, he was never distracted by the necessity of last-minute "cramming" or adding "final touches."

Eleven o'clock in the expansive sanctuary witnessed a traditional processional of pastor and participating staff ministers, as they followed the church choir into the chancel and located their seats among five ornate, upholstered chairs. Centered on the platform was a heavy piece of pulpit furniture (architecturally a *sedilia* but affectionately nicknamed the "three-seater").

Randall scrupulously avoided taking the middle seat. He also avoided the appearance of "leading" the service, normally first arising at the midpoint to deliver his pastoral prayer. Thereafter he would defer to a fellow staff minister for the reading of the sermon text, after which he would return to the pulpit.

Apparent in the dress and demeanor of a famously casual man was a Sunday morning formality. While Randall rarely robed himself for his preaching—preferring a business suit, tie, and white dress shirt—nevertheless his attire was impeccably tasteful, calling to mind the respect he held for the occasion and for the task.

The "Pulpit Bible" on the table below him already having been turned to his sermon text, he further underscored the biblical nature of his speaking by opening his personal NIV and placing it to the top left of the pulpit, visible to the congregation. Only occasionally were his opening words light, winsome, colloquial, or even transitional, as he sought to maintain the gravity and unity of his message with that of the verses that had just been read.

In the case of the *Building on Bedrock* message referenced above, Randall began by repeating the sermon title, which formed not only a word of introduction but, more importantly, a declaration of personal conviction: "I believe in the forgiveness of sins!"

Such was the first complete paragraph—a single sentence. Likewise the second paragraph: "To get a vivid picture of precisely what that means, lend me your imagination and journey with me for a while."

Randall's "journey" thus began with a 600-word present-tense narrative based on the Luke 23:18-25 text (the release of Barabbas), before segueing into a discernible but undistracting two-part sermonic outline. In fact, in the transition that followed the narrative, *outline* is the word he employed:

> Right here, in this episode from our New Testament, the Gospel—the Good News of God in Jesus Christ—is being produced! If the New Testament has an engine room, this is it.
>
> Here clearly outlined are the issues to be included in proclaiming that Gospel in our generation.

The first "issue" Randall took up was what he termed "the heart of the matter." Proceeding theologically to address the atonement for sin in terms traditionally called "substitutionary," he affirmed, "The grace possessed are the guilt possessed set free! That central, rugged, rough-hewed cross was my cross, and your cross, as surely as it was Barabbas's cross."

"But hear this," he prefaced: "They released Barabbas not because he was innocent; they released him in spite of his guilt. Here then is the heart of our Gospel. Observe the stamp Barabbas bears: 'Guilty, yet forgiven!'"

While insisting that human forgiveness hinges entirely upon one person (Christ) taking another person's place on a cross, Randall observed an important ramification of the Lord's atoning action: "Our forgiveness also involves a crucifixion—my crucifixion of me and your crucifixion of you in Christ, discovering that every promise of God comes nailed to a cross. Jesus only told us to take up two things—his yoke and our cross."

Thus forgiveness is at once painful—"It is just as much tied up with our spiritual health as a surgeon's knife is with our physical health"—and creative—"Those forgiven become forgivers. It always brings good out of evil."

The second issue in Randall's underlying "outline" entailed his answers to two obvious questions arising from the central affirmation of the sermon: "What is sin and what is forgiveness?" Referring to various words used in biblical references to the concepts, the preacher produced a comprehensive Greek and Hebrew tour de force.

"Sin" (Gk. *hamartia*), he observed somewhat conventionally, is a "missing of the mark," i.e., "our failure to be what we were meant to be. What we are and what we could be, that is the contradiction which makes us all sinners."

Other biblical words, Randall added, make the same point: "distortion, perversion, rebellion, transgression, falling, lawlessness, ungodliness, and disobedience."

All of the words, he deduced, imply the universality of sin and further suggest the bleak outcome of which the Apostle Paul had expressed certainty: "The wages of sin is death . . ." (Rom 6:23a). "This fact," Randall was quick to add, "makes the biblical reality of forgiveness even more crucial for us."

Happily, "The fact of God's forgiveness is amazingly rich and varied." Pointing to sixteen Old and New Testament words connotative of forgiveness, Randall detailed their variety and comprehensiveness: "to hide, to lift away, to send away, to pay a debt, to wipe off, to abolish (annul), to save, to heal, to loose, to wash, to purify, to take away, to cover over, to make expiation, to justify, to reconcile."

Having already established an image of atonement associated with "substitution," Randall interjected a reference to a broader interpretation of the concept:

> Vincent Taylor, famed New Testament scholar, says there are fourteen strands to describe the atonement of Jesus Christ in the New Testament. What he means is that no one idea is capable of containing the whole truth. It is a massive truth beyond the power of mere mortals to comprehend.

> The many-sidedness of forgiveness pictures the proof that in whatever situation and from wherever a person begins there is a way of forgiveness for that person.

All the same, it is clear from both the beginning and the ending of his message that Randall was personally inclined—and sought to incline his hearers—toward an assurance of a forgiveness wrought of the displacement of a guilty person by an innocent person willing to satisfy the penalty.

Randall moved toward the conclusion of his sermon by recalling the same "guilt possessed" personality and image with which he had begun, bookending the relatively conventional, two-part discourse outlined above. What rendered the sermon *unconventional* was the dramatic flair and rhetorical flourish that he applied to his overall, encapsulating narrative.

"We started out with Barabbas," the preacher reminded his hearers. They would not have forgotten. Using words that would form the title of the later, published version of his through-the-Bible series, Randall had started his sermon by inviting the congregation: "Journey with me . . . lend me your imagination."

It had been a quick journey through territory most listeners had toured before. While making liberal use of imagination, nothing in the story Randall unfolded had been implausible or in conflict with the scriptural narrative. The scene was set in first-century Jerusalem. The occasion was the annual Feast of the Passover, on the eve of the Sabbath. The actors—pilgrims, priests, and prisoners—were the same as those mentioned in the Gospel accounts.

The preacher had proceeded in a rhetorical style typically his own. Paragraphs were short—a sentence or two. Sentences were short, sometimes delivered in a staccato fashion.

"They wait. The long night wears on. It is now past midnight. Street sounds quieten."

Metaphors and other rhetorical devices were profuse. Pilgrims were "religious refugees." They had "spilled over onto the hillside" and "poured into the city." Jerusalem was "a virtual madhouse." Campfires flickered "like so many fireflies in the Judean night."

Meanwhile, temple priests had "[gone] about their duties with a lick, a promise, and a rushed up prayer." Matters of greater urgency had consumed them: "A posse has already gone out. The leaders on this night of infamy will come not from the underworld, but from the temple."

Next Randall had conducted his hearers from the temple to a Roman prison, where *three men* "await the dawn of Friday." While the thoughts of many in the congregation had doubtless moved on to Calvary with its three crosses, their preacher had carefully crafted a reminder that the third cross was not originally intended for its eventual and revered occupant.

> These three are on a death row condemned to die at dawn. . . .
>
> Street sounds quieten a bit, the chants of worshipers hush a little, the silence is disrupted only by the occasional gamut of a rat or the steady drip of condensing moisture off the dungeon ceiling. . . .
>
> A wild dog howls in the distance, the wind whistles through an ancient olive grove on the hillside of Olivet, somewhere a donkey brays. . . .
>
> Still the three men wait, condemned, never to see but one more sunrise. Then it happens.

Now "The silence is split by boisterous sounds." Randall had imagined the acoustic impact of an approaching mob, whose cries "echo through [the] dungeon." *Crucify him! Crucify him! We will take the blood on our hands! We will take the blood on our hands!* As "the doomed men simply listen . . . the dawn creeps ever closer."

> More time passes. Then the clanging of armor announces the approach of the guard. The men in their cells feel their hearts pound, lumps rise in their throats, they grow a bit pale, they bite their lips, perspiration pops out their brows. This is it!
>
> The thief in the left cell is led out to be crucified.
>
> The thief in the right cell is led out to be crucified.
>
> Then the bar in the middle cell is raised. . . .

What the preacher had described as "the most notorious prisoner of them all" was said now to step from his cell into the narrow prison corridor. "Then," said Randall (introducing a name and offering a twist possibly unforeseen), "the guard speaks": "Barabbas, you are free. Some carpenter from Nazareth will die on your cross."

Even had they been distracted by the compelling narrative, the Greensboro congregation suddenly awoke to the central force and focus of their pastor's sermon. "The cross of Christ" did not belong to Christ. Rather it belonged to a man whose name was Barabbas. Barabbas had escaped it only because the Christ had accepted it in his place.

Scripturally, Barabbas's story ends with the accession of the Roman procurator, Pontius Pilate, to the demands of the mob: "He released the man they asked for, the one who had been put in prison for insurrection and murder, and he handed Jesus over as they wished" (Luke 23:25, NRSV). But as his sermon neared its end, and following his two-part exposition of its doctrinal core, Randall returned to his original narrative by implicitly acknowledging that no one could know what became of Barabbas. Still, he ensured that his hearers might identify with the notorious character. Borrowing not from his own imagination but rather from Jewish playwright Harry Denker,[8] the preacher drew a picture of an individual who failed to comprehend the enormity of the favor he had received.

Denker's Barabbas "returns to the robber band to which he once belonged," Randall disclosed.

> They fear him. They think he is a conspirator who is now working with the authorities to give information about the members of the band. Therefore, they reject his return to their ranks.
>
> He is dejected, disillusioned, depressed. He returns to Pilate to ask why he set him free.
>
> Pilate responds, "To keep peace, you do strange things. You crucify prophets, and you let thieves go free."
>
> To which Barabbas replies, "They told me I was free, but I am not free. I am now more tragically bound than before!"

---

8. *Give Us Barabbas*, 1961.

Thus the preacher's message of good news came also as a warning: Christ's "substitutionary atonement" is offered, but it is not guaranteed. In Barabbas's case, "The forgiveness which came at such awesome price on his cross, that Friday, was apparently to no avail for him."

> You see, repentance is the key to getting God's forgiveness and our sins together.
>
> Jesus' original invitation was, "repent and believe the Gospel" (Mark 1:15).
>
> Repentance is sorrow over our previous lives, coupled with a determination to let Jesus Christ do something about them. In short, repentance is our intention to let God help us hit the mark. That is the divine dream for us at creation.

"I believe in the forgiveness of sins," the preacher concluded. "That means Barabbas's sins, my sins, your sins, and the sins of every person in this world who will let Jesus forgive them. Amen."

Chapter 4

Before You Can Preach

"Before you can preach to them, you have to be their pastor."

People "called by God" to Christian ministry in the mid-twentieth century, and in a deep Southern context, uniformly understood that they were "called to preach." This likely was Randall Lolley's initial interpretation. As late as 1959, outlining his decision to return to seminary study following his first post-graduate church position, he had written, "the call to preach is a call to prepare to preach."

Whether it was the early experience he had gained in country churches while studying at Howard College and Southeastern Seminary, the pastoral care training he had received as a seminary student, or his observation of his own pastor and boss in Greensboro that caused him to focus more on *pastoral* ministry is not known. To be sure, First Baptist's Dr. Claud B. Bowen was remembered more for his close personal and spiritual connection with his members than for his preaching.

Whatever the case, by the time of Randall's arrival back in North Carolina following doctoral study in Texas, the chair of deacons at Winston-Salem's First Baptist Church appeared to elevate his new leader's pastoral devotion to the level of his exceptional preaching. "He spoke a few words, then went straight to his work, / Preaching and visiting, and turned with a jerk, / And laying his letters aside of his phone, / Giving a nod, a'visiting he had gone"—so parodied Don Britt at a Sunday school class Christmas dinner.

Thirty-four years later, near the conclusion of his formal, vocational ministry in Greensboro, Randall would deliver a sermon introducing two New Testament letters that the Apostle Paul had written to his younger ministry associate Timothy. "Note that in these letters Paul writes as a pastor," Randall insisted, "not as an itinerant preacher, missionary, or evangelist":

> You see, the pastor is not a pioneer like the itinerant preacher, teacher, missionary, or evangelist. The pastor is a homesteader. The pioneer opens up the frontier. He hacks back the forest, cuts away the underbrush. The homesteader establishes the community—building the houses, churches, schools, and trading posts.
>
> The pastor is a guardian, a conserver of community. Pastors pass on torches. Their work is not as glamorous or as spectacular as the pioneer. But their work is crucial to the Kingdom of God. Without the pastors, the outposts are never established into frontier towns.[1]

Pastor as guardian, conserver of community, and passer of the torch is the approximate role into which Randall settled during his capstone, six-and-a-half-year ministry in Greensboro. At his arrival in early 1990, the church had concluded a laborious two years of searching for new leadership. Frustrating the search had been a complicated conclusion to the previous fourteen-year pastorate, which had produced confusion within the congregation and a need for healing and reconciliation.

All that Randall Lolley had learned about the practice of pastoring during his previous forty years of ministry came quickly into play as he stood before First Baptist Church on Easter Sunday, April 15, 1990. Six years thereafter, concluding the (1 and 2 Timothy) sermon referenced above, Randall summarized those lessons in four words. Speaking of the "faithful sayings" that Paul mentioned in the course of the two letters, he would conclude, "God help all of us to plant these true, certain, and faithful sayings in our souls: sayings about *salvation, vocation, spiritual exercises, eternal life.*"

In the body of that later sermon, subtitled "Hooray for the homesteader,"[2] the preacher expanded on his four words. First was *salvation.* "This is a faithful saying, and worthy of full acceptance, that Christ Jesus came into the world to save sinners. And I am the

1. *Journey with Me,* 289.
2. *Journey with Me,* 287.

foremost of sinners, but I received mercy." So Paul had written in 1 Timothy 1:15.

Of importance to Randall was the Apostle's movement in the verse from a general truth to a particular application: "It is nice to believe that Jesus Christ came into the world to save sinners, but it is not redemptive simply to believe that. My redemption comes by my accepting that he came to save *me!* Your redemption comes by your believing that he came to save *you!*" Salvation, therefore, is something promised to all who believe, both pastor and people.

A "salvation" of another sort came to First Baptist Church, and also to its new pastor when Randall arrived in 1990. In a letter to former Southeastern Seminary student Beth Braxton, written five years later, he would recall:

> The challenge here continues to be one that I am grateful to assume. Perhaps you know that I was at this church for two years just out of seminary as an Assistant Pastor (actually an intern). Upon my return five years ago I knew about one out of three of the people, thus, bonding was more immediate.
>
> The church was wounded when I arrived, so was I. It was good for both congregation and pastor to link up for these years.

Lay leaders' memories of Randall's time in Greensboro vary with respect to the degree of "woundedness" felt by the majority of members. During his 1989 discussions with members of the pastor search committee, Randall had responsibly inquired about possible unresolved issues.

Two of the questions he posed in a typewritten document were (1) "Is there serious division?" and (2) "Why have two [pastoral candidates already] turned away?" First Baptist Church historian Scott Culclasure noted that Randall, once his status evolved from consultant to candidate, was "cagey" in posing the questions, as presumably he "already knew the score."

What soon became apparent was the manner in which the newly called pastor undertook his ministry. Following his opening Easter Day sermonic broadside, titled "Wanted: An Open Tomb on Sunday," Randall set about establishing meaningful pastoral contact and communication with all 2,500 people on the church's active members roll. Having posed the question "Are your expectations realistic—what is job #1?" to the pulpit committee, his own "job #1" became obvious.

First came the inner leadership circle. Hal Koger, who assumed deacon chairmanship in the year following Randall's arrival, recalled, "Dr. Lolley had a carefully planned program to get to know each member personally, starting with the church leadership. I believe this was very effective. As a deacon at the time, I was invited, along with three others, to a luncheon."

Along the way, the deacons themselves were challenged to expand their pastor's outreach. On the second Saturday following his inaugural sermon, Randall assembled a "Shared Ministry Partners Breakfast." To deacons and other congregational leaders he announced:

> I am requesting that every family in our congregation be visited in the next thirty days. If possible contact them personally; if not, a letter or a telephone call will suffice. [But] please make on my behalf a pastoral call into every household. Tell them these things:
>
> 1. That your new pastor has come to Greensboro solemnly committing the best and most mature years of his life to this place and to these people. It can be a climactic time for us all.
>
> 2. Tell them that their new pastor is convinced that preaching and pastoral care go together. Each fuels the other. I pledge to preach out of my sensitivity to what is needed in my pastoral contacts. I pledge also to make pastoral contacts through my preaching. I sincerely want to be both pastor and preacher.

Randall's visitation priorities displayed a true "gospel inversion."[3] One pulpit committee member recalled, "He said at the outset of his ministry here that he first wanted to visit and get to know the homebound members, because they would be first to be *heaven*-bound. And that was what he did."

---

3. Matthew 20:16, ESV: "So the last will be first, and the first last."

"Internal healing is a heavy assignment to undertake," mused Hazel Fisher, who chaired the deacons during Randall's first full year, 1990–1991. Suggesting an interpretation of her pastor's well-known maxim "Before you can preach to them, you have to be their pastor," she noted,

> I think he meant that he needed to form personal relationships leading to the establishment of trust before congregants would be willing to listen to and follow his guidance. . . .
>
> Randall had a unique way of making everyone feel heard and appreciated. He could disagree completely with what one was saying but didn't confront or challenge, rather paved the way for further discussion with the goal of a meeting of the minds.

Relating his pastor's person-centered approach to his pulpit philosophy, Hal Koger added, "He even showed this in his preaching when he avoided being dogmatic about theological issues, saying, 'It's just my personal opinion.'"

Serving as deacon chair upon the Lolleys' arrival in Greensboro was Jack Swanson, whom later Randall invited to join the church staff as associate pastor for administration and systems.[4] Offering his own interpretation of "Before you can preach," Jack proposed,

> I think that Dr. Lolley meant that [in order] to be an effective preacher, one had to know the members of the congregation on a personal basis. This means more than just knowing their names and speaking to them when seeing them. It also means knowing about the individuals, who their family members are, what their cares and concerns are, what their faith journey had been, what their life might be like.

Virtually everyone associated with First Baptist during the 1970s and 1980s had extolled the preaching ability of Randall's predecessor. "He *was* a preacher," observed deacon and church member Robert Angell. On the other hand, "Randall was a *pastor*."

---

4. First Baptist was entering the computer age, and Jack had retired from IBM.

But Randall likewise "was a deep-thinking preacher," two-time deacon chair Robert Caldwell insisted. "Sometimes [he was] over my head and I had to review his tapes. But I never felt he was not a called pastor first. In my visits with him . . . he loved to be among the people/flock, and they loved a pastor who cared."

Still, "It was . . . a marriage of convenience," Scott Culclasure concluded, "in the sense that both parties needed healing." Their prospective pastor had received "an honest appraisal" from the search committee—even if the committee members themselves perhaps failed to fathom the depth of feeling within the congregation.

Correspondingly, Randall himself had been transparent about his own sense of injury resulting from his truncated experience of seminary leadership. He was cited in local newspaper coverage on the Monday following his unanimous election by the Greensboro congregation: "He called his decision difficult, saying he hated to leave the Raleigh church after less than two years . . . [but] he wanted to put distance between himself and Wake Forest, where Southeastern is located."[5] In the state's Baptist newspaper, the *Biblical Recorder*, the explanation was clearer:

> In announcing his resignation, Lolley told the Raleigh congregation that he is moving because he and his wife need more distance from Southeastern Seminary and because of their ties to First Church of Greensboro.
>
> He cited a lingering "total sense of pain" over the seminary. That pain has been intensified and lengthened because of the close proximity of the seminary's Wake Forest campus and his Raleigh church, he noted. . . .
>
> "Raleigh, with all its beauty and excitement, is still very near the people and the places of our common weeping. We choose to put this passage behind us, and it is our conviction that distance will help."

Another summarizing term Randall had gleaned from the four "faithful sayings" within Paul's Timothy correspondence was *spiritual*

5. Alison Davis, "Ex-seminary leader moving to Greensboro—First Baptist said to be pleased," *Greensboro News & Record*, February 12, 1990.

exercises, inferred from 1 Timothy 4:8-9: "Take time and trouble to keep yourself spiritually fit." Noting society's obsession with physical fitness, Randall said, "Perhaps no more timely word has ever been written for a weight-conscious, cholesterol-conscious, diet-conscious, exercise-conscious, calorie-conscious generation. We are perilously close to focusing on bodily fitness so much that we are choking our spirits to death."

In reality, lay leaders of the Greensboro church during Randall's tenure do not recall any clear, continuing confession of woundedness from their pastor. Rare were his personal or pulpit references to his seminary experience. Rather his focus seemed to be on aiding the members of the congregation in their own spiritual and emotional reorientation from the past to the future. Meanwhile, in such other-directedness Randall carried out his own "spiritual exercise" and enjoyed his own consequent healing.

By 1990, he was fast approaching conventional retirement age, but "I did not think of Randall as old," recalled Bob Caldwell. "His energy and his enthusiasm made him younger than his age. He was a bundle of energy seemingly willing to do all that a pastor should do."

A further summarizing word drawn from the Timothy letters had been *vocation*, reflecting Paul's assurance: "If anyone aspires to the office of bishop (minister), he desires a noble task" (1 Tim 3:1). Randall's disappointment over the culmination of his "dream job" as a seminary president notwithstanding, he never approached the pastoral ministry to which he reverted as if it were a vocational second choice. In ebullient terms he described the demand and the joy of being a pastor:

> Serving as a pastor is indeed a good work. Where else in a week's time can a human being participate in more spectacular variety?
>
> In the seven days from Sunday to Sunday regularly for 45 years, I have had the unspeakable joy of joining families at the birth of their children. This joy has been tempered by trips with other families to bury father, mother, sister, brother, husband, wife, friend.
>
> I have talked with couples about their plans for marriage, and with others about their plans for divorce. Dozens and dozens of

> persons have trusted me with counseling, where we have discussed the most intimate matters in their lives.
>
> I have had hundreds of committee meetings, and have wrestled with thousands of administrative matters. I have visited hospitals almost every day, and nursing homes, and members' houses where we have shared the agonies of dwindling health and the excitement of returning strength.
>
> I have stood with couples saying their wedding vows and talked with hundreds who are considering a church family like ours as their spiritual home. I have read and wrestled with and written weekly two sermons and a midweek worship, and have prepared for journeys out of town and out of the country for denominational meetings, mission meetings, and tours.
>
> Where else, I ask you, can such endless and infinite variety be afforded one human being?[6]

Alluding perhaps to Paul's traumatic Damascus Road encounter with the risen Lord, Randall flatly denied that he himself had "come kicking and screaming" into his pastoral calling. "I would like the word to go forth as to how my 'call' came," he said. "God got hold of my wanter! The reason I am serving you as a pastor is because I want to!"

In looking back three decades, one member of the search committee that recommended Randall had difficulty recalling that the congregation actually required much "healing"—perhaps because the new pastor brought to his task a heavy measure of reassurance and inspiration. "He was encouraging in so many areas," she recalled, "particularly missions, both home and foreign. He participated in many, such as the summer construction mission trips, and also encouraged trips to [assist FBC-related missionaries in destinations such as] Chile."

The inspiration Randall brought to a congregation requiring reconciliation and restabilization was as much personal as corporate. In autumn 1990, Hazel Fisher became the church's first woman chair

6. *Journey with Me*, 290. In a further word that anticipated his approaching retirement, Randall added, "And I would do it again if I had life to live over because I want to!"

of deacons. When invited to consider the position, she had consulted her still-new pastor and found him "particularly open to having a conversation with me. . . . He was encouraging and supportive, which helped to give me the confidence to accept the nomination. Further, he was a trusted colleague during that year, and I appreciated his guidance."

To his personal encouragement and pastoral support Randall always added a measure of pure fun and enjoyment. Hal Koger recalled monthly lunches, during his own term as deacon chair, that primarily afforded opportunity to "compare notes" prior to upcoming meetings of the diaconate. In their attempts to "out-surprise each other" with new and different restaurants, Hal remembered choosing a local "soul food" café, which Randall thereafter countered with a visit to the basement-level dining venue of an African American church.

"I was hungry," Hal reminisced, "and ordered a 'half-chicken.' Randall looked up at the waitress and said, 'I'll take the other half!' As the waitress walked away, he said, 'If you ever tell Lou that you and I ate a whole chicken, I'll kill you!'"

Near the midpoint of his six-plus years in Greensboro, Randall spoke privately of coming to understand his actual function within the congregation as that of "unintentional interim," ultimately serving as a correctional, transitional, and preparatory bridge between his predecessor and his successor.

Because his tenure was brief by comparison to that of the three pastors who had served during the eighty years prior to his arrival, some church members came to view him in the same light. They were grateful, however, for the significant work he was able to accomplish during their comparatively brief time together.

Randall himself reflected thoughtfully and thankfully on all that had transpired. In typical ordered and methodical fashion, at the time of his arrival he had jotted down an "assessment" of the church's life and health and then filed the note away. Six years later he would retrieve the assessment and update it to reflect his thinking as his retirement approached.

The note characterized April 15, 1990—the day of his first sermon—as a day of "magic" and "mystery." He had arrived in

Greensboro six weeks prior to his fifty-ninth birthday, asking himself how he could have departed his former pastorate "after only nineteen months (the mystery)," only to engage his final, formal ministry "here at a place and among a people where it began (the magic)."

Already he had sat in on his first deacon meeting. He had been pleased that forty-eight deacons (four-fifths of the total) had attended and heard him declare, with regard to the ministry they would undertake together, "It has to work!" Describing himself and the church's lay leadership as "two wounded healers," he announced his intention to gather for breakfast every deacon, individually and in small groups, during the first month of his pastorate.

His assessment further recorded that, during the subsequent breakfast meetings, Randall distributed half-sheets of paper, asking each person to write down what had been "most positive" and "most negative" thus far during their term as a deacon. More than 95 percent of them, he observed, listed "pain over former pastorate."

"Job 1" for the congregation, he concluded in a single word, would be to "Heal." His own task as pastor, he noted, would be to "Build a Bridge" (presumably between the church's past and its future). His strategy for accomplishing his task, he added alliteratively, would be (1) to [build the] *Staff*; (2) to *Stretch* [the congregation], "but just so far"; (3) to *Spend*, "but just so much"; and (4) to *Stay Together* and "Get well!"

Returning to his files six years later, Randall retrieved and updated his note. He titled his addendum "My Assessment of the General Health of FBC-G." Overall, the church's health he adjudged to be "Better (far better) if not well." While all was "not yet perfect," the "trust level [was] on the rise." Leadership, both staff and lay, was "good, as good as any time since 1990."

But was the church—following his half-dozen years as pastor—growing? "Remember," he cautioned, "there is a difference between growing and swelling." In numerical terms, the church had actually lost a net nineteen members.[7] A significant measure of loss in membership had come in the deaths of older members, as Randall

7. Randall noted total membership figures of 3,306 in September 1996 compared with 3,325 in April 1990.

recalled presiding over 245 funerals, averaging 37 per year. It was a number "larger than any one of my first five pastorates."

Still he celebrated growth of a more important kind, principally in organizational health and spiritual maturity. First Baptist was becoming a younger congregation. The median age of the members at his arrival had been fifty-eight, whereas within the "last three years" most people added to the rolls had been in their thirties. This, he concluded, bode well for the future health, viability, and vitality of the church.

"Great challenges" were indicated as "future health" and "alternative church" (a term not defined in his notes). At the bottom of the "assessment" appeared this wistful word: "I'd really like to be in my forties and be called as pastor of FBC-G—warts and all!"

While presumably Randall shared his cheerful assessment in some public setting (e.g., staff, deacon, or church business meeting), he struck an even more positive note in the concluding sermon he brought to the congregation. Selecting Acts 20:16-36 (Paul's valedictory address to the Ephesian elders) as his text, he offered a lengthy discourse titled "Finally . . . ."

In authentic pastoral fashion, the sermon offered First Baptist a strong word of encouragement to understand that healing and wholeness had resumed their residence in the congregation and that the work ahead was the same as the task of the church of Jesus Christ at any time in history: to balance the dual imperatives of "being" and "doing."

The Apostle Paul had warned the church at Ephesus to "be on the alert" (v. 31). When spiritual alertness was allowed to diminish, then people—even within strong families of faith—might begin "to split hairs over whether they are to *be* church or to *do* church."

The church at Greensboro had already demonstrated its identity as a true family of faith. Looking back to the launch of his ministry, Randall declared, "I believed it then, and I believe it now. You are family! You are grace-possessed people who belong to each other because you belong first to the Lord Christ."

Henceforth, "You have one superlative task—to live in the total fabric of your lives as if Jesus Christ is alive in you." Challenging the assembled congregation to "present the total Gospel to the total person, so as to achieve a total commitment," Randall characterized the total Gospel as "the full, complete, good news of God in Jesus Christ."

He explained, "Part of that good news must be proclaimed," while part "must be demonstrated. It is never either/or; it is always both/and. Someone else can and will always outdo you in one or the other of these. Yours is the chance to keep them properly blended, balanced, together."

As one who comprehended that "Before you can preach to them, you have to be their pastor," Randall had consistently demonstrated the balance that he recommended. Departing his pulpit weekly and periodically, he had immersed himself in the life of the congregation and community and in the lives of individual church members and their families. He had personally attached himself to the organized efforts of the local church he tended, as it sought to expand its witness to lands and peoples beyond itself. His strength to perform his task as pastor had been, he assured, shared equally among the congregation. "That is the strength of who you are," he affirmed. "You belong to Christ—and are to keep watch over yourselves and over all the flock."

Likely none had ever maintained better watch over the flock at 1000 West Friendly Avenue, Greensboro, than had Randall Lolley. A favorite memory of the mine was a hospital visit he and I paid to a dying church member during winter 1993.

Jack Maynard had been a typical, medium-profile parishioner. He had not served the office of deacon nor held significant committee chairmanships. But he and his winsome wife were frequent attenders at Sunday school and morning worship, and the two of them maintained warm friendships within the congregation.

To his pastor, Jack was one of the "grace-possessed people" who belonged to each other because they first belonged to the Lord Christ. And now Jack, beset at late middle age by unanticipated poor health, was dying.

Arriving at the intensive care unit of the local hospital, Randall sought and received permission to approach his church member's bedside. Heavily sedated and breathing with the help of a ventilator, Jack was unable to converse with his pastor. Randall nonetheless offered words of comfort and encouragement, in the event the patient still might hear and understand.

When, after long moments, time for a prayer of blessing arrived, Randall Lolley knelt on the cold tile floor beside the hospital bed. Cradling Jack's right hand in his own, he prayed softly for God's peace and presence with an individual the Lord had chosen to be his own, and whom he would shortly be receiving unto himself.

At the "Amen," Jack's pastor—as if by spiritual instinct—lifted up the man's hand . . . *and kissed it.*

Chapter 5

Pastor on Loan

For he grew up before him like a young plant, and like a root out of dry ground; he had no form or majesty that we should look at him, nothing in his appearance that we should desire him. (Isaiah 53:2)

The familiar forecast from the prophecy of Isaiah regarding the outward appearance of the Suffering Servant of Israel has always been hard to accept. Renaissance, Romantic, and popular images aside, it is difficult even in modern cinematographic depictions to locate a plain, unappealing, or otherwise unattractive depiction of Jesus of Nazareth. That is because a Jesus with "nothing in his appearance that we should desire him" defies most people's expectations.

Through the years of his pastoral and seminary ministries, Randall Lolley also had a way of defying people's expectations. This could be true from the moment of first encounter. Tom Graves, who came to teach Philosophy of Religion at Southeastern Seminary in 1979, recalled,

> In my first meeting with Randall I flew up from South Florida to meet him at a South Alabama airport. I was wearing a recently purchased three-piece suit and expected to meet a similarly attired seminary president. Instead I was greeted by a man wearing pink slacks, a very sweaty polo shirt, and unlaced tennis shoes. Randall had been playing golf that morning. He extended his hand to welcome me by simply saying, "Welcome Tom, I'm Randall."

Much could be written about people's first meetings with Randall Lolley—particularly in circumstances where individuals attired themselves in three-piece suits and sought his blessing or approval for academic or ministerial employment. In autumn 1985, Fred

Grissom was teaching Christian History at the most picturesque but smallest and remotest of his denomination's six seminaries, Golden Gate Baptist, located in Mill Valley, California, near San Francisco.

But Fred, yearning to move back east, had made inquiry at Southeastern Seminary. A "recruiting trip" (where seminary professors courted potential students) to Baptist colleges in Alabama afforded the opportunity he was looking for:

> Randall arranged for me to meet him in Charlotte on my way. This was on a hot Saturday afternoon in September. Since I was to meet with a seminary president, I dressed in a three-piece all-wool suit. When I got off the plane and walked toward those waiting to meet arriving travelers, I saw a person in a short-sleeved sport shirt and cotton pants who looked like pictures I had seen of Randall. He had come directly from a Wake Forest University football game. I was already roasting in my suit, but I got even hotter.

Southeastern, under the leadership of Randall and his dean of faculty, Morris Ashcraft, relied heavily on personnel recommendations from existing faculty. Be that as it might, Randall always took the matter of "head hunting" seriously and personally, determining to involve himself in new employment decisions.

Fred recalled that his prospective boss treated him to dinner at a good restaurant and then accompanied him to his hotel. There, Fred said,

> We talked for about three hours. We talked about almost everything, including his being from LA, Lower Alabama, and my being from Upper Alabama. We talked about our families, and it quickly became apparent to me that his wife was as important to him as mine was to me. We talked about our views on church, on education, on politics, including the politics of the SBC. I had already decided that I would be as open about my views as I could be.

Randall himself having decided to be "open," the revelation, which Randall had traveled from Winston-Salem to Charlotte in order to deliver, took the candidate by surprise. Fred explained,

> We finally began to talk specifically about Southeastern. He told me that it had quickly become apparent to him why the faculty committee at Southeastern had made me their number one candidate for the teaching position. Then, after a brief pause, he said that, nevertheless, he would not recommend that Southeastern hire me for the position and he would like to explain why. He told me that he thought it was very important that the school hire a woman for the position.

Concealing his disappointment, Fred summoned his philosophical inner self and told Randall he could understand his point of view. The young professor had served as an adviser to women at Golden Gate and "knew how important it was for women students to have role models who could help them overcome the obstacles they had before them."

Following their lengthy conversation, Randall departed, and Fred telephoned his wife to let her know they would not be moving to North Carolina. Still, he confessed he was in awe that he had conversed for three hours with a seminary president. Moreover, "This first meeting with Randall illustrated the warmth, openness, and honesty that characterized my later relationship with him, both as professor at Southeastern and as a friend." (In 1987, Fred finally joined the SEBTS faculty.)

There were other first encounters at airports. Sam Balentine was an Old Testament and Hebrew teacher at Kansas City's Midwestern Baptist Theological Seminary when Randall flew there in March 1983 to vet him for the same position at SEBTS. Surprisingly, it was the president, more so than the prospect, who seemed nervous as they met one another at the airport.

"He asked if we could go to his hotel first," Sam recalled. Randall explained that North Carolina State University was about to play the University of Houston for the national basketball championship. Back in Old Wake Forest, NC State's head coach Jim Valvano was a friend and neighbor to the Lolleys. So the competition and its outcome were important in more ways than one. Sam could join Randall as they viewed the game on TV in the latter's room.

"When we got to his hotel," Sam remembered, "he insisted on carrying his own bags. Then when we arrived at his room, he rushed in, threw his suitcase aside, turned on the television, located the game channel, jerked off his jacket, plopped down on the foot of his bed and said, 'Hot damn! Here we go!'"

Following State's unanticipated victory, Sam celebrated with his prospective boss, and then the two proceeded to conduct the employment interview. Characteristically, Randall was unhurried. Sam remembered that he finally got himself back home at 1 a.m.

Randall's solicitude for prospective and newly acquired faculty extended through the vetting process back at the seminary and even to their eventual arrival on campus. In 1977, Bob Dale was a consultant with the denomination's Sunday School Board in Nashville, Tennessee, when he grew interested in the professor of pastoral leadership and church ministries position at Southeastern.

In their initial interview, Bob asked Randall about his experience at the seminary—in particular what it had felt like to transition from pastoral ministry to seminary leadership. "What was it like to move from *retail* to *wholesale*?" Bob queried. "Well," Randall answered without hesitation, "I like to think of myself as still a pastor—a pastor on loan to the denomination."

Randall proceeded in convincing ways to demonstrate his ministry focus to his latest recruit. "He had a pastoral heart," Bob discovered—and a practical one at that. "He knew that my new position at the seminary would pay 25 to 30 percent less than I had been making at the Sunday School Board. So he made it clear that I would be free to moonlight."

Randall's encouragement of Bob Dale's "moonlighting" resulted in a professional writing career that produced multiple books on church ministry and leadership. Meanwhile, "Randall knew that the salary structure at Southeastern was too low to result in a livable retirement. Eventually he doubled the 10 percent annuity contribution to 20 percent, and supplemented it with an additional 5 percent."

As Bob, along with wife Carrie and six-year-old son Cas, moved from Tennessee to North Carolina, their moving van caught fire and damaged their possessions. Randall gave exceptional attention to helping them recover from their loss, establishing them in their new residence in Wake Forest and even entertaining their child as they unpacked. "He dropped by the house every two to three days, and would sit and read books to Cas, who amazed our new president with his own reading ability."

Bible, Greek, and Hebrew professor Carson Brisson was among professors who, in the pattern of Randall himself, launched their careers at Southeastern as undergraduates. As such, Carson's first impression came earlier than most:

> My wife and I were 21 and newly married. We had everything we owned in the wide world stuffed into an old car. We moved into a residence hall for students and spouses at SEBTS on a blazing hot August afternoon. . . .
>
> A couple a bit older than us started helping us carry things up the stairs. They introduced themselves as Randall and Lou. That's all. They never mentioned their connection with the school. We thought they were just a sweet, older, lovely couple in seminary just like us. They were both cheerful and welcoming, and worked so hard to help us unload our car. We immediately felt at home. All feeling of being strangers in a strange place melted away.
>
> About a week later school began. We went to chapel. The couple who had helped us were on the dais. . . . We wondered why. Then introductions were made. They were President and Mrs. Lolley! We were amazed.

As later he joined the faculty and viewed Randall from a collegial perspective, Carson grew ever more persuaded that his president was administratively unique. "I think it was his style. He was quite accessible. His 'door' was open, so to speak. He did not emphasize the trappings of office. Which is to say he seemed to keep his eye on service, and avoided in the main the attractions of power."

Accessible is a term employed by others of Randall's faculty members. Asked if he believed his president was unique among seminary heads, Bob Dale replied, "He was unusual as an executive leader. He was far more accessible, friendly, welcoming." Recalling his prior bosses, Sunday School Board presidents who could be almost "military" in their leadership style, Bob suggested that Randall's self-concept outweighed the office he held. "He was so well defined—he knew who he was. He was comfortable in his own skin. He could be authoritative without being bossy."

Recalling a particular faculty gathering at Eagle Eyrie, the mountain retreat center for the Baptist General Association of Virginia, Bob referred to the intellectual prowess and strength of will that seminary professors could bring to the table.

> People would try to push Randall. The Four [seminary curriculum] Areas would act as a search committee for new faculty. One group wanted more academics. The Biblical Area wanted to give him only one name, rather than three. He resisted. He heard them out, but then he explained straightforwardly the logic behind the recommended procedure.

During faculty searches, Bob added, Randall seemed more interested in the personal and spiritual quality of a candidate than in his or her credentials for a particular position. "That made for more variety" within the faculty as a whole.

Seated at the head of the table during every faculty deliberation was Morris Ashcraft, whom Randall had invited in 1981 to transfer from Midwestern Seminary to become Southeastern's dean of faculty, an uncommon position in Southern Baptist seminaries. Bob Dale described the president and the dean as "good teammates," as Randall showed himself comfortable with sharing a significant measure of leadership with another administrator.

Remembering that Dr. Ashcraft was among thirteen professors fired from the faculty of Louisville's Southern Seminary in 1958,[1] Sam Balentine suggested that—far from posing a threat to his own leadership—it was Ashcraft's strength of personality, character, and conviction that actually appealed to Randall. "Comfortable in his own skin," Randall was happy for his dean to steward faculty candidates

1. The terminations came as a result of unresolved conflict with seminary administration over the approach to faculty recruitment.

through the interview process before recommending three or four possibilities to the president.

"Randall and 'Ash' were our North Star," Sam suggested. "I never encountered another such team."

Tom Graves offered a similar view: "Randall was tremendously helped in his relationship with the faculty by Dean Morris Ashcraft. Those two worked as a marvelous team, always relating to the faculty with honesty, forthrightness, and openness. I have never worked with another administrator who was so open to public questioning and dialogue."

Church Music professor Michael Hawn described his president as "extremely collaborative and process-oriented. He could take ideas from others, and not everything had to be generated initially by him. He was hands-on in relationships, but not a micro-manager." An example supporting Michael's observation was offered by Tom Graves:

> I worked on two specific projects at Randall's request. First, the publication of our new faculty journal, "Faith and Mission," was a substantial financial commitment involving the printing of 5000 journals, secretarial time, and postage. I was fairly compensated for my time, and at every step of the way Randall continued to offer his full support and words of appreciation. Randall understood the commitment and long hours it took to pull this off, and he was very generous in his praise.
>
> Second, in the summer of 1984 Randall asked me to help organize North Carolina Baptists, encouraging them to attend future meetings of the SBC and educating them concerning convention issues. He provided additional office space, bought me a computer and printer, and then trusted me to carry on the work, reporting back to him periodically.

It was apparent that Randall—who, said Bob Dale, seemed grateful to have come from the "small world" of Lower Alabama to the place where he had arrived at SEBTS—consequently viewed himself as a debtor to all of his constituencies. These included his faculty, the hundreds of students who sought theological education at the seminary, and the thousands of churches and church members who supported his institution with their prayers and their financial support.

What Randall thought he owed faculty, in the view of many of his teachers, was the very thing for which he was later noted and awarded by the American Association of University Professors and its Meiklejohn Award: academic freedom. Such freedom implied, according to Bob, "letting the experts be the experts. It also meant freeing up their time for writing and for teaching."

During his time at Southeastern, Tom Graves taught courses "on the critics of Christianity, contemporary philosophy, and religious authority." Noting that such studies, by their nature, raised issues the discussion of which would have troubled some people in the denomination and its churches, Tom was pleased that neither his president nor the dean ever questioned his teaching. "I received nothing but encouragement and commendations from the seminary administration," Tom recalled. "I know it was not the same for persons at other Baptist seminaries."

"I knew Randall had my back," said Sam Balentine. Sam remembered criticism he had received for a lecture he gave on the distinctions that could be observed between the Old Testament and the Hebrew Bible. "But he never sought me out and asked me about it. . . . A number of us were to his left theologically, but there was no tension."

It was due to his stance on academic freedom—as opposed to "a lockstep approach to theological indoctrination"—that Randall eventually resigned his presidency, Michael Hawn concluded. "I think the faculty and Morris Ashcraft helped him understand the implications of academic freedom within the context of the SBC, but it was not a hard sell."

The idea of *partnership* in the various tasks of ministry appealed to Randall Lolley.[2] Observers noted his partnership with his dean of faculty, and he celebrated a consistent partnership of trust with

---

2. See Appendix A: Lolleyisms: A Glossary, among which was the familiar sign-off Randall attached to interoffice memos: "Thanks for your partnership in the task."

faculty members themselves. The dynamic extended also to the students who passed through the doors of the institution he led.

Indebted to their teachers, Randall counted himself likewise indebted to those who were taught. In *Servant Songs: Reflections on the History and Mission of Southeastern Baptist Theological Seminary, 1950–1988*, he wrote,

> Since I was so thoroughly convinced of it myself, I had little difficulty convincing my faculty colleagues that I believed the only reason Southeastern had a president was to help teachers to teach and students to learn. From the very beginning I contended for a genuine, in-depth partnership in the teaching/learning process. It worked. We became a community of learning.[3]

"He treated students like partners in education, the same way he treated faculty and staff," observed Fred Grissom. "I never saw him treat a student with disrespect or condescension."

In terms of felt obligation to those who were preparing for ministry, Randall thought he "owed them the best Baptist faculty he could assemble, that was free to pursue truth, and that lived the gospel they taught. He owed them an example of what it meant to combine prophetic leadership with compassion—and he delivered as long as he was allowed." So said Michael Hawn.

Tom Graves suggested that the president's openness and accessibility to his school's students influenced everyone on staff, and particularly Randall's administrators. Referring to the monthly, free coffee-and-doughnut forums that he provided in the seminary cafeteria, Graves said,

> Most any question was allowed, and Randall was frank and full in his responses. Particularly with the mounting SBC crisis, he was open to permitting conservative student organizations on campus, whose purpose was to undermine his leadership. As tricky and perilous as those times were, I don't think it could have been managed in a better way in terms of students.

3. *Servant Songs*, 35.

"We had conservative students," added Sam Balentine. They would incur their president's displeasure if they "harassed" women students, but in general they were allowed to express themselves. Meanwhile, the more moderate students were likewise afforded freedom. During and following Randall's autumn 1987 confrontation with the new, majority-conservative trustee body, he permitted his supporters in the student body to display yellow ribbons around the campus as symbols of protest and solidarity.

What Randall believed he owed his students was a by-product of his sense of obligation to the churches and people of the sponsoring Southern Baptist Convention. "I think," said Carson Brisson, "he believed SEBTS was to provide well-educated, *Baptist* ministers, who emphasized so-called Baptist distinctives such as congregational governance, the sanctity of conscience, and a version of the Gospel that emphasized forgiveness and observable sanctity."

Fred Grissom concurred, adding that Randall envisioned a seminary that would, in certain respects, also lead the denomination's churches through the pastors and other ministers it provided:

> Randall believed the seminary should lead the denomination and its churches to become more nearly what they claimed to be—the servants of Christ. That entailed helping them toward needed changes, even when those were difficult and flew in the face of tradition. One example of that was his support of women in ministry, not just for the sake of the women students but for the sake of the churches as well.

"He did believe in accountability," Sam Balentine was convinced, "but not in sovereignty." The Southern Baptist Convention and its churches owned and financially supported Southeastern and its sister seminaries. As such, the denomination was owed allegiance to its desire for ministers who shared and disseminated historic Baptist teaching. Still, the SBC was in no position to comprehend or closely control the educational dynamics of a graduate-level academic institution.

Consequently, a large measure of mutual trust was required—both by the seminary and by its confessional parent. "As a lifelong

Southern Baptist Randall understood the importance of the Cooperative Program and the denomination's support for theological education. As a former pastor he understood church life as well as any seminary president I encountered," insisted Tom Graves.

Ironically, Tom added, "It was an act of courage for Randall, along with a few other institutional heads, to challenge the SBC elected leadership and try to save the denomination from its capture by fundamentalists. . . . He cared enough for his denomination and its churches that he was willing to put his career on the line."

In the view of the late Baptist psychologist Wayne E. Oates, authentic pastoral ministry demanded personal qualifications that were clearly observable from Christian Scripture. Referring to the "right mindedness" that Jesus restored to the Gerasene demoniac (Mark 5:15), Oates wrote, "The epistles to Timothy and Titus both use the same term, which may be translated variously as 'sane,' 'sensible,' or 'of a sound mind,' 'self-controlled,' 'sober-minded.'" Oates amplified:

> Most emphasis, however, is placed upon the degree of mastery a man has over his temper. Paul says that a man should be a "master of himself." This implies that he has great strength of power and spirit, but he knows how to express his aggressions in a positive and healthy manner. . . . He is not "violent but gentle," not "quarrelsome" and continually searching out something over which to start a fight.[4]

Through the decade and a half that Randall served there, his colleagues at Southeastern Seminary witnessed this aspect of the "pastor" who labored among them as their president. The word most appropriate, in the opinion of Sam Balentine, was "integrity." Such integrity in the face of the pressures that mounted against Randall toward the end of his service was observed by Sam's colleague Carson Brisson:

4. *The Christian Pastor* (Philadelphia: Westminster, 1964), 82–84.

> It was October 1987. The trustees were meeting. Randall was getting coffee in the administration building in a back hall between the Business suite and the Registrar's suite. A "friendly" trustee from Maryland entered the side entrance and informed Randall that he was there on behalf of the trustees to ask if Randall "wanted clarity or time." I will never forget it. Those were his exact words.
>
> Randall was stirring his coffee with a little, red, plastic stirrer, the kind you can get a thousand for a dollar or two. He continued to stir. Then he looked up at the trustee. "Clarity," he said, crisply and loudly but not too loudly. "Clarity," he repeated. The trustee didn't need any other information. Randall went over to him where he still stood in the door. They hugged. The trustee left, I assume to report Randall's one-word answer. A few hours later there was clarity. Randall resigned the next week, along with his Dean, the late Morris Ashcraft, a man of great honor, who loved Randall, and whom Randall loved.

Carson Brisson believed that, in Randall Lolley, he "observed a man who had at core an irenic spirit, and believed that this spirit was the resident value of the Gospel, and was genuinely baffled when he ran into ideologues." Carson observed significant suffering in the school's president—suffering that transcended "the wounds of adversaries, friends and colleagues, students and staff"—as he witnessed the school he loved being "dismantled."

"Suffering Servant" is the designation traditionally applied to the coming Redeemer of Israel, as described in Isaiah 53. "Wounded Healer" is the term author-priest and academic Henri J. M. Nouwen attached to a minister who, looking deeply within, applied lessons gained from his own suffering to relieve the suffering of others. In Protestant and Evangelical tradition, such ministers are termed "pastors." At bottom, it may have been the *pastoral* character of Randall Lolley that most deeply impressed his colleagues at Southeastern Seminary.

People who worked alongside him at Southeastern responded to this question: Was Randall, during his time as seminary president (1974–1988), a pastor more than anything else—more than an administrator, more than an academic, more than a denominational servant and statesman, more than a public figure and spokesman for a theological and political counter-movement within his own confessional community?

"Beyond any doubt, in my opinion," answered Carson Brisson. "He saw knowledge and all forms of power as subordinate to the care of the soul standing in front of him in the moment." Added Fred Grissom:

> Randall certainly served a pastoral role to faculty, administration, and students. When students held a demonstration of their support after Randall's resignation, I watched as he walked up to a group of them, smiled his megawatt smile, spoke works of encouragement that brought smiles to their faces, then put his arm around the shoulder of a weeping young student. That kind of encounter was repeated countless times with faculty and administration.

Tom Graves cited additional examples, the recollection of which he said brought him to tears:

> The night before he resigned Randall called me at our home. It was very late. Without informing me of what he would announce in chapel the next morning, Randall was calling to see if everything was all right with me and if my plans of going to [become pastor at] St. John's Baptist Church were finalized. He later told me that his chief concern in resigning was making sure the faculty members would be secure in their future jobs. That was the kind of leader and friend that Randall was. At the biggest crisis point of his life, he was worried about us.

On an even more personal note, Tom recalled,

> I went with Dean Ashcraft to inform Randall that I had just been diagnosed with multiple sclerosis. Upon hearing the news Randall immediately reached out and grabbed both of my hands and started crying and after a while said a prayer for me. No one could have responded in a more personal and caring fashion. As time went on he continued to stay in touch with me concerning the progression of my MS. I could not have asked for a better pastor.

It was as Randall surrendered his seminary leadership and Tom Graves simultaneously prepared himself to transition from professor to church pastor that Tom received from Randall the gift of a powerful symbol, one that would guide and inform Tom's own ministry going forward.

In a column for ethicsdaily.com (now goodfaithmedia.org), Baptist Theological Seminary at Richmond (BTSR) president Linda McKinnish Bridges wrote of the history of the institution and of the origin of the "servant's towel," which became the familiar icon of the school and which was presented to each of the 800 people who received their master's degrees there.[5]

Founding president Tom Graves, Dr. Bridges wrote, had shared the story at a banquet honoring the final 2019 graduating class. It had been while Randall and wife Lou motored from Old Wake Forest to Charlotte to preach at Tom's installation as pastor of St. John's Baptist Church that an idea occurred to Randall.

A few years before, he had listened to a sermon by pastor Nancy Hastings Sehested, one where she described the call to ministry as "finding a towel with your name on it." In an action at once impulsive and deeply purposeful, the Lolleys "pulled off Interstate 85 and found a store where they purchased a hand towel and a black magic marker, which Lou used to write 'Tom Graves' on the bottom of the just-purchased towel." Bridges continued,

> As Lolley concluded his sermon on servant leadership, he presented the towel to Tom stating, "Ministry is finding a towel with your name on it." . . .
>
> We remember the life of Jesus, as recorded in the Gospel of John (13:3), he "knew that God had given all things into his hands, and that he had come forth from God, and was going back to God . . . he took up a towel."

---

5. "Virginia Seminary Leaves Behind 30-Year Legacy of Towel-Bearers," May 31, 2019, goodfaithmedia.org/virginia-seminary-leaves-behind-30-year-legacy-of-towel-bearers/ (Sam Balentine observed, "The vision that resided at Southeastern was reborn at BTSR." The Richmond-based seminary closed on January 31, 2019.)

> This is a powerful thought. Jesus, who has all of the authority given to him from the Creator of the Universe, "after supper, laid aside his garments and took a towel."

As if having not only her seminary and her presidential predecessor—but also Randall Lolley—in mind, Linda Bridges concluded,

> Our world needs towel-bearers more than ever. People who understand that service is for the common good, not for personal gain—service that creates goodness and kindness in the world, not chaos and confusion; service that repeatedly says, "Not I, but you, you go first."
>
> We need leaders who understand that service calls for bold and firm accountability and generous grace in the very same breath.
>
> We need leaders who understand that failure can mean success, that defeat can signal growth, and that suffering can serve for gain.

Chapter 6

The Most Important Person in the Room

Greg Mathis attended Southeastern Seminary as an off-campus student, commuting daily from his church field in rural southern Virginia, where he simultaneously served a full-time pastorate. Graduating in 1980 with a Master of Divinity degree, he was called to far Western North Carolina to another rural congregation, Mud Creek Baptist, near Hendersonville.

In several ways, Greg represented a minority among SEBTS students during the presidential tenure of Randall Lolley. A self-described conservative, he acknowledged that the question for a pastor like himself in the late 1970s was not whether he would attend a conservative or a liberal seminary but whether he would attend a seminary at all.

However, having completed an undergraduate degree at North Carolina's Gardner-Webb College, Greg concluded that he would profit from a graduate-level theological education. He chose Southeastern Seminary in "Old Wake Forest" for one of the primary reasons for which it was founded in 1950: proximity to Baptist pastors who were serving in the southeastern United States.[1]

A busy pastor, Greg was also a busy student. While the seminary recommended that commuting students enroll for no more than ten hours per semester, he managed a full eighteen hours, graduating in the typical three years that were necessary for a master's degree. Because he was dually focused on classes and church ministry, he deprived himself of most of "campus life." Greg never became personally acquainted with the seminary president. He never attended the

1. Thomas Bland, ed., *Servant Songs*, "In the Beginning," 2–3.

popular once-a-month Friday morning coffee-and-doughnut forums with Dr. (and sometimes Mrs.) Lolley in the seminary cafeteria.

Still, he came to appreciate Randall Lolley. "I guess I learned more about him later, through his brother Tom," Greg said. Tom Lolley, himself an SEBTS graduate, had pastored North Carolina churches and eventually served the Baptist State Convention as an "area missionary." Tom represented the convention to churches and associations in the western part of the state, including Mud Creek Baptist and its host Carolina Association.

"Both those guys [Tom and Randall] were great," Greg said. "Everybody respected Dr. Lolley. He was sharp, he was good at what he did, and he served faithfully. His brother also had a high opinion of him, although Tom was maybe a little more conservative."

Meanwhile, Tom harbored candid observations of his older sibling, some of which he reserved for members of his own family. His son Tim (SEBTS Class of 1988) recalled that his father had a "pet peeve" regarding his sibling. When the latter would, for example, conclude a sermon or other speech at a Baptist meeting, he would quickly be surrounded by congratulators and other well-wishers. Randall would become so preoccupied with anyone with whom he was conversing that his brother lamented, "You couldn't get anywhere near him. He'd talk as long as somebody wanted to talk."

Ginger Graves (Class of 1987) had decidedly more than second-hand knowledge of Randall Lolley. Daughter of Baptist State Convention Executive Director-Treasurer Roy J. Smith (who along with Randall was part of the Class of 1957), she remembered the June 1973 meeting of the Southern Baptist Convention in Portland, Oregon. There the Smiths eschewed hotel accommodations to camp outdoors alongside the Lolleys. Through such encounters, Ginger discovered early that Randall supported women with great enthusiasm and embraced their calling to church ministry. Unsurprisingly, when she sensed her own calling, she chose to prepare at the seminary that he was soon to lead.

Ginger viewed Randall's idiosyncrasy and his brother's pet peeve from a positive angle. "I remember so many times seeing him on campus, and he never failed to stop, talk, and inquire how I was doing, as well as my family. He was [originally] called to be a pastor and demonstrated this over and over as he would listen intently, and offer care and guidance with great compassion and love."

Denominational leaders made various impressions. Late and prominent pastor Carlyle Marney is recalled to have said of one Baptist seminary president of his day, "He was a royal processional of one man." But students from the Lolley era remember Randall in a different light. Larry Hovis (Class of '87) said, "He was the opposite of my image of a seminary president. He was open, friendly, engaging, welcoming. When you were with Randall, you were the most important person in the room."

Bob Ballance (Class of '88) was headed across the campus toward the cafeteria one day when he sensed a tug at his sleeve. It was none other than the president, who offhandedly inquired how Bob came to choose Southeastern for his ministry education. Recalled Bob, "He listened intently as I awkwardly told him my story, embarrassed that it wasn't more impressive. I realized that, to him, I was not just a nameless face; to him I was created in God's image and was someone to be known and respected equally."

"Everybody respected him because he respected everybody," Greg Mathis said. Bob Ballance agreed, referring to an expensive fire engine that the seminary purchased for the town of Wake Forest. "Randall led the way in raising money for that truck because he respected first responders."

"He would," Bob continued, "embrace the janitor at the seminary with the same gusto he embraced the school's chair of trustees, a donor who had made a large contribution, or a faculty member with advanced degrees."

George Spencer ('78) was a North Carolinian who contemplated a choice between studying in Louisville, Kentucky, at the oldest Southern Baptist seminary, or at the relative newcomer Southeastern in Old Wake Forest. The two were, he understood, the "most liberal" of the six SBC seminaries. Deciding to visit both campuses, he and his wife traveled first to SEBTS and inquired at the administration building. "Dr. Lolley came walking through. He stopped and introduced himself. We liked him immediately—so well, in fact, that we had decided by the time we arrived back in Concord that Southeastern would be our choice."

Never inaccessible, the SEBTS president "made himself available to everyone," according to Mike Queen ('81). When Mike arrived on campus in 1978, he was a member of a pulpit committee for his home church in Huntington, West Virginia. The committee was becoming frustrated in its search, and its chairman had asked Mike to investigate possibilities in North Carolina.

Randall's secretary allocated fifteen minutes from his late-afternoon schedule to afford the young seminarian an opportunity to talk to the president about his church's history and make a "ten-minute spiel" about its desires regarding a new pastor. "I finished," Mike recalled, "with three minutes to spare, and asked Dr. Lolley if he had any questions. Of course, he did. But at the fifteen-minute mark I stood to leave. . . . He asked me to sit back down. After another fifteen minutes, I stood again to leave.

"In exasperation he asked me if I needed to pee, and offered his bathroom. Of course, he was simply interested in my church and what we were looking for. After forty-five minutes he seemed satisfied. He asked me to return in two days, and he would have a name or two for me. When I went back, he gave me five names . . . each one an excellent candidate."

Far from delivering an impression of royalty or nobility, Randall's "speaking and relational style were totally free of any air of superiority," in the opinion of Bob Ballance. "There simply wasn't an aloof bone in the man's body."

In a handwritten reflection dated May 2010, Randall averred, "I was a plain vanilla Alabama boy who made it halfway to the top of the country [North Carolina]; and on the journey experienced some family things, some pastoral things, and some presidential things that molded and marked my life in Christ for eternity."[2] A similar self-estimate was present at a fall convocation attended by entering student John Pierce (Class of '81), who heard the seminary president describe himself as "a simple guy from L.A. [Lower Alabama]."

---

2. This single sentence is the nearest to an autobiographical statement I discovered among Randall Lolley's files, papers, and other memorabilia.

"Then," added John, "he gave a brilliant and inspiring theological presentation. I made a note to myself not to fall for that 'just a good ol' boy' idea again."

C. F. McDowell ('81) marveled that "Every word that was spoken from [Randall's] mouth was worth hearing, listening to, contemplating, and living."

Oratorically gifted as he was, however, many people who encountered him through the years agreed with Ginger Graves: Randall Lolley was, in every calling and in every setting, first of all a pastor. He had said it himself: "Before you can preach to them, you have to be their pastor."

As at the various churches he served through the years, this was also the case at the seminary. Steve Sumerel (Class of '78), who participated with several former theater majors in a drama troupe that formed at the campus, said, "I suppose it was because Dr. Lolley was a lover of the arts that he took great interest," attending some play rehearsals and "always there on opening nights."

It was after the final performance of the play *J.B.*, recalled Steve, that "Dr. Lolley sought me out for a very affirming talk. He told me that drama was an all-but-untapped resource for bringing folks into God's narrative. . . . He encouraged me to use my gifts toward that end."

Steve, who told Randall he enjoyed writing as much as acting, dropped two playscripts by the president's office. "Later that week I got a note in my mailbox, again very affirming of my gifts." Enjoying the lead role in another drama, *The Diary of Adam and Eve*, Steve experienced his seminary commencement two weeks thereafter. "Well done, Adam!" said Randall as he handed the new graduate his diploma.

"I was so energized by his affirmations," Steve added, "that I made drama a signature aspect of my ministry."

Defining the pastoral charisma typically associated with Randall Lolley, Doug Murray ('81) called it "the gift of making you feel valued and taken seriously." Recalling an appointment he once made to consult with the president about his future ministry, Doug related,

> I went into what seemed to me to be a huge office, but soon forgot that as I talked with Dr. Lolley. . . . We talked about everything. He even talked about the challenge of figuring out where a young couple would spend the holidays, whether with the husband's parents, or the wife's, or both. He finally let me go—after 45 minutes! . . . Again, I don't remember [all] we talked about. But I do remember how he made me feel: a valued person, a colleague in ministry. I'll never forget that.

Larry Hovis concluded that it was because Randall was comfortable in himself that he had a gift for making others comfortable. John Pierce reminisced about the universally recalled and extolled monthly Friday morning coffee-and-doughnut forums in the campus cafeteria. No subject of concern to students was off-limits to Randall, said John, or too trivial to claim his attention. "He was interested in everything from traffic issues to textbooks."

Jack Glasgow ('80) added, "His Friday morning forums in the cafeteria were so pastoral—every student heard and respected, every answer coming from a place of genuine caring."

C. F. McDowell noted that Randall's proclivity toward personal and pastoral attention over other requirements of ministry would follow him from his seminary leadership back into local church ministry, where he would continue teaching it to students in other settings. Recalling his own participation in a mid-1990s "Young Leaders" seminar sponsored by North Carolina Baptist Hospital's Center for Congregational Health, C. F. wrote,

> Dr. Lolley was nearing the end of his tenure as senior pastor. . . . He shared with us that due to the "closed door" style of pastoral leadership of [a] predecessor, he saw it of utmost importance that he take the opposite approach and be available and present for the congregation. I well remember he shared with us that he went to the office very early (before dawn) and got his studying and administrative work done and all laid out on his secretary's desk. Then he opened his office door and spent several hours present and available for [church] members prior to going home and being in bed very early to do the same the next day.

In what doubtless was his darkest hour as Southeastern president, Randall extended the equivalent of pastoral care to students who stood by in an attempt to defend him and his leadership. Referring to the infamous autumn 1987 meeting of a (by then) majority-conservative trustee board, Bob Ballance recalled, "The trustees had called for an executive session that morning to meet with Randall about his leadership performance. . . . While all of the other students present at the meeting . . . left and returned to their classes, [fellow student] Peggy Haymes and I chose to stay put."[3]

New trustee chairman Robert Crowley, Bob recalled, "was not happy that we were choosing to stay. We were quietly protesting the executive session." At that point,

> Randall got up, came over to us, and very quietly thanked us for our support and care; but then told us he thought it would be best if we left. While he embraced us for our concern, at the same time he showed no disrespect to the trustees, remaining calm and retaining his always-optimistic demeanor. To us he was an embodiment of self-confident, faith-filled pastoral leadership.
>
> He had told the entire student body the previous week, at a president's forum in the cafeteria, when he realized things may not go so well at the upcoming trustee meeting, that we should all view this as a "learning opportunity." He taught us well by example.

Jack Glasgow referred to a particularly strong example, one confirming a hard decision he made during his first year as a student. Christmas was coming, and that year December 25 fell on Sunday. Choosing to stay over and participate in a dramatic dialog sermon at the church he was serving as a staff member, Jack delayed his departure for his home:

> After worship I started the drive home to Atlanta. It was a drizzly, cold and foggy day. I stopped for a restroom break at the Georgia Welcome Center at dusk. Standing next to me in the men's room was, you guessed it, Randall Lolley. . . . We went to the lobby and he introduced me to Lou. He told her, "Honey, this is one of our

---

3. Trustee meetings were open to the entire seminary community.

> Southeastern boys. He stayed in Zebulon to preach with Charles Edwards at Zebulon Baptist this morning, and now he is headed home to Atlanta."
>
> Dr. Lolley said, "Son, if you cared enough about the church to miss being home at Christmas so that you could celebrate the birth of Jesus with your people, you are going to make a great pastor."
>
> Lou told him to tell me why they were traveling so late on Christmas Day. They were headed to the Wiregrass Region of Southeast Alabama, his home. . . . Lou said, "Randall is doing an interim at a little church in the Tar River Association, and he did not want to miss preaching on Christmas morning with them."
>
> President of a seminary, he had delayed going home for Christmas to preach for a small church he served in interim. He bought me a cup of coffee from the vending machine and sent me on my way with a hearty "Merry Christmas."

The hot cup of coffee presented on a cold day to Jack Glasgow was illustrative of a certain sense—not only of appreciation but also of obligation—that Randall felt toward the hundreds of seminary students he encountered during his presidential years. In his introduction to his letter to the church at Rome, Paul wrote, "I am a debtor both to Greeks and to barbarians, both to the wise and to the foolish—hence my eagerness to proclaim the gospel to you also who are in Rome" (Rom 1:14-15, NRSV).

The idea is that Paul would be remiss, or in violation of God's purpose for his life and his stewardship of his gifts, if he did not preach the good news. Paul delivered a similar assertion to the church at Corinth: "If I proclaim the gospel, this gives me no ground for boasting, for an obligation is laid on me, and woe to me if I do not proclaim the gospel!" (1 Cor 9:16, NRSV).

Whether Randall Lolley felt a sense of actual *indebtedness* to those constituencies he served while presiding over Southeastern Seminary is unknown. But people who studied there agree that he did approach his task as if he were responding to a sacred obligation.

Part of it related to his feeling that those who populated Southeastern Seminary were extensions of his own family. Referring to theology professor Robert Culpepper's biography, *God's Calling: A*

Missionary Autobiography, Bob Ballance cited a chapter wherein the author recounted a phone call he received from the seminary president. The two discussed the possibility of Culpepper's leaving the denomination's foreign mission field to join Randall's faculty.

"The reader," Bob asserted, "is left with the impression that Randall viewed faculty members as members of his own family. As best I could tell, he was unwaveringly loyal to them all, and to the administrators who were part of Southeastern as well."

Randall's felt "obligation" to his faculty family might be described, according to LaCount Anderson (Class of '80), in a single word: *freedom*. That is, he wanted the seminary he led to be "a place of learning, not indoctrination; a place where ideas freely flowed, without intimidation, should those ideas not necessarily agree with Baptist doctrine."

"Academic freedom" was a term employed repeatedly by pastoral care professor Richard Hester, representing SEBTS faculty as spokesman for their newly formed chapter of the AAUP (American Association of University Professors), in interviews with local news media during the "firestorm" of autumn 1987. It was also his own defense of the cherished principle that resulted in Randall's AAUP Alexander Meiklejohn Award the following year.

Their president's emphasis on freedom was not lost on his students. Said Roger Nix, "He wanted SEBTS to be unique and not a cookie-cutter SBC seminary. He sought to provide an atmosphere of acceptance and openness for all views to be taught and discerned in the classroom."

In pursuit of that objective—and especially in the face of denominational critics of certain faculty members—Jack Glasgow observed that Randall "had their backs. He defended their integrity and commitment in the face of brutal attacks." Such a posture toward faculty, Randall had concluded, was necessary for the maintenance of authenticity and excellence in the classroom.

Moreover, it served to ensure the possibility of a high-quality theological education for students. Randall also counted himself a debtor, many of his students believed, to those who arrived at Southeastern to prepare themselves for Christian ministry. "He [thought that he] owed us the best and most honest education possible," observed Doug Murray, "that would truly prepare us for service in a local church."

Mike Queen reflected on the occasion when Randall came to Huntington, West Virginia, to preach at Mike's home church, Fifth Avenue Baptist:

> When Dr. Lolley preached at Dr. [R. F.] Smith's installation at FAB, he met my dad. Dad said to him, "Dr. Lolley, my son has left our family business, and I had to give him up. He is yours now. He is a good man. Please don't mess him up."
>
> Dr. Lolley assured my dad that I would get a great theological education, and I believe I did.

Yet it was more than quality classroom education that Randall ensured for students. "He provided the students at SEBTS," Ginger Graves was quick to add, "a role model for what it means to be a minister":

> He did so with such grace and laughter. During the difficult years at SEBTS, he remained loyal and protective of the place. He was on the front line advocating for all, while protecting those who walked the campus and taught in the halls.
>
> The word "owed" is interesting to me, because I believe Dr. Lolley's authenticity is grounded in his total commitment to what God had told him to do, and therefore we were all beneficiaries of him living a dedicated life.
>
> As president he encouraged diversity, and particularly during my time, as it pertained to women in ministry. He embraced our calling and supported women with great enthusiasm. He never failed to take interest in the church I was serving, and really made me feel as if I was the most important person possibly in the history of mankind, doing ministry.

Randall's sense of obligation to students extended beyond their seminary graduation, beyond even his service as president. At Greensboro's First Baptist Church his administrative assistant, Jo Covert, recalled that a preponderance of the letters she prepared for her boss's signature were letters of recommendation of former students to churches where they were (or wanted to be) under consideration for service.[4]

Bob Ballance recalled pastoring in the western US and becoming "homesick for the South":

> There was a church open in North Carolina, one that I knew well. I called [Randall] and said, "Would you be willing to put my name in there?"
>
> "Send me your resume NOW!" [he said]. I emailed it to him. He hand-delivered my resume to the chair of the pastor search committee later that afternoon, and she called that night to set up a time to talk. He [was] that kind of guy.

Not only recommendations and referrals but also advice and counsel were among Randall's continuing bequests to his former Southeastern charges. Mike Queen reminisced,

> Many years after graduation, he and I were in conversation just before Holy Week. I told him that I struggled to prepare a sermon for Easter. Everyone knows the story—it is hard to be fresh, interesting, etc.
>
> He said, "Boy, if you cannot get excited about preaching on Easter, something is wrong. You may need another line of work." I was shocked. Then he said, "You do not need to make it interesting. It is already the most interesting story in the history of the world."
>
> My Easter preaching was never the same after that.

In the minds of some students, Randall's range of holy obligation extended also to the churches to which he recommended them and to the Southern Baptist denomination to which they related. "I sensed that he felt great pride in the seminaries the denomination

---

4. While serving on Greensboro FBC's staff, I once entered the parking lot of a local Taco Bell at lunchtime. Visible through the plate-glass window of the restaurant was Dr. Lolley, who had finished his typical meal of a chicken burrito and Diet Pepsi. His lips moved as he held in one hand a Dictaphone and in the other a sheaf of letters from former students.

had created," said Bob Ballance, "and that he was honored to be a part of that educational delivery system. He did his best to accommodate all the constituents demanding a voice in that educational process, until the point came he could no longer accommodate the fundamentalists' rigid demands."[5]

Former students concurred with the suggestion that their president, in his dealings with the various parts of the Southern Baptist constituency, displayed a convictional willingness to host and respect religious perspectives that were different, in some ways, from his own. Bob Ballance remembered,

> As some of the moderate-minded trustees rotated off the board, replaced with fundamentalists who had a very different view of what the seminary should be teaching, Randall took extraordinary measures to get to know these new trustees. He visited with them in their homes, and if they were pastors, he visited with them in their churches. No one could have done more to accommodate their demands with integrity than Randall.

Greg Mathis went from seminary graduation to serve a growing rural congregation in Western North Carolina. Rising in prominence and engaging in denominational politics at the state level, he eventually became president of the Baptist State Convention (1996–1997). As the state convention and its churches followed the SBC in dividing along theological and political lines, Greg was associated with the conservative side.

He also counted himself among conservatives who studied at Southeastern during the Lolley era. While much of his education there he considered to be theologically well rounded, he believed he did hear "unorthodoxy" from certain professors who were "more influenced by less-conservative opinions."

---

5. The new conservative majority typically framed their demands in terms of *parity*, i.e., equitable representation of conservative professors among seminary faculty. Randall, however, viewed their actual objective as *conformity*, both to language (primarily the use of the word "inerrant" in reference to Scripture) and to doctrine (strict adherence to confessional statements).

On the other hand, Greg said he was comfortable with Dr. Raymond Brown, who "always gave both sides," and Dr. James Leo Green, who seemed to be conservative in his theology. But these, Greg assumed, represented a minority of the total SEBTS faculty.

Randall handed Greg Mathis his Master of Divinity diploma at graduation in spring 1979, just as the Southern Baptist Convention braced for a decade-long period of conflict and division. Greg said that intimations of the "gathering storm" had already been felt on the campus of Southeastern Seminary.

As Christmastime neared, Greg found himself at a Brendle's jewelry and electronics catalog showroom in Greensboro. Several aisles apart, he spotted his former seminary president, who was waiting as his wife Lou shopped. Deciding in the moment to broach a question long on his mind, Greg approached Randall, exchanged greetings and small talk, and spoke briefly of the possible turmoil within the denomination and its seminaries.

"I believe," suggested Greg, "if you could balance us up—get more teachers like Dr. Green and maybe a sprinkling of Dr. Browns—this controversy would go away." Greg recalled that Randall, while indicating his agreement with Greg's assessment, noted he would encounter resistance from faculty.

Greg understood that Randall had been committed to principles of shared governance of the seminary and faculty consensus in matters of the hiring of classroom teachers. But he inferred that the faculty ultimately asserted such influence in employment and other matters that the president's hands were tied.[6]

To Bob Ballance it appeared that Randall invariably sought the role of diplomat. "He shook every hand, friend and foe alike." Mike

---

6. Regarding his "Plan of Action," initially presented to and endorsed by SEBTS trustees in spring 1987, Randall said he had "addressed and promised balance in the selection of faculty, chapel speakers, and lecturers on campus." However, when the "new majority" conservative trustee body reassembled in autumn, "they ignored the Plan of Action completely and set out on an abrupt new course for the seminary" (*Servant Songs*, 58–59).

Queen agreed: "He tried to bridge the divide. No one could. I know. I tried to do it in N.C."[7]

As the strife in the national convention intensified into the 1980s and conservative influences set their focus increasingly on Southeastern Seminary, Randall manifested what Larry Hovis termed a "non-anxious presence":

> [As student council president] I worked closely with Randall. It was the 1986–1987 academic year, which was a very tense time. . . . Trustee meetings were extremely tense times that seemed to put everyone on edge. . . .
>
> In spite of the tremendous pressure he was under, it never seemed to break Randall's spirit. He remained a positive, upbeat person, not only in public, but in smaller, more intimate gatherings. . . . I'm sure he was anxious about all that was happening to the seminary, but at least in front of me, Randall never let his anxiety show.

"He preached hope in conflict," recalled LaCount Anderson.

Said Roger Nix, "He was never swayed to compromise his convictions in order to save his job." John Pierce agreed: "He was courageous and more protective of the institution and ideas than his own job." Nevertheless, Bob Ballance observed, Randall began to approach "a time of painful discomfort regarding his convictions. Demands were being made by fundamentalist students and trustees he could no longer accommodate."

Randall "threw down the proverbial gauntlet," Bob said, in a chapel sermon preached following the infamous autumn 1987 trustee meeting: "He was emotional—there was frustration, anger, sadness. We all knew what this sermon meant. His resignation was imminent."

> He did resign a short while later. . . . He held one last "President's Forum" in the cafeteria. . . . He talked at length about giving up

---

7. As president of the General Board of the Baptist State Convention, Mike joined with Greg Mathis in 1999 in the promotion of a "shared leadership plan," a proposal defeated that year by vote of the convention.

> this "job of his dreams." He also offered a blessing for the female students who were present, as his support for the ordination of women had been a major point of criticism by the trustees. And then he started to weep. . . . It was like a death for us all . . . .

Southeastern students, present and former, returned their own expressions of blessing and support in a rally they held in Binkley Chapel. Randy Hall (Class of '77) drove from his ministry post in Lexington, North Carolina, pausing in nearby Durham for supper at a Chinese restaurant. Breaking apart his fortune cookie at the end of the meal, Randy noticed a message he thought would be apropos for the occasion later that evening. "If I get close to Dr. Lolley, I'll give this to him," he told his car mate.

As it happened, Randy entered the chapel at the same moment as Randall. "I got this in a fortune cookie this evening, but I think that it was meant for you," he said to the president. Unfolding the small slip of paper, Randall read it and responded, "May I keep this?"

The "fortune" read: "There is no use speaking to those who have no ears."

In the course of conflict, the labeling of principals by their opponents appears unavoidable. Thus before, during, and following the rift that occurred among Southern Baptists in the 1980s, the now-familiar labels *liberal*, *moderate*, *conservative*, and *fundamentalist* became associated with personalities and groups forming the denominational constituency.

As Southeastern's president, Randall Lolley was termed a "liberal" by some (e.g., Paul Pressler in *A Hill on Which to Die*), a "moderate" by others (e.g., Cecil Sherman in *By My Own Reckoning*), and a "moderating conservative" by himself (see "Appendix B: Rolesville Retrospective").

But how did students at Southeastern during Randall's term view their president?

"Such terms [as *liberal*] only have meaning in comparisons," according to John Pierce. "He [Randall] was more conservative than some theologians and less conservative than others."

"I did not see him as a theological liberal," said Doug Murray. "He was person-focused and church-focused" but still "a substantial scholar in his own right."

"Liberal?" Jack Glasgow queried. "I would say 'yes.' He was very accurate in his scriptural exegesis and devoted to Scripture. But he was open to new ways of thinking about God and salvation. That openness is true of a liberal in the best sense of the word."

But Bob Ballance insisted, "He was not a theological liberal. I did some graduate and post-graduate work at . . . Drew University, where I encountered theological liberals. Comparatively speaking, Randall was conservative and traditional in his theological thinking and beliefs—at least so it seemed to me."

Randall was "not a liberal in the classical sense," Roger Nix clarified. But, he added, the "goal posts were moved" such that liberalism was defined by "a few specific doctrinal issues."

Borrowing a term from pastor/theologian Brian McLaren, Larry Hovis suggested Randall Lolley exhibited "a generous orthodoxy." He was deeply devoted to the Scriptures, and especially to the Gospels. "But he was so devoted to the Christ of the Gospels (an orthodox position)" that he "sought to elevate and affirm those whom Jesus elevated and affirmed."

Consequently, Larry concluded, "He was sometimes labeled as a liberal by both friend and foe."

Fight or Flight

"No one ever loathed conflict more than Jesus."

So observed Randall Lolley as he addressed the congregation on Sunday morning, in the early months of his First Baptist Church pastorate in Greensboro.

On the other hand, he added, "Crucifixion is not the product of serenity."[1]

Randall was referring to an inescapable paradox for a Christian believer. While Christ in his Sermon on the Mount had counseled meekness, nonresistance to evildoers, and turning the other cheek, still "For Jesus, from prelude to postlude was a thousand days' journey marked by constant confrontation."

He preached the sermon in late summer 1990. Operation Desert Storm, marking the onset of the First Gulf War, had just been launched under the administration of President George H. W. Bush. "What a weekend to talk about conflict and controversy!" the preacher marveled. Then he asked, "Have you noticed that these [conflict, controversy] seem to be the common thread which courses through humankind's experience? In fact, our psychologists tell us that we develop strong personalities, not by the absence of conflict, but rather by the constructive handling of it."[2]

Conflict and confrontation are stressful experiences for most people, especially for those who enjoy other people and who clearly like to be *liked* by other people. Randall Lolley was always—in the view of those who knew him long and well—a "people person" par

---

1. From the sermon "Conflict," preached August 12, 1990, as the twelfth of a thirteen-part series titled *Beginnings*.

2. Randall had majored in psychology while an undergraduate at Howard College (later Samford University).

excellence. Maintaining happy and peaceful relationships was high on the list of his personal values.

As a consequence, whenever he encountered opposition or unpleasantness in other people, he would often choose "flight" over "fight" as a stress response. Assuredly this was more in the manner of the "meekness" that Jesus counseled (Gk. *praus*, "mildness," sometimes interpreted as "strength under control") than reticence or timidity.

Baptist church pastors know that interactions with church deacons can, under some circumstances, become stressful. As an "area missionary" for the Baptist State Convention of North Carolina, Randall's younger brother Tom was occasionally invited to lead local church deacon retreats. During one such gathering at FBC Greensboro, Tom conducted the group through a study of the biblical origins of deacon ministry and the delineation of deacon qualifications, as outlined in Paul's first letter to Timothy.

Reminding everyone that the word "deacon" means "servant," Tom encouraged the body to abandon the familiar temptation to function as a ministry watchdog or a board of directors and instead to begin looking for ways to serve as ministers to the congregation while setting before its members appropriate examples of model churchmanship.

The admonition did not "take" with everyone. At a subsequent monthly meeting, one member of the Greensboro diaconate rose to enter what (for him) was a standard and oft-repeated observation—that there were too few baptisms and that church membership figures for the current year showed a slight decline from the year before. What was the explanation, and what could be done about it? (When attending and observing as a ministry staff member, I anticipated some defense or other response from my pastor. But as on previous such occasions, it did not come.[3])

---

3. In their introduction to *Bold Preaching about Christ: Sermons by J. Clyde Turner* (Nashville: Broadman Press, 1978), Randall and co-compiler Alton H. McEachern recalled a church member's observation that Turner (FBC Greensboro pastor, 1910–1948) "could remain silent in more languages than any man he had ever known."

Randall was not always so "serene." In the course of his message on conflict, he had warned, "Now hear this—the New Testament does not give us permission to be angry . . . . [Rather, under the correct circumstances] the New Testament gives us a *mandate* to be so." Still, anger—if indeed he experienced it—was a response that Randall kept judiciously suppressed, displaying it only when an occasion seemed to require it.

Miranda (not her real name) was a young woman who attended Sunday morning services for a brief period during Randall's time in the Gate City. She had a pronounced need for attention—particularly from church ministers. Having arisen from a Roman Catholic background, Miranda would often approach Randall in the hallways, address him as "Father," and proceed to confess some behavior or attitude that she believed to be sinful.

Habitually late for services, when Miranda did arrive, she would make noisy entrances into the room and position herself ostentatiously on a front pew. Once when Randall was leading a Communion service during early worship, she entered the church chapel from a side door to the altar, coffee in hand, whispering audibly to worshipers as they prepared to receive the bread and cup.

Randall proceeded with the service and concluded with a prayer of blessing, appearing unfazed by what was an obvious distraction. As worshipers departed for Sunday school, however, he approached Miranda, took her by the hand, and asked me to come along as he conducted Miranda from the room and upstairs to the pastor's study.

Once inside, Randall closed the door, went down on one knee, clasped both of the young woman's hands tightly in his own, and addressed her: "Miranda, I don't know if you understand what you did downstairs just now. What you did was interrupt the most solemn and sacred observance that we Christians have together. In the process you spoiled the entire experience for many of the people who were there."

Miranda remained silent and appeared stunned as the pastor continued. "And this is how serious it was, and I want you to hear me when I tell you how serious *I* am. You are and will remain a welcome and valued part of this congregation. But if you ever, *ever* do anything like that again, I am going to call the police! Do you understand what I am saying?"

Miranda understood, for she never repeated the infraction. The episode illustrated the disinclination of Randall Lolley to respond angrily to any frustration or irritation—except in the most egregious circumstances.

People develop strong personalities, Randall had said, "not by the absence of conflict, but by the constructive handling of it." Whether in the course of his *Beginnings* sermon series he sought to prepare his Greensboro congregation for inevitable conflict in the unfolding of their lives as pastor and people, or whether he was in reality dealing with as-yet-unresolved emotions stemming from a previous personal experience of conflict, is unknown. It may be that both objectives were in play or that his intention was to borrow from a chapter of his own past and apply its lessons to challenges that might lie in the church's future.

The principal conflict in the life and ministry of Randall Lolley dealt not with deacons or difficult church members but with the painful conclusion to an otherwise happy and fulfilling fourteen years as president of Southeastern Seminary. Randall offered a thoughtful and carefully crafted retrospective of the experience in a 1994 publication, *Servant Songs*, subtitled *Reflections on the History and Mission of Southeastern Baptist Theological Seminary, 1950–1988.*[4] As second in a collection of a dozen essays penned by people associated with the institution prior to its 1988 transition from moderate to conservative leadership, Randall's chapter was titled "Years of Pleasure and Pain: 1974–1988."

Still, the temptation—and occasionally the summons—to reflect on his seminary experience in the years immediately following his resignation from the seminary and his return to pastoral ministry must have been present. While the 1990 sermon "Conflict" (in the series *Beginnings*) made no direct mention of the strife and turmoil that had recently affected the Southern Baptist Convention, its

4. Edited by Thomas A. Bland, 31–69.

institutions, agencies, and churches, it nevertheless appeared in some respects to be a veiled response to individuals and groups who had precipitated the conflict.

Drawing upon two encounters that Jesus of Nazareth had with opponents, as chronicled in the Gospel of Mark (2:23–3:6), Randall set out to develop and outline a faithful Christian strategy for dealing with one's adversaries. He began by underscoring the "fight or flight" dilemma traditionally suggested by the discipline of psychology. Turning to memorable lines from Shakespeare's *Hamlet*, the preacher quoted:

> To be, or not to be, that is the question:
> Whether 'tis nobler in the mind to suffer
> the slings and arrows of outrageous fortune,
> Or to take up Arms against a Sea of troubles,
> And by opposing end them . . . .

In the course of his familiar soliloquy, the character Hamlet mused whether it was better ("nobler"), in human life and relationships, to accept injustice or to fight back. Referring to injustices inflicted upon oneself, Jesus had counseled the former: *Blessed are the meek.* Nevertheless, since the Lord's own life ended violently as he became a victim of Roman crucifixion, Randall pointed to what he thought should be obvious: *Crucifixion is not a product of serenity.*

From early in his sermon, the preacher set out to demonstrate Jesus' tendency *not* toward acquiescence but rather toward resistance. The targets of his resistance were "hardliners" (a term Randall used elsewhere to describe denominational opponents)—people who opposed Jesus, "whether from the left in the form of the Sadducees, or from the right in the form of the Pharisees."

"They were always coming after him," he continued in the sermon. "Their weapons did not change. Throughout the entire three years [of Jesus' earthly ministry] the weapons were always the same: Legalism, Literalism, Chauvinism, and Intimidation."

The words "legalism" and "intimidation" appropriately attach themselves, in the thinking of scriptural commentators, to the machinations of Jesus' opponents in the Gospels. "Literalism" applies as long as it is understood that the opponents' legal authorities included not only the elements of the traditional Law and Prophets (i.e., the Old Testament) but also what Jesus termed "human precepts" or "human tradition" (Mark 7:7-8, NRSV).[5]

"Chauvinism," on the other hand, seemed out of place in Randall's list of the familiar weapons of Jesus' opponents. Understood as excessive nationalism or patriotism, it might have applied to Sadducees or Herodians or perhaps to the Zealots of Jesus' day. But it applied imprecisely to the Pharisees in Randall's sermon texts, whose loyalties lay more with adherence to religious requirements and less to national identity. (In the minds of 1990 congregants, "chauvinism" likely would have connoted the familiar idea of "male chauvinism," which Randall later came to conclude motivated most of the conservative movement within the Southern Baptist Convention.)

Yet aside from subtle indications that the preacher may have had in mind recent events in the denominational struggle and in his own life, his sermon proceeded narratively and masterfully to make a general case for a Christ-like approach to the difficult matter of dealing with conflict. "Watch it take shape first in Mark 2:23-28":

> Here the hardliners seek to take the high ground. The Torah, at its heart, enforced the obligation of Sabbath observance. After all the fourth Commandment of the mighty Ten was "Remember the Sabbath day to keep it holy" (Exodus 20; Deuteronomy 5). In time, therefore, Sabbath law became the most important law of all to Pharisaic Jews. It gave them their identity. It set them apart from Gentiles.
>
> No wonder, then, they felt so deeply on this Sabbath issue. If this bastion fell, then all was lost. The whole truth of the Torah was shattered. This had to be protected at all cost.

In a real sense, Randall was *listening* to the Pharisees here, seeking to "put himself in their place" and so comprehend their point of view.

---

5. Randall referred to this "oral law" at the midpoint of his sermon, noting that the Pharisees likely concluded Jesus and his disciples violated "Rabbinic rules #586 and #587" when they chafed heads of wheat and ate the kernels as they walked through a certain field on a Sabbath day.

But in calculating Jesus' response to their objections, he identified a Christian value that in his mind rose above the Pharisees' determination to honor a single day of the week above all other human or godly concerns.

Noting Jesus' counterpoint that David himself had appeared to tread upon otherwise holy ground when he and his hungry men consumed the "consecrated bread" (1 Sam 21:4, NIV) from the altar of the sanctuary at Nob, Randall explained,

> Yet David, Jesus said, was blameless, not because the law did not hold, but by the grand release of a higher obligation. The priests were hungry, really hungry; [but] so was David. The law gave way to meeting human need. Mercy is better than the letter of the law. And mercy mandated that day in the temple that David and his friends eat the Sabbath food on the Sabbath Day.

To be sure, "Jesus did not destroy the law," Randall maintained. "He left it intact completely. The Sabbath is still holy, but there is something holier. It is a higher grace. Mercy envelops law; and mercy no longer forbids this activity [hungry people procuring and eating food] on that holy day."

The "higher grace" of which Randall spoke corresponded with what later in the sermon he would term "a fresh vision of the kingdom of God." Jesus, he insisted, proposed such a vision to his adversaries when he concluded, "The Sabbath was made for man, not man for the Sabbath."

The freshest aspect of the vision, it seemed, lay in Jesus' final word, "So the Son of Man is lord even of the sabbath" (Mark 2:28, NRSV). Insisted Randall,

> That did it. That really did it. If you wanted to get into holy trouble fast at that time with those hardliners, just say that you are the lord over the holy day . . .
>
> Here, the issue is not the interpretation of the Torah, but the very nature of the Torah—over against the nature of this young Messiah. Jesus claims lordship over the Torah, no matter who

interprets it or how it is interpreted. Jesus was not annulling the Sabbath law, he was subjecting the Sabbath to his Messiahship.[6]

Turning to Mark 3:1-6, Randall noted that Jesus once again sought to engage his detractors, who "watched him to see whether he would cure [a man with a withered hand] on the sabbath, so that they might accuse him" (v. 2). Posing a question to which he received no response (was it lawful to do good, or harm; to save life, or to kill?), Jesus did what Randall believed was mandatory: "He looked around at them with anger; he was grieved at their hardness of heart" (v. 5). Randall elaborated, "Now it is pure anger, simple anger. It is not, however, bitter, personal resentment. It is rather an anger which tapers off into pity more than to hostility or to spitefulness or revenge. It is an anger born of a grief over their hardness of heart."

Ironically, for Pharisees who were looking to see whether any "work" would be performed on the sacred day, Randall noted that they must have been frustrated:

> Jesus bids that man do a thing which is forbidden for no one. In fact, that is a common gesture with worshipers in the synagogues on the Sabbath: to stretch out their hands. . . . The man follows the word, and the man's withered hand is healed. The work is done, but there is no "work" actually done. Jesus healed with a word, and there is no prohibition against such a word in a synagogue on a holy Sabbath.

Baffled and stymied in their attempt to entrap Jesus, his enemies did what Randall counseled against. They demonstrated resentment, hostility, and spitefulness as they "went out and

---

6. "The very nature of the Torah" were words that seemed to echo SBC conservatives' phrase "the nature of Scripture" as the focus of their argument for inerrancy. While they agreed that Jesus, as Lord of all (Acts 10:36), was Lord also of the Scriptures, they insisted that Jesus "the Word" could be understood and interpreted only through the words of Scripture. (R. Albert Mohler, aligned with denominational conservatives, was quoted: "Pray what do we know of Jesus Christ apart from the Scriptures?")

immediately conspired with the Herodians against him, how to destroy him" (v. 6).

Meanwhile, reiterated Randall, Jesus "embraced a fresh new vision of the Kingdom of God, and he refused to negotiate that vision on the hardliners' terms":

> What boldness for the healed and the healer. Jesus stung his foes to madness and set the man free from a system petrified and rigid. He placed himself squarely on the side of human worth over against a depersonalized legalism. Jesus Christ, that Sabbath day, set free more than a man. He set free a system. And he did something forever, to more than the stump of a hand on that day in the synagogue. He healed religion too! . . .
>
> Meanwhile, Mark says in 3:7: "Jesus withdrew from his foes." Their hatred prepared its next blow. He is too fearless to come to terms with them. He will strip the mask from their face. He will rake the green scum from their lives. He is still their ultimate threat.

Concluding his sermon, Randall recalled how, in the two accounts of confrontation, Jesus set forth a strategy for his followers to use in dealing with conflict. "Listen," Randall said:

1. He heard the hardliners out. Over and over Jesus listened to them.
2. He countered with his own fresh vision of the Kingdom of God.
3. He called the hardliners exactly what he perceived them to be and refused to negotiate his fresh vision of the Kingdom on their terms.
4. When all else failed, he quietly walked away.

Whether or not Randall Lolley, in his later sermon to a local church congregation, was subtly and perhaps subconsciously reflecting on unhappy experiences of the preceding decade, it is instructive to explore the ways in which his responses to those events conformed to the four principles above.

He heard the hardliners out. Not everybody that Randall would in later years label a "hardliner" appeared so in the beginning. Thus it may be that "hearing them out" initially was an easier and more natural thing to do.

The clearest case in point would be a Southeastern Master of Divinity student who visited his president during fall semester 1982. The student's appearance in Randall's office followed a string of four consecutive conservative victories for the presidency of the Southern Baptist Convention. At that point, in a publicized design for altering the direction of the agencies and institutions of the convention, new and more conservative trustees were soon to arrive on Southeastern's campus.[7]

His visitor, whom Randall described as "a bright, articulate student from Winston-Salem and a graduate of the U.S. Naval Academy," sought the president's blessing for the formation of a new student organization.[8] The proposed group would bring together conservative, evangelical students for fellowship and discussion of ideas that the student claimed were omitted or misrepresented in other seminary venues.

Randall listened and initially pushed back, suggesting that existing student groups should provide an adequate platform for an airing of alternative viewpoints.[9] When his visitor persisted, however, the president "supported approval of the organization, all the while knowing the risks for division inherent in such action. My sense of openness and fair play," Randall explained, "motivated me to give these students their forum."[10]

It proved, however, one of several decisions relating to the rising conservative-moderate controversy that Randall, by his own

---

7. The plan, originally devised and proposed by Paul Pressler, called for conservative convention presidents to nominate conservative committees-on-committees, who would thereafter nominate conservative committees-on-boards, who would in turn nominate conservative trustees to SBC institutions and agencies. Each nominating cycle required a year and a sustaining vote by the subsequent convention in session.

8. See Bland, ed., *Servant Songs*, 43.

9. See Appendix B: Rolesville Retrospective.

10. *Servant Songs*, 44.

admission, would live to regret. Soon discovering that similar student organizations had simultaneously been advocated at sister seminaries, he became suspicious. In semesters to follow, he noted "confrontation after confrontation" between his administration and faculty and the Conservative Evangelical Fellowship (CEF) leaders.

"Repeatedly I got the distinct impression that the CEF leaders were being counseled and funded by persons off campus," Randall observed. "In retrospect, I was wrong to support the formal recognition of such a militant and divisive group of students on our campus."[11]

His dealings with the petitioning student and other objectors to the theological climate on the SEBTS campus illustrate, however, Randall's propensity for hearing and responding to dissident voices. "With rare exceptions," he wrote, "I responded to every letter, received or returned every telephone call, and granted every appointment requested by persons who wanted to talk about some facet of the SBC controversy."[12]

While he invariably heard people out, Randall did not always or ultimately accede to their requests. When the newly approved and constituted CEF organization aimed, as one of its first initiatives, to invite Judge Paul Pressler to address the seminary community, the president objected:

> If Mr. Pressler is invited to speak it should be in the area of his expertise—i.e., the law and courts system. Otherwise, you will be placing him in a position of being an authority quite outside his field and his opinions will be judged accordingly. In short, he is not a theologian or an expert in Biblical studies. Naturally, he has opinions on these matters, but they are scarcely informed by a lifetime and/or career in these disciplines.[13]

---

11. *Servant Songs*, 44.

12. *Servant Songs*, 43.

13. Judge Paul Pressler, *A Hill on Which to Die* (Nashville: Broadman & Holman, 1999), 155.

Subsequently, however, when members of the dissident student group met secretly with representatives of an SBC Peace Committee[14] and issued a list of twenty-seven concerns related to statements taught or published by Southeastern Seminary faculty, "President Lolley asked each faculty member to reply to the relevant concerns." The professors' answers were thereafter "communicated by President Lolley to the subcommittee [of the Peace Committee]." When the subcommittee asked for further clarification of some answers, Randall returned to relevant faculty for additional statements, even as he expressed "dismay that nothing had been heard from the subcommittee or its chair or from the Peace Committee about the earlier reply."[15]

Throughout, Randall Lolley displayed a characteristic willingness to engage in and maintain dialogue with detractors of himself and of his institution. Such willingness prevailed throughout the steady unfoldment of the decade-long transition of the convention and its institutions and agencies from moderate to conservative control. As late as autumn 1986, Randall gathered with presidents of the other five Southern Baptist seminaries prior to a Peace Committee prayer retreat at the denomination's Glorieta Conference Center in New Mexico.[16] The purpose of the preliminary meeting was (in the opinion of one observer) to "defuse the ticking bomb in Baptist life" by issuing "a reassuring statement."[17]

There Randall joined his fellow seminary heads in hammering out what came to be known as "The Glorieta Statement." The statement asserted "the supernatural origin of Christianity and the inspired, 'God-breathed' character of the Bible," while "reaffirming the seminary confessional statements, and committing [the presidents] and their institutions to balance in the classrooms, to respect

14. Established by the Southern Baptist Convention in 1985.

15. "Academic Freedom and Tenure, Southeastern Baptist Theological Seminary (North Carolina)," *Academe* (Journal of the American Association of University Professors)(May–June 1989): 37.

16. New Orleans, Southwestern, Midwestern, Southern, and Golden Gate.

17. Paige Patterson, *Anatomy of a Reformation* (Ft. Worth: Seminary Hill Press, 2004), 9.

for the convictions of all Southern Baptists, and to renewed awareness of evangelism, missions, and the Baptist heritage."[18]

The statement further affirmed the presidents' conviction that the Bible is "utterly unique. No other book or collection of books can justify that claim. The sixty-six books of the Bible are not errant in any area of reality. We hold to their infallible power and binding authority."

It became the statement's usage of the language "not errant" that prompted Peace Committee member Cecil Sherman, an early leader of the moderate resistance movement within the convention, to resign his committee membership in protest. "They caved in to their Fundamentalist critics," Sherman said of the six presidents. He explained,

> The Glorieta Statement fairly reeked with words designed to appease Fundamentalists. They were begging Fundamentalists to get off their backs. And it worked . . . but not for long. Within a few years, the men who wrote the Glorieta Statement were forced from office or fired. . . . The very people we had struggled for six years to protect were abandoning us and crossing over the line to snuggle up to their critics.[19]

In early 1993, Cecil Sherman, as first coordinator of the national Cooperative Baptist Fellowship, appeared at a North Carolina "state group meeting" at Greensboro's First Baptist Church, where Randall was entering his fourth year as pastor. As they took an elevator to the third-floor pastor's study, Randall turned to Sherman and said, "Cecil, you were right about what we did at Glorieta. You were right, and the rest of us were wrong."

I heard the exchange, but I don't recall Dr. Sherman's response. What I continue to believe, however—based on close observation of Randall then and through years to follow—is that his part in the Glorieta Statement would have in no way constituted a capitulation.

---

18. *Academe* (May–June 1989): 37.

19. Cecil Sherman, *By My Own Reckoning* (Macon, GA: Smyth & Helwys, 2008), 206–207.

Even if ultimately shown to have been ill-advised, the statement and its language demonstrate a patient and dogged determination to "hear out" his adversaries and respond to such concerns as were honestly and honorably held.

"Nobody believes in the truth of the Bible more than I do," Randall told Dr. William Friday in a late 1987 television interview.[20] What classical inerrantists (evangelicals who formulated declarations such as the Chicago Statement on Biblical Inerrancy) were looking for, he opined, was a confession that the Scriptures were entirely trustworthy. During a Conference on Biblical Inerrancy (one of three Scripture conferences that the six authors of the Glorieta Statement had promised that their institutions would sponsor), Randall had heard the words "perfect," "trustworthy," and "infallible" in reference to the Bible, and he was comfortable with such language.

He was persuaded, however, that the actual word "inerrant" had—in Southern Baptist circles—come to represent more than a simple declaration of scriptural truth. Instead it had become "part of a politicized party system" that applied the word to "a pre-packaged agenda of several items" of a social and political nature.

In an intriguing retrospective on the eventual institutional fallout from the denominational schism, Randall enumerated three "Lamps in Dark Places."[21] Recalling "an old kerosene lamp" that his Alabama family had used when retreating from an approaching tornado to their subterranean "storm pit," he observed, "There are other kinds of lamps being lighted in dark places. The lights are coming on all over the Baptist landscape in North America."

Randall identified "Lamp 1" as the journal in which he was writing, the *Review and Expositor*, a "new, broad-based Baptist consortium journal" that succeeded an organ formerly published by the faculty of The Southern Baptist Theological Seminary in Louisville. "Lamp 3" comprised the "new Baptist alliances," such as the Alliance of Baptists and the Cooperative Baptist Fellowship.

Meanwhile, "Lamp 2" *celebrated* (he used the word) "new Baptist organizations" that included conservative spin-offs from existing

---

20. *North Carolina People*, WUNC-TV, taped November 4, 1987.

21. *Review and Expositor* 94 (1997): 11–12.

state conventions: e.g., Southern Baptist Conservatives of Virginia (SBCV), Tennessee's Conservative Baptist Alliance (CBA), and similar movements in Missouri, North Carolina, and Texas.

"These Baptists," Randall conceded, "have moved in their states very much like many of us [moderates] have moved on a national level . . . . It is honorable for structure to reflect vision. Our institutions must embody our ideals. This is the Baptist way."

He countered with his own fresh vision of the kingdom of God. Ground was seldom yielded, however, on the issue of appropriate language to describe the truth of the Bible. Repeatedly through the years of the conservative-moderate SBC controversy, Randall called upon friends and adversaries alike to confess and to employ the Bible's own terminology.

In an address to the 1990 Southern Baptist Forum in Atlanta, Randall referred to Psalm 19:7-10, where the "law of the LORD" (also the *testimony*, the *precepts*, the *commandment*, the *ordinances*) is described. "Here in one Old Testament text," he pointed out, "are nine words describing the Word of the Lord—perfect, sure, right, clean, true, righteous, desirable, and sweet. And the word 'inerrant' is not among them. *Inerrant* is a man-word, not a God-word."[22]

Inerrancy language had been misused, Randall was persuaded, to subvert the width and breadth of God's calling of individuals to Christian ministry. In the 1987 television interview with Bill Friday, Randall had noted that fully a fifth of the students then studying at Southeastern Seminary were female. "We've always asked of a student, what is the direction God is calling you to? If she says the pastorate, we say great! We'll help you prepare."

Meanwhile, "These inerrantists say 'You can't be a pastor.'" Admitting that "a couple of verses on the back side of the New Testament could be interpreted that way," Randall insisted that such interpretation did not do justice to the overall message. "We have to be careful about telling a young woman she can't respond to the urgings of the Holy Spirit."

---

22. "Lest a Bramble Rule over Us," a sermon that appeared earlier in the SEBTS journal *Faith and Mission* (Spring 1984), where it was titled "Some Kinds of Baptist Boldness Needed Now."

In an early observation that would be echoed in SBC internecine disputes emerging a generation later, Randall had called the convention controversy "a test to determine whether Southern Baptists will remain a convention of conservative Christians freely cooperating within their local congregations to do evangelism, missions, education, and benevolences or whether they will become a coalition of independent fundamentalists torn asunder by power plays and party spirit."[23]

Disagreements over the role of women in preaching and church leadership would return to beleaguer Southern Baptists, lending credence to Randall's warning that the convention's rigid stances could risk further division and highlighting his alternative vision of a conservative but freely cooperating Christian denomination of churches.[24]

Perhaps the *apotheosis* of Randall Lolley's "fresh vision of the Kingdom" appeared in his authorship of a "Plan of Action" for the future of Southeastern Seminary, as by 1987 it came increasingly under the influence of an ever more conservative board of trustees. While acknowledging that the plan "satisfied neither side," the AAUP bimonthly publication *Academe* opined that Randall had "skillfully attempted to maneuver through the conflicts that surrounded him":

> He reaffirmed the Baptist heritage, the historic mission of Southeastern, and the essentiality of scholarship and the commitment to seeking truth. He upheld the seminary's confessional norm as "historic and adequate," while promising that charges relating to it would be dealt with seriously and in full accord with due process. He emphasized that faculty selection was the outcome of a partnership of trustees, administration, faculty, and students. He called for steady monitoring in annual evaluations to assure the maintenance of fairness and openness in classrooms. He rejected all forms of "caricature, intimidation, or attack of persons for their theological

23. *SBC Today*, March 1985.

24. Katherine Burgess, "Debate over women's roles breaks out on eve of Southern Baptist meeting," *Memphis Commercial Appeal*, June 9, 2019.

> beliefs" and promised that invited speakers would represent the whole theological spectrum of the Baptist constituency.[25]

The *Academe* article further noted, "At its meeting in March 1987, the board of trustees by majority vote endorsed the Plan of Action, but nothing was heard of it thereafter."

He called the hardliners exactly what he perceived them to be and refused to negotiate his fresh vision of the kingdom on their terms. For the most part, Randall, throughout the convention controversy and the resultant transition of trustee leadership at Southeastern Seminary, resisted the prevailing moderate tendency to call members of the denomination's conservative faction "fundamentalists."[26] During the Bill Friday interview he called them "inerrantists," and in the course of his "Conflict" sermon (in the *Beginnings* series), he employed the word "hardliners."

Randall seemed to respect the reality that *fundamentalist*, in most social and cultural contexts, was a pejorative term.[27] This realization did not, however, dissuade him from "calling the hardliners exactly what he perceived them to be."

In his concluding 1987 autumn convocation address at Southeastern, the president appeared to compare the function of the emerging conservative trustee majority with that of forces complicit in the crucifixion of Christ. The academic freedom that had theretofore characterized the seminary, he suggested, was the opposite of "theological indoctrination wherein truth is determined always by majority opinion. We recall all too vividly that our Lord was crucified with the majority agreeing."[28]

---

25. *Academe* (May–June 1989): 38.

26. He did use the term in later years, suggesting that the SBC inerrantist faction so self-identified. See Appendix B: Rolesville Retrospective.

27. A footnote from the *Academe* article cited above observed, "There are evidently strong objections to the use of the term 'fundamentalism.' In an article in the *Raleigh News and Observer* (November 23, 1987), a Southeastern trustee, William D. Delahoyde, wrote: 'To call someone a "fundamentalist" in this day and age is the shortened way of saying they are an anti-intellectual moralist, possessing the sophistication of Gomer Pyle and the sensitivity of Darth Vader.'"

28. Ironically, the title of the 1987 fall convocation address, *Quo Vadis, Southeastern?* (Where Are You Going, Southeastern?) was the same as that of

Later in the semester, and following his announcement of his resignation as president, Randall penned a farewell letter titled "Au Revoir," wherein he used stronger language: "I commit from this day forward every moment of my time and every millibar of my energy to restoring this school into the hands of her friends and out of the hands of her foes—so help me God!"[29]

His pushback to conservatives who were coming into the leadership of the denomination drew their ire. With a typically Lolley-esque flourish, Randall had conducted a group of dissident moderates in a march from the convention center in San Antonio to the historic site of the Alamo, following the closely contested election of conservative Jerry Vines to the SBC presidency in 1988. Conservative leader Paul Pressler reflected,

> In what I considered a sophomoric, melodramatic gesture, Randall Lolley led a few messengers to walk several blocks from the convention hall to the Alamo, where they burned their ballots. They said that freedom was being extinguished in the Southern Baptist Convention. This seemed an odd position to take, since Southern Baptists had already freely voted ten times in all parts of the convention territory to elect a conservative president.[30]

Jerry Sutton, a leading conservative chronicler of the Southern Baptist conflict and its aftermath, noted that they were not ballots that were burned at the Alamo but rather copies of a resolution that Sutton had written as chair of the convention Resolutions Committee and that the convention messengers had just adopted. The resolution, titled "On the Priesthood of the Believer," maintained that the historic doctrine had not been intended to eliminate or diminish the primary authority of a local church pastor. Randall,

---

Randall's presidential inaugural address of March 11, 1976.

29. Quoted by Joni Hannigan in "Most SBC Entity Heads Stayed True to Moderate Convictions," *Baptist Press*, June 9, 2004.

30. Pressler, *A Hill on Which to Die*, 141.

Sutton recalled, "argued that it was one of the most un-Baptist [sic] things ever adopted by the Southern Baptist Convention."[31]

Randall's own ire was evident throughout the early days of his seminary post-presidency. Having accepted the pastorate of the First Baptist Church of Raleigh, he made plans to lead the church's contingent of messengers to the San Antonio SBC meeting:

> [Randall Lolley] said that if conservatives elected Jacksonville, Florida, pastor, Jerry Vines, as SBC president this year he would suggest to moderates that they divert their contributions from normal denominational channels. . . . [In a Baptist Press release] Lolley intimated, "I am not going to finance Jerry Vines' type of leadership if I have anything to do with it as a pastor of a local church. And if I have any influence in North Carolina, I'm going to see to it that the state of North Carolina doesn't do it either. That's not a threat, that's a promise."[32]

Two years later, in 1990, in what was styled his "Bramble Bush Sermon" to the SBC Forum in Atlanta, Randall reflected on Vines and other conservatives who had borne the convention presidency since 1979:

> Our leaders recently have been elected, and they have led us with a dinosaur rhetoric. And their rhetoric is soon to die out in three crucial areas (biblical authority, pastoral authority, and Christian femaleness) as the fresh winds of a recovered biblical free-church rhetoric displace the very forces which have fueled the past.

The SBC Forum sermon was preached shortly after Randall transitioned from Raleigh to become pastor of First Baptist, Greensboro. During his six years in the Gate City, he reflected infrequently on the division within the denomination—and even less on the events that

---

31. Jerry Sutton, *The Baptist Reformation: The Conservative Resurgence in the Southern Baptist Convention* (Nashville: Broadman & Holman, 2000), 189.

32. Sutton, *Baptist Reformation*, 186. Sutton wrote that Randall, speaking again to Baptist Press a week before the San Antonio convention, *walked back* the comment, explaining, "I popped off."

had foreclosed his seminary presidency—while devoting the bulk of his attention to local church matters.

But in late 1995 he received a letter from Paige Patterson, his second-in-line successor at Southeastern. Representing the SBC Council of Seminary Presidents, Dr. Patterson was inviting Randall and wife Lou to join him and other presidents, current and past, for a dinner during the upcoming 1996 SBC meeting in New Orleans. Patterson, in typical style, had headed his invitation with the salutation, "Dear Lolley." Randall replied,

> Dear Patterson,
>
> Get real! Your pen can be honey. Your pen can be poison. Your letter of December 1 was cordial, even nice. But we have felt your sting. Lou and I have made our choice. We do not intend to be "window dressing" for you and your colleagues to claim any deep change in relationships and rapport.
>
> I still hear the words of your previous life (before you had such exclusive power); and frankly, I think your words then were much more consistent with your spirit than your words now. Sorry, but we cannot accept your invitation and we will not be in New Orleans.
>
> Sincerely, W. Randall Lolley

When all else failed, he quietly walked away. Randall's reply to Paige Patterson notwithstanding, he did come to terms with "the handwriting on the wall" regarding both the seminary and its sponsoring denomination. If he didn't at first "quietly walk away," he did eschew bitterness, he did restructure his personal ministry in positive and productive ways, and he did direct other, similarly disappointed Baptists away from their lamentable past and toward a brighter future.

Randall had repeatedly referred to an "alien vision" for Southeastern Seminary, which had arrived with newer and more conservative trustees and which conflicted with the vision he had implemented during his fourteen-year presidency. "So what will become of your vision?" Bill Friday inquired in the 1987 television interview, recorded only days after Randall's resignation. "Will academic freedom and openness of inquiry now be challenged?"

"Exactly," Randall replied. "As for my vision, it is gone with the wind."

Friday wondered whether Randall had found the loss of the seminary to be a difficult *personal* experience.

"The worst I've ever been through, Bill," Randall confessed. "Because I loved my school. I meant to stay there until I retired. I'm not trying to be melodramatic when I tell you it's been a tough, tough time."

Nevertheless, he added, the news wasn't all bad. For he had come to "a certain peace" within himself—although it was a "pained peace." Referring to a chapel sermon that he preached subsequent to his resignation, he recalled the experience of Jesus of Nazareth in Jerusalem's Garden of Gethsemane. "I got the feeling Jesus' disciples said, 'Hey, you got us into this—now don't you run out on us.' In a sense, in Gethsemane I heard him saying, 'the only way I can ever really be with you is to leave you for a while.'"

As the two—Bill Friday and Randall Lolley—prepared to sign off, Randall referred to Rev. Robert Crowley, the conservative Maryland pastor who had recently assumed the position of chair of Southeastern's board of trustees.

"Get my chairman on [your program]," said Randall. "He deserves a chance to respond to all I've said."[33]

---

33. Friday did interview Crowley during a later episode of *North Carolina People.*

Pastoral portrait at Greensboro's First Baptist Church, painted in spring 1999 and dedicated by the congregation on Sunday morning, September 12, with the Lolleys in attendance (Tom Edgerton, artist)

Roscoe Lolley family (Roscoe and Mary, Randall and Tom)

Roscoe Lee Lolley

Mary Nunnelee Lolley

Young Clara Lou Jacobs

Baseball glove used by second baseman "Lightnin' Lolley" at Samson High School, later at Howard College

Wedding Party, Westside Methodist Church, Geneva, Alabama, August 28, 1952: (l–r) Porter and Emma Jacobs, Clara Lou and Randall Lolley, Mary and Roscoe Lolley

The Rev. and Mrs. W. Randall Lolley, August 28, 1952

Dedication of Pine Ridge/Poplar Spring church parsonage, Pilot, North Carolina, 1955

Southeastern Seminary Master of Divinity Class of 1957
(Randall Lolley is right side, second from top)

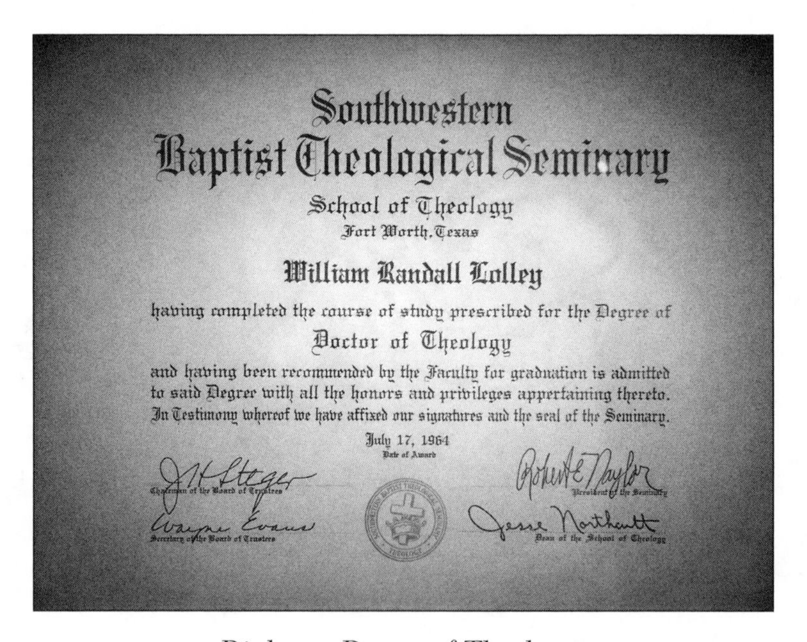

Southwestern
Baptist Theological Seminary
School of Theology
Fort Worth, Texas

William Randall Lolley

having completed the course of study prescribed for the Degree of
Doctor of Theology
and having been recommended by the Faculty for graduation is admitted to said Degree with all the honors and privileges appertaining thereto.
In Testimony whereof we have affixed our signatures and the seal of the Seminary.

July 17, 1964
Date of Award

Chairman of the Board of Trustees

Robert E. Naylor
President of the Seminary

Wayne Evans
Secretary of the Board of Trustees

Jesse Northcutt
Dean of the School of Theology

Diploma, Doctor of Theology,
Southwestern Baptist Theological Seminary, 1964

The First Baptist Church,
Winston-Salem, North Carolina (1962–1974)

Publicity photo, First Baptist Church,
Winston-Salem, North Carolina (1962)

Lolley family, FBC Winston-Salem church directory photo (1963): Pamela Jo is to the left, and Charlotte Lynn is to the right.

Randall with his immediate predecessor Olin T. Binkley, Presidential Inauguration, Southeastern Baptist Theological Seminary, March 11, 1976

The ceremony was postponed for one year to correspond with the 25th anniversary of the seminary's founding.
(courtesy Archives and Special Collections, Library at Southeastern, Southeastern Baptist Theological Seminary, Wake Forest, North Carolina)

Randall and Clara Lou receive well-wishers at his SEBTS presidential inaugural reception

(courtesy Archives and Special Collections, Library at Southeastern, Southeastern Baptist Theological Seminary, Wake Forest, North Carolina)

Preaching in Binkley Chapel, Southeastern Seminary

(courtesy Archives and Special Collections, Library at Southeastern, Southeastern Baptist Theological Seminary, Wake Forest, North Carolina)

President Lolley in his office, Southeastern Seminary

(courtesy Archives and Special Collections, Library at Southeastern, Southeastern Baptist Theological Seminary, Wake Forest, North Carolina)

Lou and Randall Lolley at Southeastern Seminary

(courtesy Archives and Special Collections, Library at Southeastern, Southeastern Baptist Theological Seminary, Wake Forest, North Carolina)

Christmas at the President's Home, Southeastern Seminary

Southeastern Seminary President's Home, Durham Road, Old Wake Forest, North Carolina

Randall and Lou with Jimmy and Rosalynn Carter, volunteering with Habitat for Humanity

SEBTS fire truck donation to the Town of Wake Forest

(courtesy Archives and Special Collections, Library at Southeastern, Southeastern Baptist Theological Seminary, Wake Forest, North Carolina)

"The Lolleyday Inn," Valle Crucis, North Carolina

Randall and SEBTS faculty dean Morris "Ash" Ashcraft, relaxing at the Lolleyday Inn

Randall sharing a moment with Lou

President Norman A. Wiggins presenting Randall Lolley the Doctor of Humane Letters (HL.D.) at Founders Day, Campbell University, January 16, 1986

(Randall also received honorary doctorates from Samford, Wake Forest, Mercer, and the University of Richmond.)

Tom and Randall Lolley (standing), with their father Roscoe at SEBTS

University of North Carolina Chancellor William C. "Bill" Friday (*North Carolina People*, UNC-TV) interviewing Randall Lolley after the latter's October 1987 resignation as president of Southeastern Seminary

(courtesy Special Collections & University Archives/Wake Forest University)

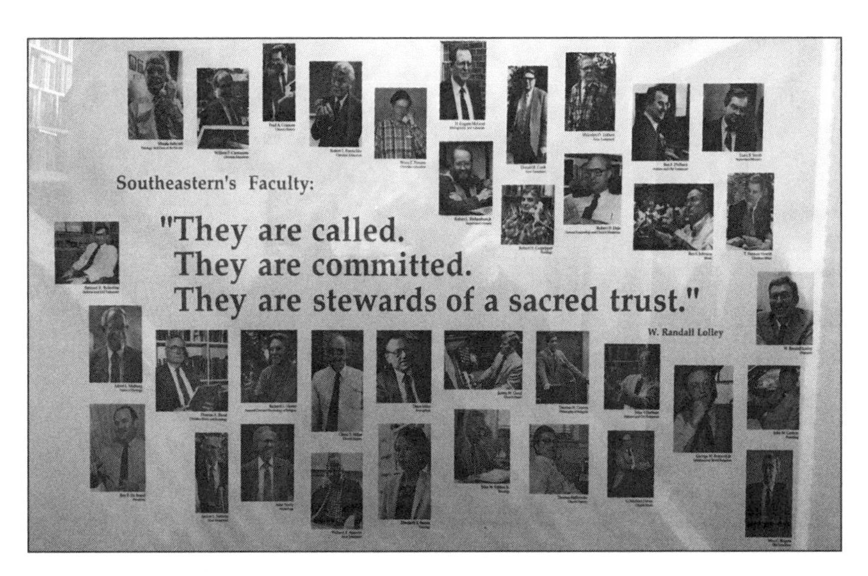

The faculty of Southeastern Seminary during Randall's final year as president (1987)

The Alexander Meiklejohn Award for Academic Freedom,
presented by the American Association of
University Professors, 1988

Tim Lolley receiving his M.Div. diploma from his uncle, as
Randall presided at his own final SEBTS graduation, Spring 1988

Ribbon-cutting for the SEBTS women's dormitory

In summer 1988, Randall bade farewell to Southeastern Seminary
(George W. "Joe" King painting)

The First Baptist Church of Raleigh, North Carolina (1988–1990)

Randall listening intently to
nine-year-old parishioner Janet Barnes.

(Not long after this late-summer encounter, Janet lost her life when an F4 tornado struck Raleigh, November 28, 1988. Photo courtesy FBC Raleigh.)

Sunday school at Maranatha Baptist Church (Plains, GA),
with Jimmy and Rosalynn Carter

The First Baptist Church of Greensboro, North Carolina
(1990–1996)

The "Good Ship Lolley-pop," Children's Library mural painted by FBC Greensboro custodial supervisor Tyrone Smith

"Coach Lolley," prepared to lead the FBC Greensboro staff to victory over the deacons

Lou douses Randall in an FBC Greensboro game of "Flush-em."

Ninety-seven-year-old Greensboro FBC member Bill Lusk with Randall's 2015 publication, *Journey with Me*, featuring sermons introducing every book of the Bible

Randall Lolley's 36-volume lifetime collection of mostly handwritten sermons

Ribbon cutting for the Lou and Randall Lolley Room, Baptist Theological Seminary at Richmond (BTSR)

Touring Egypt via camel

Representative souvenirs from Randall's "bucket list" travels

Randall teaching at Capernaum's "White Synagogue"
(Israeli tour guide Gila Yudkin to his left, in cap)

Randall teaching in Jerusalem's Garden of Gethsemane
(Eastern "Golden" Gate and Dome of the Rock to the rear)

Assisting fellow Holy Land pilgrim and FBC Greensboro member Dr. Helen Stinson aboard a tour bus in Bethlehem, as she reads the Nativity story from Luke's Gospel

Lou and Randall lunching at The Cypress, their retirement community in Raleigh

Chapter 8

Randall Lolley and the Bible

Lou Lolley and her daughters have maintained that, of the many awards and recognitions that came to their husband and father through his years of active ministry, the one he cherished most was the Alexander Meiklejohn Award, presented by the American Association of University Professors. The AAUP website reads,

> The Alexander Meiklejohn Award for Academic Freedom is given to an American college or university administrator or trustee, or to a board of trustees as a group, in recognition of an outstanding contribution to academic freedom, preferably during the preceding year. . . . The award is made only when the contribution to academic freedom is judged to be truly outstanding.

The recognition followed Randall's 1987 resignation from the presidency of Southeastern Baptist Theological Seminary. During the prior fourteen years, he had presided over a faculty and an institution suspected by some observers as manifesting academic freedom in the form of theological liberalism.[1]

Whether the liberalism was real or imagined, and whether Randall himself was "liberal" or whether, as a matter of philosophy and personal principle, he simply was comfortable hosting a variety of theological viewpoints—these are disputable matters. His happiness with the Meiklejohn recognition, however, seems to point to the latter option.

---

1. Grady Cothen, *What Happened to the Southern Baptist Convention?* (Macon, GA: Smyth & Helwys, 1993), 280.

"Let the experts be the experts" is the amplification that one former SEBTS faculty member gave to Randall's interpretation of "academic freedom."[2] But the latter's tendency to permit expertise to define itself and pursue its own direction rankled people who believed seminary-based research and teaching should be confined to the parameters of commonly held convictions of churches and church members cooperating with and contributing money through the parent denomination.

In his book *A Hill on Which to Die*, Judge Paul Pressler, acknowledged as one of two original "architects of the conservative resurgence," enumerated a "Delineation of Possible Problems" within agencies and institutions of the SBC.[3] Pressler wrote that he had compiled the list in 1985 at the request of a former state Baptist convention executive secretary. Of the fifty-three examples of "possible problems" cited by Pressler, a majority referenced seminary teachings and the published or publicly expressed opinions of seminary faculty members.

Four examples related to Southeastern Seminary. John E. Steely, formerly Professor of Historical Theology, had been quoted in the Virginia Baptist newspaper *The Religious Herald* (in reference to Paul's counsel about women teachers in the church, 1 Tim 2:11-15): "Paul, your logic doesn't persuade me." Steely had said he would never use the word "wrong" in reference to Scripture, but he believed that the Apostle himself was "fallible."

Next, Robert G. Bratcher of the American Bible Society, who for one term was employed at Southeastern as a summer school faculty member, was quoted as having told a 1981 SBC Christian Life Commission seminar, "Only willful ignorance or intellectual dishonesty can account for the claim that the Bible is inerrant or infallible. . . . No truth-loving, God-respecting, Christ-honoring believer should be guilty of such heresy."

Pressler wrote that Bratcher continued, "We are not bound by the letter of scripture, but by the spirit. Even words spoken by Jesus in Aramaic in the thirties of the first century and preserved in writing

2. Robert D. "Bob" Dale, who served during Randall Lolley's presidency as Professor of Pastoral Leadership and Church Ministries.

3. Nashville: Broadman & Holman Publishers, 1999, 323–52.

in Greek, 35 to 50 years later, do not necessarily wield compelling or authentic authority over us today." Christian authority, Bratcher added, rested not in scriptural words but rather in Jesus Christ as "THE Word of God."

A third example, which Pressler attributed to "institutional liberalism," took the form of "a litany used in the Seminary chapel worship service at Southeastern Seminary on March 17, 1983." The litany invited women in the congregation to affirm: "The gospel is liberation . . . . Jesus broke the law and tradition in his treatment of women . . . . Jesus was a feminist." Men attending the service were invited to concur: "The gospel is liberation . . . . We need to discard our masculine role and discover who we really are."

A fourth and final example bearing specifically upon Southeastern related to Old Testament professor John I Durham's contribution of lessons on the book of Job, submitted for publication in the Sunday School Board adult Sunday school curriculum *Life and Work.* In the first lesson, dated July 7, 1985, Durham had been represented as stating, "There is in the Old Testament no concept of an empire of evil opposed to God. God was in charge, and 'the one who accuses' was His loyal servant."

As Randall Lolley earlier acknowledged, this had provided some general readers, and especially critics of the seminary, the impression that his professor had denied "the reality of Satan or evil." What Durham had originally written and submitted for publication was materially different: "There is here no question of any save God being in charge, and 'the one who accuses' is his loyal servant." The claim about "no concept of an empire of evil opposed to God" having a presence in the Old Testament was said to be an editorial addition not approved by Durham.[4]

Meanwhile, unhappiness with certain teachers and teachings at Southeastern Seminary showed itself not only in anxious and accusatory inquiries from outside the campus but also in the formation and

---

4. Bland, ed., *Servant Songs*, 49. Pressler disputed the contention that the editorial addition altered Durham's overall meaning. He quoted Sunday School Board president Lloyd Elder: "A more complete review of the entire lesson shows the manuscript by Durham is not unlike what appears in print."

function of a student group known as the Conservative Evangelical Fellowship (CEF). During autumn 1982, Randall became aware of the group's desire to organize and receive formal seminary recognition. The impetus for the organization, he learned, was the sense on the part of some students that "'the conservative viewpoint' on most issues was either omitted or misrepresented in seminary circles."[5]

Randall wrote, "Throughout the process I supported approval of the organization . . . . My sense of openness and fair play motivated me to give these students their forum." He later came to regret his compliance, however, as CEF "became a controversial, divisive presence on our campus." A year before his resignation as its president, the seminary placed CEF on administrative probation in response to a secret, off-campus meeting it had held with visiting members of what was known as the SBC Peace Committee.[6]

The question is fair: did Randall as a seminary president accommodate within the academic community points of view regarded by critics as "liberal" because he necessarily concurred? Or was it rather because of the "sense of openness and fair play" that he celebrated within himself—the same *liberality* (as opposed to liberalism) that likewise led him initially to support the existence of an adversarial organization, which ultimately, in his view, became detrimental to the fellowship, morale, and core values of his teaching and learning community?

Moreover, was this liberality what he later understood to be recognized by the American Association of University Professors in their conferral upon him of the Meiklejohn Award for Academic Freedom?

Disagreement over the nature of Christian Scripture and the implication of such disagreement were central to the division that arose in the Southern Baptist Convention and widely manifested itself beginning in the late 1970s. Was the Bible "inerrant" (without mistakes of any kind as originally written)? Or was it, even though "inspired" by the Holy Spirit, nonetheless a product of the temporal and cultural circumstances under which it was composed—and

5. *Servant Songs*, 43.

6. *Servant Songs*, 44.

therefore subject to certain anomalies that required careful interpretation in all cases, and revision in some?

There is no known record of the conversation that took place between the newly called Randall Lolley and the forty men who constituted his Samson, Alabama, ordination council in 1951. The ordination certificate simply indicates that the candidate was examined with respect to his "Christian experience, call to the ministry, and views of Bible Doctrine," and that his performance on the examination was deemed "satisfactory."

What may be ascertained, however, is the way in which the newly minted minister came to flesh out his calling and propound his understanding of Scripture and its teachings. What was his essential regard for that expansive body of literature known as the Bible? With what manner of reverence did he approach its sixty-six books, and how did they function to inform his preaching, teaching, and institutional leadership throughout his forty-five years of vocational ministry and his continuing ministry after retirement?

Did his attitude toward the "inerrancy"—or the absence thereof—of holy Scripture make a material difference in the content of his teaching or in the authority he ascribed to the Bible's presence in Christian life?

During the concluding year and a half of his formal, vocational ministry, Randall Lolley pursued an ambitious and suggestive project. His closing proclamation to his final congregation was to be a lengthy series of Sunday morning sermons, each devoted to a complete book of the Bible.[7] In the preface to a later, published version, Randall wrote, "The purpose of these sermons was to review the entire biblical landscape, and to discern once more the interconnectedness and interrelatedness of the Holy Scriptures. Hopefully, the redemptive threads woven from Genesis to Revelation have come to light in these sermons."[8]

---

7. Some were combined according to genre, e.g., 1 and 2 Kings and 1, 2, 3 John. The series repeated, with minor modification, one preached in Raleigh in the late 1980s.

8. *Journey with Me* (Macon, GA: Nurturing Faith, Inc., 2015), preface.

Randall's lengthy, capstone pulpit project formed a ministry bookend with a shorter series he had presented six years earlier. Soon after arriving in Greensboro in 1990, he preached thirteen sermons from the four Gospels, appropriately titling that series *Beginnings*. A cursory search of the total seventy-one collected sermons from the two series sheds significant light on the preacher's agreement or disagreement with positions attributed to some of the professors serving with him during the days of his seminary presidency. The two sets of sermons were preached within eight years of Randall's departure from Southeastern.

Regarding Robert Bratcher, onetime summer school professor at Southeastern and later head of the American Bible Society, Randall thought well of him. In 1993, he hosted Bratcher for a Winter Bible Study at First Baptist Greensboro. Nevertheless, his position on the authority of Scripture, while not entirely dissimilar to Bratcher's, was sufficiently nuanced to correspond with the understanding of Baptists as a whole.

Bratcher had been quoted by Paul Pressler as saying, "We are not bound by the letter of scripture, but by the spirit," adding, "It is Jesus Christ as THE Word of God who is the authority for us to be and to do." In his introduction to his through-the-Bible series—a sermon titled "The Primacy of Scripture"—Randall appeared to agree, opining that Baptist belief was not related primarily to the printed words of the Bible but rather to "the Word behind the words." However, he added a significant qualification: "There is simply no other place [other than the Bible] where we can go to hear God speak."

An earlier version of the same introductory sermon recalled a "simple commitment" the preacher had made when "clouds of controversy" first descended upon the Southern Baptist Convention. The commitment was a handwritten statement kept in the desk drawer of the president's office at SEBTS, there to be examined by any who cared to inquire.

The first article of Randall's commitment stated, "I accept unequivocally the scripture as the WORD OF GOD." Then came his pledge that, while he would willingly use any word the Bible used to describe itself, he would not employ other language that some might attempt to force upon him. Thus Randall's resistance to the use of the word "inerrant" echoed Bratcher's (although Randall would later appear to acquiesce).[9]

In the well-documented controversy surrounding a Sunday school lesson prepared by Southeastern professor John I Durham and published by the Sunday School Board, Durham had been understood by some to question the concept of an "empire of evil opposed to God" in the Old Testament, and perhaps even to deny the existence of Satan as later presented in the New Testament. While a reading of the Old Testament portion of Randall's through-the-Bible series fails to turn up clear references to Satan, the sermon on Job noted, "*Hasatan* stripped him." (*Hasatan* is Hebrew for "accuser," one of the Bible's terms for the devil.) Randall further stated, "Job is not fictional. He is fact. Job is not an imaginary man. He is real."

In all instances of his preaching, where people are portrayed in Scripture as actual, historical figures, Randall assumed that they were such. Where episodes are presented as having occurred in actual time and space, he assumed that they did. In his Gospel series titled *Beginnings*, he turned to Matthew's account of Satan's temptations of Jesus, following the latter's baptism in the Jordan River. There Randall took for granted the ontological reality of the devil, even observing, "You simply have to admit the devil quoted scripture too!"

With regard to the allegedly "feminist" litany at Southeastern, "Randall has always been very pro-woman" (so explained wife Lou in a mid-2019 private conversation). It is therefore unsurprising that he would have found comfort hosting a seminary chapel service where a reading proclaiming that "Jesus broke the law and tradition in his treatment of women" appeared in the worship order.

He resisted, however, the suggestion that this inclination on his part was either liberal or unbiblical. Recalling a 1986 visit of members of the SBC Peace Committee to the Southeastern campus for the

9. The Glorieta Statement of 1986, drafted by Randall and his fellow SBC seminary presidents, used the phrase "not errant in any area of reality" with respect to the Scriptures.

purpose of investigating allegations made largely by the Conservative Evangelical Fellowship, he said,

> These students brought these radical, rigid, weird charges, with no focus at all—it was just broad charges. One, for example, that I remember so vividly, levied against John Steely . . . . The students said that he supported women in ministry. . . . The Peace Committee spent a good bit of time wanting to explore what it meant on our campus to support women in ministry—as if that were a mortal sin.[10]

Following his 1996 retirement from active pastoral ministry, Randall accepted a Cooperative Baptist Fellowship invitation to teach English as a second language (ESL) in the south-central Siberian city of Irkutsk, Russia. He noted at the time that a secondary motivation was to visit local churches and experience "pristine Christianity." Asked, upon his return, what aspect of the experience made the deepest impression on him, he expressed his surprise and disappointment that women in that setting were given little or no opportunity to teach or to preach in the churches.

Whether or not such practice was constitutive of a "pristine" expression of the faith, Randall took profound issue with it. He understood that the Apostle Paul had placed limitations on women in the churches with whom he corresponded (e.g., 1 Tim 2:11-15), but Randall was persuaded that responsible interpretation required reading such texts in light of strictly local problems faced by the churches and not as dictates that would bind the church as a whole in centuries to follow.

While opponents of Southeastern Seminary and its president counted a pro-women-in-ministry posture as but one among several of the institution's "problems," Randall himself came to see his and the seminary's position as altogether central to their critics' concern. Nineteen years following his retirement, in a 2015 homecoming sermon to Raleigh's Longview Baptist Church, he described the

10. Cothen, *What Happened to the Southern Baptist Convention?*, 211.

historic growth and expansion of Baptists in their various expressions as "both a bane and a blessing."

"Paramount" among the reasons, he said, was that "there arose a group of hardliners among us who operated on a very simple dictum: 'Our way or the highway!'" Randall recalled that he was "doing the job of my dreams" in the mid-1980s when hardliners assumed control of the Southern Baptist Convention and its institutions and agencies. "They came to a meeting in March [1986] with a plan in place—a plan that they said would guarantee the 'purity' of our school."

The "plan," as Randall described it, called for him to tell women studying at Southeastern that the Bible prohibited their ordination to pastoral ministry. They might serve as missionaries or in other areas of ministry not requiring ordination, but local church pastorate was scripturally limited to men.

"I protested!" Randall recalled.

> And [I] asked them where in the Bible was this prohibition. It was then that I realized how they cherry-picked scripture. They could pick a verse here and a verse there, cobble them together, and make the Bible say just about anything that they wanted it to say. I warned them of that and came to believe that is precisely what they intended to do. They did NOT want women to be Preachers.

Concluding the thought, Randall in characteristic fashion observed, "Accurate understanding of the Bible demands that we read a text in its context. That means in the womb of all the Scripture surrounding it, taking into account the connections between the texts."

Another 2015 sermon, marking the installation of a female pastor at Raleigh's Crabtree Valley Baptist Church, approached the issue of women ministers head-on. Referencing 1 Corinthians 12:4-11 (Paul's discussion of variety in spiritual giftedness) and 2 Timothy 4:1-5 (the Apostle's charge to a person possessing the gift of preaching), Randall concluded, "I leave you with this: the Scriptures teach that our God in Jesus Christ calls some to be priests, some to be prophets, and some to be guardians in the house of the Lord—all to the edification of the Saints. Not once in these texts does the Bible disfranchise women."

Along the way Randall informed the Crabtree Valley congregation of "the most significant and painful decision of my life: to resign . . . as President of my Alma Mater on the principle of Christian Femaleness within Ministry in Jesus Christ's name." (In a handwritten note found loose among his files at his home office in Raleigh was this: "I would not want it my legacy to disfranchise over ½ the human race from the highest calling to SERVANTHOOD in Christendom. Jesus Christ obliterated that practice by his example.")

While on issues such as women in ministry he appealed to Jesus' example from the Gospels and Paul's words from his New Testament letters, Randall never disregarded or untethered himself from the Hebrew Scriptures. His attitude toward their veracity and their revelatory uniqueness is apparent from his treatment of several Old Testament works in the course of his book-by-book preaching series.

Important to remember is that a portion of the SBC controversy around the Scriptures pertained to the "historicity," or absence thereof, of the first eleven chapters of the book of Genesis. The initial publication of the 1969 Broadman Bible Commentary's first volume, *General Articles/Genesis–Exodus*—where the Genesis portion appeared to disavow the idea that Adam and Eve and Noah were historical people or that the events surrounding them actually occurred in space and time—was ultimately withdrawn, rewritten, and replaced.

While Randall appreciated the scholarship of G. Henton Davies, the writer of the original commentary on Genesis, his preaching did not echo Davies's opinion. And while he did not position himself on the precise historicity of the narratives, neither did he deny that the named personalities and their "stories" were real. Adam and Eve were cited alongside the later Noah and the Hebrew Patriarchs as actual people. "To ignore them, to deny their stories and the foundational truths they hold, is to cut ourselves loose in a sea of chance," he wrote.

With regard to the book of Exodus, Randall in his sermon on Genesis had already acknowledged the actual personhood of lead character Moses: "Moses may well have written huge portions of the Pentateuch, but there is evidence that these earliest books of the Bible are not the single work of any one person." Then, in his treatment of

Exodus, he contextualized the book's account of God's call of Moses within extrabiblical history regarding the Hyksos kings of Egypt—thereby assuming the historical truth of Exodus.

Randall's tendency to assume the reality of Old Testament historical narratives comes especially to light in his acceptance—and seemingly his justification—of the conflicts engaging the children of Israel with the Canaanite nations in the book of Joshua. "These wars of possession," he noted, "were terrible surgery, but they were surgery, according to the Bible. For here, moral tumors were being cut out of history, so that the healthy part might survive."

"History" was an important concept in Randall's treatment of the Law and the Prophets. From his sermon on 1 and 2 Kings: "The prophets interpreted the events of Hebrew history in light of their white-hot allegiance to Yahweh, the God of Israel." In only limited instances was his reception of historical reality tempered by the notion that an account may have been filtered through the recollection of contemporary observers. Of Elijah and his "translation" into heaven aboard a fiery chariot, Randall wrote, "Even in death he could not be tamed. His countrymen testified that he disappeared in a whirlwind and left no grave."

"Esther: For Such a Time as This" presented the preacher with an opportunity to explore in Old Testament proclamation his New Testament preoccupation with women as men's equals, particularly with reference to their ability to serve God. Located within the sermon is a four-paragraph paean of praise for women and how they should "break all the molds" that have been "prepared for them by men and culture."

While the book of Esther does not mention God, one "mold" that Randall apparently believed had been prepared "by men and culture" was Scripture's consistent reference to deity by use of masculine pronouns. Whereas his preaching prior to his time as president of Southeastern Seminary made use of "he," "his," "him," and "himself" in reference to God as Father, all sermons after 1988 illustrate that he dispensed with the practice, preferring to repeat the word "God" as often as necessary. He continued, however, to quote passages from his typically used NIV preaching Bible with the masculine pronouns intact.

In his sermon "Job: Declaration of Independence," Randall observed that the author is unknown. However, "There may be reason to believe that this is an autobiographical drama in which a nameless Jew relates his own struggles through the pen-name of Job." All the same, "Job is not an imaginary man."

Randall was careful to exercise caution and even a certain humility in addressing what many commentators and observers regard as the more fanciful portions of the Old Testament's narratives. Arriving at the book of Jonah in his through-the-Bible series, he sought to drive straight through to the prophetic message underlying the story line. But along the way he acknowledged what he termed "incidentals," which though incidental were nonetheless important:

> The incidentals are the ship, the ticket, the storm, the fish, the gourd, the wind. If we focus on them, we miss the essential message. Now let me hasten to say that just because they are incidental, that does not make them unimportant. I am not prepared to say that these existed only in the imagination of the writer. This is no fable we are dealing with.

Arriving at the New Testament and its four Gospels, Randall dealt with them unconventionally. There he focused on what might be discerned from the Gospels about the lives and testimonies of the named writers, Matthew, Mark, Luke, and John. These "autobiographies" he believed were enclosed within the overarching biographies of Jesus of Nazareth, and with the necessary effort could be detected there.

Authorship of the Gospels was assumed from their titles. Even Mark was not taken to be pseudonymous in the usual sense: "Behind these pages that bear the name and reveal the hand of John Mark stands a story warm and human in its weakness, lofty and soaring in its strength." (Typically controversial issues attending Gospel interpretation, such as the Virgin Birth, the miracles, and the nature of the Atonement, were approached in the series *Beginnings* and are dealt with below.)

Departing the Gospels, Randall pursued the biographical theme in his regard for Acts and Romans, both of which he understood to have the Apostle Paul as their primary subject matter. While Acts does indeed detail the "acts" of the apostles and the "action" of the Holy Spirit, Randall presented Paul as the primary subject matter in the mind and intention of the writer Luke.

In Romans, Paul was regarded as his own biographer, as he employed his memory of his own experience in order to detail four great themes of his missionary message: God's initiative in Christ, humankind's great need, Christ's offer of salvation, and humankind's great opportunity of service to God and the world.

Using his sermon "Romans: Keep the Faith" to introduce itself and succeeding sermons on the Epistles of Paul, Randall offered a cautionary word that, as he moved forward, would guide his interpretation of the total Pauline correspondence. "In the letters," he reminded, "we hear only one side of a conversation." What the churches were saying back to Paul was largely unknown and mostly to be intuited. It is the Scripture interpreter's task, therefore, to reconstruct circumstances and situations and then to apply consequent lessons to the lives of individuals and churches in the present time.

As a reminder, by the time Randall arrived at Galatians, listeners were encouraged not to regard Paul's letters as "theological treatises." Utilizing the services of a fast-writing *amanuensis* (stenographer), and only occasionally adding a postscript in "my own hand" (Gal 6:11), Paul was engaged in actual correspondence, with no apparent assumption that the church would eventually receive his writings as authoritative Scripture.

It may or may not be significant that Randall did not, in his treatment of 1 and 2 Timothy, deal with the implication of 1 Timothy 3:16-17 ("All scripture is God-breathed . . ."); and all the more since verse 17 ("that the man of God may be thoroughly equipped for every good work") was the scriptural watchword for Southeastern Seminary, appearing on every graduate's diploma as part of the seal of the institution.

Since, however, his preaching focus in the Pastoral Epistles was pastoral ministry and not the nature and purpose of Scripture, one may return to the introduction of the overall through-the-Bible series. In "The Primacy of Scripture," Randall included strong, unambiguous language:

> But add to that the Bible's clearest, cleanest, noblest, most climactic word about itself. That word is found in 2 Tim. 3:16. . . . The word Paul uses is theopneustis—theos, "God," and pneustis, meaning "to breathe." Put the word together and Paul is saying "Timothy, scripture is God-breathed; it is inspired by the very Spirit, the very breath, the very wind of the Lord . . . ."
>
> The entire matrix of origination, transmission, translation, canonization, interpretation, and proclamation of the Scriptures is caught up in that amazing word: that all Scripture is inspired, God-breathed by the Lord.

Given Randall's eager (if careful) preparedness to embrace the truth of the Old Testament in a way reminiscent of its normal and traditional acceptance by Baptist people, it is unsurprising that he would approach the Gospels in the same manner.

The clearest illustration lay in the earlier, thirteen-part series titled *Beginnings*, which the preacher used in mid-1990 to launch his capstone ministry in Greensboro. In the course of the series he dealt—sometimes incidentally and other times intentionally and directly—with convictional matters that some had used to assess whether or not the Bible was being regarded as "truth, without any mixture of error."[11]

In an introduction appended to a printed and bound copy of the completed series, Randall noted that Jesus' own "beginnings," experienced at various points throughout his earthly ministry, were used as a paradigm for "our pilgrimage as pastor and people." Moreover, he said that the several sermons had served to "hint" of "the direction of my own Christology."

The lead sermon, titled simply "Birth," dealt with the Virgin Birth not as an incidental matter but as a divine declaration: "God

11. The language is from the first article of the confessional statement of the Southern Baptist Convention, *The Baptist Faith and Message*, 1963.

wants us to believe that one time, in one moment in history, God made a baby God's way. . . . That is the miracle of history." Alluding to ways in which people "make" babies in an age of scientific and medical advancement, Randall marveled, "Then we argue with Matthew, Mark, Luke, and John when they tell us God made this baby God's way."

Throughout the "Birth" sermon, Randall used the term "supernaturalism" uncritically. Noting that the Gospel writers assumed the miraculous in the Lord's birth and that people in the first century believed in miracles, Randall stated, "If few do now, it's our problem, not theirs."

In a later sermon titled "Miracles," a Communion meditation based on the story of Jesus' transformation of water into wine at a wedding in Cana of Galilee (John 2:1-11), Randall quoted St. Augustine: "Everything is natural to God." Miracles, he deduced, "are not contrary to nature. Miracles are simply contrary to what we know of nature. Miracles are contrary to human nature, not to divine nature."[12]

"Tell these stones to become bread," Randall quoted Satan in the sermon "Temptation" (Matt 4:3). Speaking specifically of Jesus' ability to work miracles, the preacher was insistent: "You have to believe he [Jesus] could do it. If you do not believe Jesus Christ could have done that, then you do not have a temptation."

Regarding the historical factuality of the Gospel narratives, Randall demonstrated from the first of his *Beginnings* sermons his preparedness to expand on stories and imaginatively fill in missing details, particularly topographical and geographical details. Speaking of the holy family's "Flight into Egypt" to escape King Herod's "Slaughter of the Innocents" in Bethlehem, he noted, "They had to travel from Nazareth to Bethlehem, at least eighty miles by foot, to have this child. Now they must travel hundreds of miles more just to save this baby's life."

Continuing, he pondered,

---

12. While leading a 2007 Holy Land pilgrimage and passing by the traditional site of the biblical Cana of Galilee, Randall told his motorcoach passengers that the miracle might best be viewed as "mystery."

> Why was this trip necessary? Why must God's great breakthrough come so quickly to this? Why would father, mother, and holy child be forced to face the never-ending threats of the desert where the winds howl ceaselessly and blow stinging sands into the eyes of would-be travelers; and where the slippery, sandy stuff stretches endlessly ahead like so many mountains of brown sugar?

As one who, in the course of his pastoral and educational ministries, studied the holy lands in detail and conducted at least a dozen student and church member pilgrimages, Randall was in a position to know distances, directions, and relationships among geographical features of the biblical landscape. Moreover, his sharing of these details implied his conviction that the Gospel narratives were true and authentic, as presented.

Turning to Matthew's account of the baptism of Jesus in the Jordan River (Matt 3:1-17), Randall once more retold a familiar narrative in a way that communicated his conviction of its historical reality and factuality. In the sermon titled "Baptism," he began to rely on the concept of "record."

There was in Luke "the record" of Mary's visit to her kinsman Elizabeth, mother of John the Baptist (Luke 1:39ff.). Recalling John's hesitancy to honor Jesus' request to be baptized, Randall wrote, "Listen to the *record* (Matthew 3:14): 'John would have prevented him, saying . . . .'"

"Here is the *record*," he wrote, pertaining to Matthew's story of Jesus' wilderness temptations. While all three synoptic Gospels related the story, "No Gospel writer could have *recorded* the events had not Jesus disclosed them. Jesus told them about this moment."

Speaking of the original dozen disciples, Randall observed, in a sermon titled "Discipleship," that "Matthew, John, and Peter all wrote in the New Testament, and their *records* are amazingly diverse."

Enunciating a predominantly ethical (as distinct from evangelistic) view of Christian mission, Randall focused on Jesus' demands in his Sermon on the Mount. Titled "An Ethic of Salt and Light," and based on Matthew 5:13-16, the preacher's message addressed what it might mean to be Christian. "Christianity—when does it begin?" he asked, answering, "It begins when the salt salts." It begins, that is, when the earth is enhanced and improved through the presence and activity of Christian people.

Jesus' own mission, meanwhile, Randall viewed as the atonement for sin brought about through his crucifixion. The sermon was titled "Pain," and there the preacher continued to fill perceived gaps in the scriptural narrative. Thinking of the imprisoned John the Baptist and what might have been a more straightforward appeal to Jesus (Matt 11:1-6), Randall used his own imagination to put words in the latter's mouth: "My dear cousin John, I can no more deliver you from your prison than I can deliver myself from my cross, not and be true to the mission."

In the same passage, the Lord's words, "Blessed is he, whosoever shall not be offended in me" (v. 6, KJV), are taken to mean "Blessed is he who is not offended in the way God finally delivers God's children."

As he neared the conclusion of the thirteen-sermon *Beginnings* series, Randall appeared to be alluding to the pain of losing the seminary he had headed, as a consequence of the controversy in the Southern Baptist Convention. In a sermon from Mark 2:23–3:6, titled "Conflict," he regarded the account of Pharisaic opposition to Jesus' healing and his disciples' picking grain on the Sabbath as a warning about "religious hardliners."

Finally, in "Freedom," a Communion meditation based on John 8:31-32 ("the truth will set you free"), Randall closed his sermon by making an appeal for a freedom that acknowledges other people's right to be "wrong"—but that commits to gathering about the Lord's table with them anyway.

The First Baptist Church of Greensboro, like many churches, maintains and displays portraits of past pastors in a particular location within the church building. There one may view images of pastor-leaders going back to 1910. The congregation cherishes a tradition of long pastorates, so only five portraits appear. In two of the paintings, men are pictured in business suits, seated alone. In a third, the man stands in his pulpit robe, clutching a folder in his hands. In another, the preacher stands back of the pulpit.

In the remaining portrait, the preacher stands with his preaching Bible in his grip. He is handsomely attired (as he always was) in a white shirt, business suit, and tasteful tie, and his hands communicate strength and tenderness as they cradle the book close to his chest. His gaze through his glasses is warm and penetrating, and his smile is welcoming.[13]

The Bible, a leather-bound New International Version that he preferred for preaching (because, he said, it lapped comfortably over his hands), was the same Bible he used when he preached his concluding through-the-Bible series to the Gate City congregation.

When Randall launched the series in early 1995, I marveled that he would undertake so grand a project. How would he ever hope to complete it?

"I'll just start whackin' away!" came the answer.

His "whacking away" at sermon after sermon, book after book proved to be tedious for some listeners in the congregation. Some even suggested that people visiting the church midstream of the series might be put off by it.

But the product of the effort has proven over time to be invaluable. For one thing, the eventual book, *Journey with Me*, is on the study shelves of innumerable Sunday school teachers and seminary students, where it serves as a friendly and approachable introduction to specific Scripture passages from particular Bible books.

As important, however, is the reality that the simple fact that Randall Lolley would conceive and preach such a series indicates beyond argument his commitment to the Bible as the word of God and his conviction of the truth expressed therein.

---

13. The portrait was painted by Greensboro artist Tom Edgerton.

Chapter 9

The Strength to Believe

Randall Lolley's attitude toward Scripture and its interpretation was clearly on display in an eighteen-sermon series on the historic Apostles' Creed, presented to the Greensboro congregation midway through his six-year ministry there. Labeled *Building on Bedrock*, he had presented the same series twenty years earlier to the Winston-Salem congregation, when it was titled *The Strength to Believe.*

The fourteen-year presidency at Southeastern Seminary (and Randall's hosting of and exposure to a range of Baptist scholarly opinion) lay directly between the two pastorates and the two versions of the same sermon series. Significantly, when the two series are compared, only cosmetic and doctrinally inconsequential differences appear.[1] Whatever contact (if any) with heterodox theology Randall may have had while leading Southeastern appeared not to have impacted his core doctrinal conviction.

The ancient Apostles' Creed (AD eighth century) presented a number of affirmations and propositions that centuries later became controversial among liberal and mainline Protestants in Europe and the United States. Did God as Creator make heaven and earth, or has "creation" come about through other means? Was Jesus born of a virgin, or is such a "miracle" untenable? Was Jesus both man and God, possessing two natures; or was he solely human—albeit uniquely in harmony with God?

Was his death on the cross an atoning death or largely a personal tragedy? Did Jesus, following his crucifixion, "descend into [a place called] hell," or is hell a figurative term for death? Did Jesus "[rise] again from the dead," literally and visibly, or is resurrection to be conceived primarily in spiritual terms? Will there be a future, visible,

---

1. E.g., the later edition of the series employed gender-inclusive pronouns in reference to God.

and actual "Second Coming" of Jesus, or is this *Parousia* to be understood as the eventual repair and renewal of a distorted and damaged world?

There appear in Randall's Apostles' Creed preaching series several interpretive nuances that might, at first glance, seem to diverge from conventional, evangelical conviction but that, on closer examination, are at most ambiguous. For instance, in the sermon "I Believe in God . . . Maker of Heaven and Earth," Randall first addressed the "how" of creation in biblical terms: "What is in the Bible is a direct statement that God did it and a word is all that it took."

But then (diverging from the implication of a completed work in Gen 2:1-3), "It is a creation with a series of infinite potentialities, and it is still going on." What was being said was that human beings may be understood to be God's "co-creators" in a figurative way, as when parents birth a baby or scientists introduce a new treatment for a dreaded disease.

Another instance: in his sermon "Jesus Christ . . . Who Descended into Hell," Randall initially appeared to equivocate on the question of the extent of salvation. Citing 1 Peter 3:18-19 and 4:6, he said, "The central witness of these texts is that those who lived and died before Jesus Christ received the same grace in his salvation experience at the cross as those of us who have lived and died since then."

But later in the sermon came the qualification: "This means that for those *who love Jesus Christ* there is no limit in space, or time, or experience to the grace of God."[2] Later still, in "I Believe in the Forgiveness of Sins," Randall expanded the clarification: "That means Barabbas's sins, my sins, your sins, and the sins of every person in the world *who will let Jesus forgive them.*"[3]

Thereafter, in "Jesus Christ . . . Who Shall Come to Judge the Quick and the Dead," the preacher fully dismissed "That view [that] holds that the final salvation of all humankind is caught up in the grace of God." Randall assured his listeners, "I do not believe the Bible teaches that."

---

2. My emphasis.
3. My emphasis.

A further example of a possible variation from a traditional view: In "Jesus Christ . . . Who Ascended into Heaven," the preacher stated that the ascension signified that Christ is "freed now to be lovingly and powerfully present with every person, at every place, in every age and every experience." Did this mean that the resurrection and ascension were only figurative realities? No, for "The Savior's greatest work is to prepare a place and to prepare the people for that place so that those who believe in him can enjoy each other and him together forever."

Occasional ambiguities and their explanations aside, the totality of Randall's Apostles' Creed preaching forcefully affirmed the language of the creed itself and tied it firmly to clear scriptural claims. In "Maker of Heaven and Earth," Randall was strong to attest that the ancient formulation continues to give voice to "the original, biblical faith."

Addressing the Greensboro congregation in summer 1994, the pastor appendaged an introduction to his printed compilation of the series, which he titled "Building on Bedrock: Beliefs to Withstand Every Wind of Doctrine." In that introduction, which referenced the Apostle Paul's warning to the Ephesian church to withstand "every [deceitful] wind of doctrine" (Eph 4:14), Randall put forth a warning:

> These wild winds blow furiously through lives wreaking havoc, toppling homes, and ripping away personal spiritual foundations. At no time have the winds blown more fiercely than during the last decade of the 20th century. Nowadays these winds of teachings sweep across our community, our country, and our world. Persons are being swept away from moorings which have anchored them for years.

Then, following a description of his sermon series and a brief summary of the origin of the Apostles' Creed, he asserted, "It is without doubt the foundational statement of the faith of New Testament believers and Christians through the ages. It provides the blocks for building on bedrock."

Following are selected sermon titles and brief observations from the series, which together illustrate the preacher's endeavor to restate "beliefs we can count on to withstand every wind of doctrine."

I Believe in God . . .

Addressing the first four words of the initial article of the Apostles' Creed, Randall maintained, "The great legacy of the Hebrews to the ancient world and to us was simply to believe in God's existence and not try to prove it." Enumerating "evidences" that "well-intentioned people have used for all these centuries to assist persons on their belief in God," the preacher settled firmly on the evidence of "revelation"—both natural and written—as that which would move God from the conceptual to the experiential: "But there is an awesome movement from God in the head to God in the heart. When one believes in God in the heart, that one comes to confess that God is God for me. You see, we have more than reason, you and I, we have revelation too."[4]

Underlying texts for the sermon were the Gospel of John and Paul's letter to the Romans.

> Listen to what Paul wrote the Romans: *For what can be known about God is plain because God has shown it to us. Ever since the creation of the world, God's invisible nature, namely his eternal power and deity, have been clearly perceived in the things that have been made* (Romans 1:19-20). There was no doubt at all in Paul's mind that a person could actually move from believing in the real world to believing in the real God.

The principal revelation, however, was God-brought-to-light in the person of Jesus Christ: ". . . through revelation God takes away the veil, removes the cloak and shadow, turns on the light and says, 'Here am I!' And God did it in Jesus! In Jesus of Nazareth, God

4. In the earlier version of the sermon and series (1974), Randall referred to both Old and New Testaments as "revelation": "God has revealed himself to us through prophet, priest and king, and ultimately in Jesus of Nazareth."

finally and ultimately got a name and an address. He had a shirt size and a blood-type. He walked where you walk."

The latter conclusion Randall based squarely on John's record of Jesus' words to "the eleven faithful left in that upper room on Thursday night before the cross claimed him, 'I am in the Father, and Father is in Me. He that has seen me, has seen the Father'" (John 14:9, 11, KJV).

I Believe in God . . . Maker of Heaven and Earth

Intriguingly, the presuppositional backdrop of the sermon dealing with God as Creator had already appeared in the message "I Believe in God." There, given as the third of nine evidences for God's existence, was "The Evidence from Design." Referencing eighteenth century English philosopher and Christian apologist William Paley's argument ("I have found a watch; somewhere there must be a watchmaker"), Randall expanded it: "I have found a world. Somewhere there is a world maker."

> You and I might just as well expect to get the Gettysburg Address that was delivered by Lincoln at that graveyard by putting the twenty-six letters of our alphabet into a bucket, shaking them up and throwing them up into the air, so as by sheer chance they would come together like they came together in the words of that address. We could just as much expect that to happen as we could expect this world to happen by sheer, blind chance.

The dismissal of "chance" as a factor in producing "creation," however, did not eliminate God's choice of multiple means to bring about—and continue bringing about—the world as human beings experience it.

> There is nothing in the Bible about God's method or methods. What is in the Bible is a direct statement that God did it and a word is all that it took. What that affirms is that the creation we know is not a ready-made creation. It is a creation with a series of infinite potentialities, and it is still going on. The way God created it then leaves it open for new creations every single moment since.

"When we build on bedrock," the sermon concluded, "we start where the Bible starts. 'In the beginning God . . . .' Accept that, start there, and everything else becomes an adventure of faith. Start anywhere else, then everything else becomes a hodgepodge of competing little systems."

I Believe in Jesus Christ, God's Only Son, Our Lord

Confidently declaring that he saw the incarnational affirmation of the creed as "the rock," Randall alerted his listeners to the probability that some people would see it as "sand." Some, in fact, would fail to see it at all.

"It's like that classic spiritual says:

> Just seems we can't do right;
> Look how we treated you.
> But please, suh, forgive us Lord,
> We didn't know who you was."

Yet the creed's Christological affirmation fully identified the man Jesus of Nazareth—by name (Jesus), title (Christ), genre (Son of God), and role (Lord). Human beings were inclined to trip, Randall observed, at the latter two designations, caught up in the phrases "God's only Son, our Lord."

The Sonship declaration affirmed "God in Christ" and "Christ in God." Randall confessed that this idea was challenging not only for the hearers but also for their preacher:

> I must say to you that it is right here that this whole thing runs into a cloud-bank of mystery for me. I cannot tell you; I cannot explain to you; I do not know how this Jesus was all the God there was, and yet, in emptying himself to be a man, he was perceived and described as God's only Son. But we can understand a bit imperfectly that this sentence does not say that Jesus was *a* son of God. The sentence affirms that Jesus was *the* Son of God; the only one like him ever.

Apparent in this paragraph was reference to Paul's familiar "kenotic" teaching from Philippians 2:5-11, where Jesus simultaneously "empties" himself of divine glory (v. 7), thereupon to be "highly exalted" (v. 9, NRSV) and commended by God for worship by humankind.

The ultimate obstacle arrives in the naming of Christ as "Our Lord" and the insistence that all must finally confess his lordship, "to the glory of God the Father" (vv. 10-11). "Now hear this," Randall warned:

> It is a bit of a cliché, a tad trite, but it is the Gospel, so help me God, if Jesus Christ is not Lord of all in your life, he is not Lord at all. . . . Being Christian does not mean being interested in Jesus. Being Christian means being surrendered to Jesus, involved in Christ with your life in time in Greensboro, and in eternity.

Not only does his lordship call for total, obedient allegiance to Jesus as Lord and Master; it also suggests that "In Jesus alone, we approach God. That is what his Lordship means," Randall insisted. "His Lordship means that you are so related to him that he can get you in to see divinity itself. . . . Jesus Christ introduces us. Jesus Christ guides us, leads us, opens for us access to all God is."

Conceived by the Holy Spirit, Born of the Virgin Mary

In an act characterizing both his humility and his preparedness to trust people called to support his total ministry, Randall invited me, as associate pastor, to sustain the "Building on Bedrock" Apostles' Creed series on Sundays when the pastor was absent from the pulpit. The sermon dealing with the "virgin conception" and birth fell to me.

Meanwhile, Randall's own, wholly orthodox interpretation of the subject was already on record through his sermon "Birth," presented as part of the summer series *Beginnings* preached in Greensboro during his inaugural year 1990 (see the brief discussion of the series and sermon in the preceding chapter).

Jesus Christ . . . Who Descended into Hell

Did Randall Lolley profess belief in a literal "hell"? His exposition of the Apostles' Creed strongly suggested that he did. "There is most certainly in our Bible a conviction about Hell as a place, a space, an experience of torment for those separated from God." Recalling one of several words employed by Christian Scripture, he elaborated, "When the Bible uses *Gehenna* it is talking about the results, the torment, of those who are cut off and separated from God. It is the worst possible place to have to live . . . for a minute, must less for eternity."

But did he concur with the Apostles' Creed in its declaration that Jesus, the obedient Son of God, died and descended into hell? The answer is yes, but the unfoldment of Randall's sermon suggested a quandary. Was the "hell" of the creed to be understood as "a place, a space, an experience of torment"? Or was the use of the word simply shorthand for the human experience of death?

Midway through his message Randall observed, "Our Creed is saying that Jesus Christ descended into the very place where everybody else who died went. The place of the dead. In that sense it is another way of saying that Jesus Christ was really dead." A few paragraphs later, after confessing to "meager scriptural evidences for what the Bible people believe happened during those hours from sunset Friday to sunup Sunday" (1 Pet 3:18; 4:6; Eph 4:8-10), the preacher concluded:

> [The Apostles' Creed] is saying that Jesus Christ was really and truly dead, and that while he was at the place of the dead experiencing what all the dead experience, he was not merely marking time. He was declaring there his nature as Messiah, his mission as Redeemer, and his purpose of reconciliation to God. All those who were separated by death and estranged from God were told of Jesus by Jesus.

Lest there be confusion about the implication of this, Randall recalled what most hearers regarded as the traditional view:

> No person ever misses the Savior's chance to be saved and to become what God's dream for that person was from the beginning. Do not worry about Hell. And in small print do not worry about Heaven either. God has it covered—both of them if you believe in Jesus Christ. I must say to you that you must take stock of the fact that the scriptures are unequivocal. Life goes on, and you will either spend it totally separated, severed, alienated, and tormented forever and forever out of God's company, or you will spend it with God eternally.

Jesus Christ . . . Who the Third Day Rose Again from the Dead

In his treatment of the creed's assertion of Christ's resurrection, Randall insisted that belief in the literal, bodily resurrection of Christ is not optional. Indeed, it is "one of the only doctrines of our Christian faith that we simply must agree upon." Surveying a number of contrary suppositions about "what happened"—e.g., Jesus "swooned" and then revived, friends stole the body and made a false claim, enemies stole the body to prevent its veneration, the disciples suffered mass hallucination, etc.—Randall dismissed them one by one.

> So, then, it boils down to this. You in these pews are as free as anybody has ever been on this planet to make your mind up. . . . Your options are three, just three. First, fiction. Was it sheer fiction that was deliberately devised—a great lie? Or was it delusion? Were those people then so in love with this Christ that they were deluded into believing something that did not really happen at all? If so, everything that is Christian and everything in Christendom is founded on a hallucination. Is that the way it is for you? Or is it fact? The most firm and confirmed fact in history. A fact that divided, split time, history, into two parts: before him and after him. It baffles your mind and befuddles your language, but for me it is a fact! It is the bedrock fact of our belief. Jesus Christ rose again the third day from the dead! For me, it is a fact!

Jesus Christ . . . Who Ascended into Heaven

Is heaven an actual place, visually describable and dimensionally measurable, a place in space if not in time, a location that can be traveled to? Or is it more a state of human thinking, a dimension of human consciousness, a quality of human/divine relationship?

In his sermon on the Christ of the Apostles' Creed, who ascended into heaven, Randall explored various interpretations holistically, with an eye to incorporating them into a larger but necessarily limited picture accessible through the words of holy Scripture. The Bible, he observed, is far from reticent on the topic. He counted 240 times that "heaven" is mentioned in the span of the New Testament, Matthew through Revelation—more times in fact than "earth" is mentioned.

Yet even the inspired writers of the twenty-seven books seemed to understand they were wrestling with a subject that eluded certain description or clear definition. The matter of Jesus Christ, forty days following the resurrection, "ascending" into heaven was suggestive of the problem. Might a person in an age of interplanetary travel actually ride a space vehicle from earth to the place where the risen and ascended Jesus dwells?

Or was the matter of "ascension" better understood relationally? "Here is what it means," Randall said: "The ascension means that the final liberation of Jesus Christ has come. The liberation of all limitations of time, and space, and experience so that Jesus Christ can be freed now to be lovingly and powerfully present with every person, at every place, in every age, and every experience."

Still, the object or destination of the ascension he took to be as real and concrete as earth itself, and infinitely more durable. Referring to Jesus, he said,

> The perfect earth man shows that all of us earthlings are not finally made for this earth or the grave, but finally and eternally we are made for more. Do you believe that? You do not have to. There are folks who think it is all over when you breathe the last. That the worms and the good earth will take care of the rest of it. You can believe that if you choose, but the good news is that you do not have to, you can believe this! I say the ascension is God's certificate

> that you and I are meant for more. And that more is to enjoy the presence of God forever and forever. That is your proper destiny. That is your destination.

And then, as if to ensure that no hearer would assume he was nevertheless spiritualizing the idea of heaven, Randall commended the contributions of the Apostle John, both in the Gospel bearing his name and also in the book of Revelation.

> Nowhere in all of the writings of the New Testament does anybody speak as crisply, succinctly, and sufficiently as John does in John 14:1-3. . . . "Let not your hearts be troubled, believe in God, believe also in me," Jesus said. "In my Father's house there are *monai pollai*. If it were not so, would I have told you that I go to prepare a place for you?"

The Greek *monai* Randall translated as "staying places," a term fully complementary to the "place" that Jesus told his disciples he was going to prepare for them. "Two things stand out for me," the preacher observed. One was "a promised place," an actual location, one that positioned the disciple in the presence of the Master, "that where I am, there you may be also."

The other outstanding thing, in Randall's view, was that "promised presence":

> Only God who has prepared heaven for us can prepare us for heaven. Jesus Christ does both of those things. . . . Heaven is you and Jesus together forever. Heaven is Jesus and I together forever. Heaven is the family of God gathered at home finally forever. . . .
>
> The pain of this life, its sin, and its separation, they cannot go on forever. That is not the end. There is more. The present will yield to the future because Jesus Christ will make it so. The conqueror of one death historically will become the conqueror of every death eventually. The Savior's greatest work is to prepare a place and to prepare the people for that place so that those who believe in him can enjoy each other and him together forever.

Jesus Christ . . . Who Shall Come to Judge the Quick and the Dead

Randall's discourse on belief in Jesus Christ as one who, though currently seated "on the right hand of God the Father Almighty," will at some point "come to judge the quick and the dead" dealt more with the coming than the judging. In the earliest paragraphs the preacher identified polarities in the importance that Christian people attach to the teaching. Some, he observed, make little or nothing of it, while for others it is the central doctrine of faith:

> Many take these texts [Matt. 24 and Acts 1:11] and this part of the Creed and say, "Well, that is no longer a part of my doctrinal repertoire. It has vanished. It has no meaning. If it is even in my circumference of belief, it is certainly not the center of it. . . ." For other people, on the other hand, it is not only key, it is core. It is central. It is the absolute dominating belief about Jesus.

Confessing that it is difficult to produce a balanced view, Randall offered, "I think the biblical view is the balanced one." Questioning what a belief in a *parousia*—in a second coming—does for the believer, he suggested that most importantly it "lock[s] us into the reality that history is going somewhere. . . . The belief in Jesus' second coming is anchored in the belief that history is not accidental, nor incidental, but really is 'his story.'"

Randall cited a comment from one observer, "who out of his despair wrote: 'This universe is indifferent. Who created it? No one knows. Why are we here on this puny mud heap spinning in infinite space? I have not the slightest idea, and I am quite convinced that no one else has the slightest idea either.'"

This, insisted Randall, "flew right into the teeth of one of the New Testament's greatest pieces of bedrock. Belief in the second coming of Jesus is as integral and as central in the Scriptures as belief in the first coming of Jesus. The Parousia is as important as the Advent. The consummation of history is as critical as the beginning of history."

Noting that the idea of a second coming, while present in the Gospels, actually "saturates the letters of Paul," Randall proceeded to summarize the available interpretive categories as "realized," "personalized," and "futurized" eschatology. The latter, he asserted, is what is in view in the affirmation of the Apostles' Creed. Moreover, it is "the overwhelming view of most Christians," and it is "my view of the matter."[5] Elaborating, he said,

> Those who hold this view in reading scripture believe that Jesus Christ will actually return to this earth again a second time exactly like he [came] to this earth the first time. The first time as a baby, the second time as the Messiah of glory. Those who believe like this take Acts 1:11 very literally. The role of believers in this view is to watch, and wait, and pray, and be vigilant, and be steady in their service, ready for the Lord whenever the Lord comes.

The preacher was quick to offer four caveats "for those who might embrace this view along with me." First was the temptation to zero in on a specific time for the event in question. "Stay as far away from the date setters, chart drawers, and calendar makers as you possibly can. . . . Our Lord said he did not know when it was. . . . I am willing to be as ignorant as Jesus was on the matter."

Second, "Do not sweat the details." Noting that "It is awfully hard for us to sort out what is literal and what is figurative in the scriptural speaking about Jesus's second coming," Randall confessed, "I have a problem with those who are cock-sure, draw their charts, and make everybody believe it has to be exactly this way."

Third, "You had best not make a particular brand of millennialism a test of faith or fellowship." Describing a popular approach known as *premillennialism* and how some interpreters are persuaded of its truth, Randall mused, "That would be wonderful if just as good a group of people with just as much sense and just as much spirit did not read the very same texts and come away saying, 'No, we are convinced of a postmillennial point of view in scripture.'"

5. In keeping with his typical, tolerant attitude in matters of doctrinal disagreement, Randall inquired (while referring to the "realized" view), "Is that the way you feel about it? Fine, a lot of good people do."

Briefly describing *postmillennialism* along with the non-literal, figurative approach known as *amillennialism*, the preacher faced his congregation and said:

> You need to know where your pastor stands. . . . I am amillennial. When it comes to trying to find out how a 1,000 year period fits into the second coming of my Lord, I simply do not know. . . . Therefore, I have concluded that a millennial typology for me is not the best way to interpret the New Testament message . . . .

Having directed three-fourths of his sermon to the *coming*, Randall did not ignore the creed's mention of the *judgment* aspect of the Lord's return. Speaking of the general meaning of the term, he observed that "Judgment is that side of God's love experienced by a rebel." Its function is both curative and preventive. "The Bible says that God judges both to punish and to cure."

The ultimate judgment of the living (the "quick") and the dead, however, Randall took to be different:

> God's final judgment for the living and the dead will involve an eternal separation with its attendant torment by those who do not accept Jesus Christ as Savior. That is my position. I read the scriptures and cannot come away with any other conviction than all are judged, and that if you and I do not respond while there is time to the love of God by accepting Jesus Christ as Savior and Lord, then you and I will be eternally separated from God, and the torment that goes with separation is the ultimate outcome of God's judging the living and the dead.

Randall cautioned that some Bible interpreters reach other conclusions. *Annihilationism* (where those who reject Jesus Christ face extinction) and *universalism* (where redeeming grace extends throughout eternity to the salvation of all) were briefly described. In both cases, Randall entered his own denial: "I do not believe the Bible teaches that."

In a concluding acknowledgment of the complexity and controversiality of the subject of his sermon, the preacher reassured his hearers:

> Reading and re-reading and pondering and struggling and saturating your life with prayer will guide you and give you what for you is the correct conviction. For me, the powerful truth of this promise [within the Apostles' Creed] is, you can count on it, Jesus is the Lord of history. It is all going somewhere, and you and I, through our faith in Christ, can be a part of God's great future. Let's!

I Believe in the Life Everlasting

At the conclusion of his 2008 autobiography, the late Dr. Cecil Sherman wrote:

> All my life I have been told there is life after death. . . . Sometimes I wonder about the afterlife. I don't know as much about heaven as I would like; I surely don't know as much as some preachers claim to know. There are occasions when I have doubts about immortality. . . . But most of the time faith wins over doubt, and I think like a Christian again.[6]

Randall Lolley appeared to have "thinking like a Christian" firmly in mind when he wrote and preached his penultimate sermon from the *Building on Bedrock* series.[7] Recalling First Century Jerusalem he noted that there were essentially two options regarding the matter of what was to become of those who died:

> The best solution the people in the first century could come up with was a hunch, just a hunch mind you, that the soul might

---

6. *By My Own Reckoning* (Macon, GA: Smyth & Helwys, 2008), 279.

7. The final sermon, "The Difference that Belief Makes," utilized the Acts 16 story of the Philippian jailer to establish the familiar ethical theme of behavior and relationship as functions of "belief." Nevertheless, Randall reiterated the christological elements of the Apostles' Creed to describe the content of the belief that Paul and Silas commended: "Believe on the Lord Jesus, and you will be saved, you and your household" (Acts 16:31, NRSV).

> survive the grave in Sheol, but that, too, was risky business because Sheol was a cold, shadowy place somewhere beneath the earth in the underworld that really was scarcely better than no survival at all.
>
> In the Gentile sector of Jerusalem the funerals were different. The bodies were always cremated in that part of town because their bodies were bad business. Their spirits, only their spirits, were perceived to be good. Death to the Greeks and to the Romans was a sort of graduation exercise where the poor body, the prison and fetter of the soul, perished and the immortal spirit ascended to the world of pure forms. But after it got there no one seemed to know exactly what happened next.

Meanwhile, "Into this city of God-talk and graveyards a new breeze one day began to blow, and on the winds of that breeze floated a message. It was the message that the young man from Nazareth, who had been crucified on Friday and locked securely in a borrowed tomb, had come back to life again!"

Recalling John 3:36, Randall expanded the message into good news for all who would hear it and receive it: "He who puts his faith in the Son of God has hold of eternal life. But he who rejects the Son of God shall not see that life." This "eternal life" possessed the dimensions of resurrection and subsequent durability:

> On Easter morning . . . Christians wrote a word that had never appeared in anybody's dictionary on this planet before. That word was RESURRECTION! The message was that on Easter morning Jesus Christ signed death's death certificate. It was determined that the cause of death for death was resurrection. And ever since Christians have believed profoundly that we do, indeed, live twice. We live before we die physically in Christ, and we live after we die physically in that same Christ.

Thereafter, relying heavily on 2 Corinthians 5:17, Randall expanded the theme of eternal life to emphasize "quality" over "quantity"—an emphasis he maintained throughout the second half of his sermon:

> Right about here is the second truth we must pin down. His living again has made it possible for you and me also to live again. . . . Like Paul said, "When we are in Christ, we are new creations. Everything old has passed away, and new things take their place." Resurrection came to those original New Testament folk just as they were, where they were. And once they responded to their resurrected, living Christ, everything for them was changed.
>
> In him, they really did live twice—before their deaths and after their deaths.

Its ethical and relational dimensions aside, the preacher left no doubt in the minds of his hearers of his persuasion of resurrection's historicity:

> It comes to us as historical event. We believe in Jesus Christ's own resurrection and his provision of life after death for himself; and we also believe that through our faith in him we can connect, we can tap on to that self-same life he promises us. "I believe in the life everlasting!" He lived after he died; we can live in him after we die!

Chapter 10

And Quit the Fighting

At fifty-seven years of age, Randall Lolley departed his presidency of Southeastern Seminary and returned to pastoral ministry, first in Raleigh and afterward in Greensboro, where he retired in 1996. During these years and in years to follow he focused his attention on local church leadership, interim ministry to a dozen congregations, and the encouragement and development of new denomination-like entities.

The following draft letter was dated November 1, 1995, shortly before the annual meeting of the Baptist State Convention of North Carolina.

> Dear Mark,
>
> From Murphy to Manteo I have heard it said that among North Carolina Baptists you and I represent the classic polarity. After reading your letter to "Pastors" which I received today, I can understand why persons perceive us in this way.
>
> Mark, why keep up the fight?
>
> Why continue to go to the Convention every November until the Lord returns, for a battle?
>
> It is unseemly!
>
> We both believe what we believe deeply. Neither you nor I—nor our respective kinds of Baptist brothers and sisters in North Carolina—are going to change very much in our lifetimes.
>
> Why don't you run for president; I will also run for president. If you are elected, then I will try to get my kind of North Carolina Baptists to form another state missions delivery system, cooperating with the CBF. If you are defeated, then you try to get your kind of North Carolina Baptists to form a different delivery system in our state—whereby the relationship to the SBC continues.

> I am ready for an end to the continual bickering. Let's you and me offer ourselves to Baptists to lead them one way or another, and quit the fighting.
>
> What do you say!
>
> Devotedly, Randall

"Mark" was Mark Corts, longtime pastor of Winston-Salem's Calvary Baptist Church. Corts had served the BSCNC as president from 1977 to 1979, and he had held several leadership positions within the Southern Baptist Convention. He and Calvary Baptist were associated with the conservative side of a struggle that had extended to the BSCNC, mirroring the conflict that had by then overtaken and divided the SBC.

At the time of writing, Randall had entered the final months of his six-and-a-half-year capstone ministry as pastor of Greensboro's First Baptist Church. Already he had witnessed the formation of an alternative "missions delivery system" (the Cooperative Baptist Fellowship) at the national level, and he had led First Baptist to identify as a contributing CBF church.

At the state level, things were more complicated. The moderate-conservative struggle, which would come to a head with the defeat of a "shared leadership plan" in 1999, was well underway. Doctrinal disagreement and political infighting reminiscent of what had occurred at the national level was growing more intense. Moderate churches that throughout its 165-year history had invested money, leadership, and prayer in the BSCNC were strongly resistant to the possibility of ceding control to conservatives.

But clearly Randall Lolley, who had witnessed denominational turmoil from the perspectives both of church pastor and institutional head, had grown tired of the strife. "It is unseemly!" he had written. What he suggested in its place was a final, climactic political contest. The recommended scenario would bring about a quick conclusion to what had become a civil war and a public relations debacle for the state convention. The end result, he proposed—to be agreed upon *a priori*—should be winner-take-all, with the loser agreeing to depart the field of battle and begin something new and different.

At the bottom of the draft of his letter Randall inscribed in his own hand a note to "Gene"[1] It read, "What do you think? Should I mail it?"

There is no indication of Gene's response or that the letter was ever mailed. Nor did either Mark Corts or Randall have his name placed in nomination at the convention that November.

Actually, the foundation for a projected *state missions delivery system* relating to the national Cooperative Baptist Fellowship had already been laid. Two years previously, in March 1993, Randall had invited like-minded North Carolina Baptist pastors and laypeople to attend a "Cooperative Baptist Fellowship State Meeting" in the sanctuary of his Greensboro church.

Since the 1991 organization of the national CBF, moderate Baptist pastors in North Carolina had been meeting informally. Many had participated in a grassroots political group called Friends of Missions, which had arisen in opposition to conservative inroads into the national and state conventions. These pastors, now joined by members of their churches, were among 1,500 people who responded to Randall's invitation.

Following his departure from Southeastern Seminary in 1988, Randall had mostly attempted to subordinate denominational involvements to what he viewed as the greater call of church pastoral ministry. In Greensboro he kept himself aware of the changing landscape within state and national conventions, and he responded as necessary to a denominational relations committee that was in place prior to his arrival at the church.

But such matters rarely colored his preaching, teaching, pastoral care, and administrative leadership. Repeatedly he bypassed opportunities to return to national, denominational, or academic leadership roles. Invited by a search committee to offer himself as a candidate for the deanship of the new Wake Forest Divinity School in Winston-Salem, he declined.[2]

---

1. Probably close confidant R. G. "Gene" Puckett, editor of the *Biblical Recorder*, news organ of the BSCNC.

2. The invitation came in a letter from the school's development director, Bob Spinks, on April 10, 1996.

Some of Randall's responses were surprising. Charles Deweese, Director of Baptist Publishing for a new venture named Providence House, invited him to read and endorse a new account of the SBC conflict. Randall consented and praised the work, but offered a caveat: "My impression is that it will have a limited market because so very many people with whom I have talked are weary of reading yet another analysis of our pain. So many want to get on past it."

Nevertheless, as he implied in his letter to Mark Corts, many pastors and church people across North Carolina continued to look to the two of them for leadership of their respective causes. C. F. McDowell III, who studied at Southeastern from 1986 to 1989, recalled the emotional impact his former president had on the state convention following his resignation as president:

> On that Tuesday morning in the Greensboro Coliseum in November, 1987, the program noted the fixed order of business was the election of president. . . . The moderate candidate Leon Smith had asked Dr. Lolley to nominate him . . . . He walked to the microphone and said, "I am Randall Lolley," and before he could say, "I rise to nominate . . . ," the loudest and longest applause and standing ovation I have ever witnessed or been a part of followed for several minutes. . . . The applauding and standing messengers were saying, "We thank you. We love you. We need you." He gave the denominational leadership needed in the face of the fundamentalist takeover of SEBTS by resigning, and with his actions said to all Baptists, "be strong, let's take a stand together and you can follow me."

However, regarding any actual, future denominational leadership, "Getting on past it" became Randall's default position. This did not seem to imply an attitude of passivity or resignation. Rather he turned his attention to the alternative course suggested in the letter that likely was never mailed: helping to form *another state missions delivery system, cooperating with the CBF.*

Establishing a new state Baptist group as an alternative to the Baptist State Convention had not been on the minds of pastors and other leaders descending upon FBC Greensboro, according to Alfred

Ayscue, who served as president of the Friends of Missions organization. Still, the 1993 gathering that he, Randall, and others hosted bore the character of a traditional denominational meeting, with multiple meeting days, pre-session music, theme interpretations, missions challenges, informational breakout sessions, and inspirational sermons.[3]

A single business session produced an eleven-person steering committee, charged with returning a recommended slate of officers to a formal, organizational meeting the following year.

The next year's gathering took place in Wait Chapel, on the campus of Wake Forest University. Elected first moderator of what was thereupon named the Cooperative Baptist Fellowship of North Carolina (CBFNC) was one of Randall's successors as pastor of the host city's First Baptist Church, David Hughes. (Randall subsequently dubbed Hughes "Mr. CBFNC.")

Borrowing terminology recalled from his seminary days, Randall delivered a keynote address titled "CBF Seedbed: Flowers or Weeds?"[4] In the course of his sermon he admonished the assembled Baptists to set their minds on a future that would transcend denominational strife, carefully avoiding "the temptation to become negative or reactionary."

Whether the new organization was already—or would become—a "convention" in the style of the BSCNC quickly became a concern. Randall was soon to begin assisting the recently organized CBF in researching the question at the national level. As chair of an ad hoc study group, he and others would in 1996 issue the result of their work in a CBF publication titled *Findings: A Report of the Special Study Commission to study the question: "Should the Cooperative Baptist Fellowship become a separate convention?"*

In one of the initial CBFNC newsletters, moderator David Hughes wrote that the new organization existed for the purpose of promoting the national CBF and its principles. But as he and others found themselves participating in an identity struggle similar to that

---

3. Stephen Pressley, *A Decade of New Beginnings: CBFNC and the First Ten Years* (Winston-Salem: CBF of North Carolina, 2004), 6.

4. "Seminary" is a word whose Latin root means "seed-bed."

which vexed the national group, Randall encouraged them to "take some time to sift it out." Already, in Hughes's thinking, Randall had approximated a satisfactory identity statement with his oft-quoted "We believe that there is a Christian way to be human, a Baptist way to be Christian, a CBF way to be Baptist, and a North Carolina way to be a CBF'er."[5]

The new Cooperative Baptist Fellowship of North Carolina also wrestled with whether to "get on past" denominational angst and infighting, or to begin employing its organizational clout politically, in order to sustain the struggle within the state convention. David Hughes's successor Cathy Hartsell encouraged CBFNC supporters to remain involved in the BSCNC, attend its annual meetings as voting "messengers," and work to keep it from falling victim to a possible conservative takeover.

However, Alfred Ayscue, who in 1996 was employed by the national CBF as its North Carolina field representative, inclined more toward Randall's view. Ayscue considered the new state organization to be "an opportunity to move beyond" political activity and a get-out-the-vote mentality.

During the organization's formative years, successive CBFNC moderators echoed Hartsell's concern for "staying interested" in the Baptist State Convention—if not for political purposes, then for the purpose of partnering with state convention entities in carrying out missions projects that were mutually supported.

Randall kept himself apart from official CBFNC leadership until 1997, when he accepted confirmation as the fellowship's "moderator-elect." Some North Carolina Baptists simultaneously encouraged him to run for president of the state convention, but he declined, indicating that he preferred to concentrate his energies on the new fellowship.

As part of a three-person leadership component (moderator, past moderator, moderator-elect), Randall's influence was evident in the decision to launch a three-to-five-year planning process. He regarded the resulting "strategic plan" as a transformative development in the growth of the fellowship toward maturity and functionality.

---

5. *A Decade of New Beginnings*, 22.

At the March 1998 CBFNC "General Assembly," which met at his former church in Greensboro, Randall segued from moderator-elect to the position of moderator, and the strategic plan on which he had labored was adopted. "The plan," he later remarked, "yielded a three-to-five-year vision statement, a logo, a [redesigned] newsletter, an enhanced funding effort for the CBFNC, and a commitment to employ permanent personnel."[6]

In his first newsletter column as moderator, he identified the three tracks that would mark his leadership. They included (1) the restructuring of the main governing body—the coordinating council—to include task forces focused on missions, leadership, communication, administration, and fellowship; (2) the definition of a role for a full-time, paid executive officer to be called "coordinator"; and (3) the development of a strategy for contacting and involving CBF-friendly churches.

The third track expressed Randall's eagerness to begin fulfilling the organization's new mission statement: "Bringing Baptists of North Carolina together for Christ-centered ministry." In a later newsletter article, he outlined the thinking that lay behind the mission statement:

> BRINGING: A Special Method
> "Bringing" is a gentle force whose engine room is love. Its twin sisters are "leading" and "guiding." Its mortal enemies are "driving," "forcing," "coercing." The first word in our mission statement stands with arms outstretched shouting, "WELCOME" to everyone. It is positive, not negative. It is proactive, not reactive. "Bringing" is the work of a shepherd not a cowboy. . . .
>
> BAPTISTS: A Special People
> CBF of North Carolina is incurably Baptistic. In fact, one of the prime features of the fellowship is to celebrate our Baptistness. There is abroad in the land a terrible idea—to remove Baptist from the names of our churches. Not so for CBF. We want to restore that noble name to a place of respect and honor. Ours is a worthy Baptist heritage and hope.

---

6. *A Decade of New Beginnings*, 25.

In 1607 Baptists entered history as freedom fighters. To this day, being Baptist means freedom—free churches, free consciences, free classrooms all within a free country. Baptists stand for integrity and authority of the Scriptures, along with soul competency to interpret them. We stand for the autonomy of local congregations, the equality of every church member, and priesthood of every believer. We stand for religious liberty and the separation of church and state. . . .

NORTH CAROLINA: A Special Place
. . . Our focus is ministry in the Old North State. From Murphy to Manteo we are shaping the present and future of the Baptist presence in our home state.

. . . We are determined to be an embodiment of Jesus Christ, an extension of Christ, in our time, in our state. We mean to be what Christ was while he was on this earth.

On the North Carolina state seal there is a Latin phrase: "Esse Quam Videri." That means "To Be, Not To Seem." We dare to be North Carolina Baptists for now, for tomorrow.

TOGETHER: A Special Relationship
In 1 Corinthians 3:9, Paul tells the Corinthians and us that, "we are laborers together with God." This means that we are "together," not alike. Our diversity enriches us.

Here is what we stand for together:

A free church hermeneutic
A free church theology
Pastor/Laity partnership
Male/Female equality
Church/State separation

And we stand for all this under the Lordship of Jesus Christ. The sole parameter for our faith and fellowship is "Jesus Christ is Lord."

FOR CHRIST-CENTERED MINISTRY: A Special Purpose
Ours is a new way to be Baptist and a new way to do missions. The focus for our missions endeavor internationally is World

> A—the people on Earth who have the least opportunity to know Jesus Christ. The focus of our work in North Carolina is the Jesus agenda in Luke 4:18-19.[7]
>
> We pack light and travel lean. Our thrusts are to start churches, train leaders, develop disciples, and foster fellowship.
>
> We are not a denomination, a convention, an association, or an alliance. We are a fellowship of Christians bent "on bringing Baptists of North Carolina together for Christ-centered ministry."

However, it was Randall's first two tracks (organizational restructuring and role definition for a coordinator) that constituted the focus of his personal strategy, as moderator, to usher the nascent organization toward the coming new millennium. He was persuaded that the coordinating council needed expansion and strengthening in order to accomplish the variety of tasks that were mandated by the strategic plan. The projected five task forces would incorporate, he said, "additional persons . . . in order to involve more people, and to expand geographical representation."

Nevertheless, there remained, in his thinking, a missing ingredient in the overall culture of the fellowship—and that was full-time, paid coordination. At the national level it had been first Cecil Sherman, followed by Daniel Vestal, who had fulfilled that requirement. North Carolina had to that point "made do" with volunteer leadership, inspired by a succession of elected moderators and coordinated part-time by CBF national's North Carolina field representative.

But now Randall believed "it was time to go shopping for a Renaissance mind with a Reformation heart, an individual with that strength of piety and that array of aptitudes needed for 'herding cats.'"[8]

---

7. Jesus said, "The Spirit of the Lord is upon me, because he has anointed me to bring good news to the poor. He has sent me to proclaim release to the captives and recovery of sight to the blind, to let the oppressed go free, to proclaim the year of the Lord's favor."

8. *A Decade of New Beginnings*, 27. The term "herding cats" had been suggested by moderate Baptist ethicist Robert Parham as descriptive of the challenge of leading a diverse group of Baptists.

In characteristic fashion, he did his "shopping" through a fellowship-appointed search committee, while taking an acutely personal interest in the outcome. Emerging as the leading candidate by late 1998 was fifty-five-year-old Texas native Bob Patterson, retired from the military and soon to be ordained to the Baptist ministry.

At their initial face-to-face encounter in November of that year, Patterson recalled listening as Randall extolled the virtues of the organization Patterson would soon head. From its coordinating council with its attending task forces to the quality of the Baptist volunteers at its core, Randall seemed certain that CBFNC would soon have everything necessary to offer itself to like-minded North Carolina churches as their primary "denominational" support.

Of particular interest to Patterson was Randall's emphasis on what he termed "positive presence." The new fellowship coordinator understood that he would need to work with the various volunteers and the people of the churches they represented in ways that encouraged them to avoid negativity in their attitudes toward erstwhile denominational opponents.

To Patterson, that initial conversation and the spirit behind it marked "the real turning point from reactivity to proactivity" in CBFNC life.[9] In a manner typical of insurgent movements, "moderates" in Southern Baptist life had previously been characterized more by what they opposed than what they supported. But Randall, now joined by many others in North Carolina, had grown uncomfortable with the spiritual implication of such negativity. "The first word in our mission statement stands with arms outstretched shouting, 'WELCOME,'" he had written. "It is positive, not negative. It is proactive, not reactive."

In 2004, shortly before his retirement, and looking back on a five-year chapter of life that saw CBFNC's operating budget and list of contributing churches expand impressively, Patterson conferred comprehensive credit on Randall Lolley. "He gave the [strategic] plan, he gave the task forces, he gave the plan to hire a coordinator. He is the engine of CBFNC to this day."[10]

---

9. *A Decade of New Beginnings*, 27.
10. *A Decade of New Beginnings*, 28.

Engine or not, Randall's influence would enrich the Cooperative Baptist cause well beyond his year as moderator. While primarily interested in his home state, he never lost sight of the empathetic connection between the new North Carolina organization and its spiritual parent, CBF national. Late in his term he organized "The First CBF Missions Blitz," a week-long, statewide canvass of moderate-minded churches whose aim was to familiarize them with the Cooperative Baptist alternative to their traditional Southern Baptist identity.

On the occasion of CBFNC's ten-year anniversary, Randall reflected on his own term as moderator and "spoke of the desire of many within the new fellowship to develop strategies for working with the Baptist State Convention 'when feasible, and completely [leaving] the SBC behind.'"[11] By 2003, however, that ambition had been undermined by the growing electoral dominance of conservatives within the BSCNC.

Still Randall sustained his interest in the life and work of Cooperative Baptists in general, and CBFNC in particular, attending annual meetings and supplying advice, assistance, and encouragement wherever he could. Bob Patterson's successor Larry Hovis recalled,

> In 2005, CBFNC launched a new governance structure which divided our large Coordinating Council into one smaller Coordinating Council as the legal governing board, plus three ministry councils charged with overseeing our three broad ministry areas. Randall agreed to serve on the initial Leadership Development Ministry Council. That group was responsible for all of our theological education efforts, plus ongoing continuing education for ministers.
>
> Randall's participation in that council served two primary purposes. First, he provided valuable insight and guidance for the work of the group, given his extensive experience both as a theological educator and as a pastor. Second, he provided legitimacy to the new structure. His participation on a ministry council sent a strong signal that the ministry councils weren't "second tier"

11. *A Decade of New Beginnings*, 43.

> groups but an important and vital part of how we sought to adapt structures for changing times.
>
> The second major contribution he (and Lou) made was in agreeing to lend their names to a new CBFNC endowment fund called the Randall and Lou Lolley Fund for Theological Education. They not only agreed to give their names, but to help with the initial promotion (and to place the fund as one of the beneficiaries in their will).

Throughout the aftermath of denominational schism at national and state levels, new moderate agencies, organizations, and institutions found the "Lolley name" to be helpful in raising popular and financial support. Simultaneously, endowments such as the *Randall and Lou Lolley Fund for Theological Education* honored their namesakes, "whose courage and commitment of integrity, freedom and educational excellence laid the foundation for a new era in the education of men and women for ministry and service."[12]

Concurrent with his continued interest and involvement in the changing shape of the Baptist movement, Randall sustained his passion for leadership of local congregations. Despite a professed unwillingness at the time of his retirement from pastoral ministry to "keep right on preaching," he straightaway contacted his local Baptist associational executive and inquired about churches in need of interim pastoral leadership.

Fifteen years thereafter, and in response to a questionnaire from a former SEBTS student, Randall wrote,

> As I mentioned, I retired in 1996. We built a house in and moved to Raleigh. I began thinking, however, that I was healthy, so I talked to Roger Nix, Director of Missions for the Raleigh Baptist Association, about being an interim pastor. It wasn't my goal to be an intentional interim which helped troubled churches; I just wanted to be a "plain, old-fashioned, vanilla" interim.

---

12. "Lolley Fund helps students prepare for leadership and ministry," *Baptists Today*, July/August 2017, 14.

I've had twelve interim positions. The first was Snyder Memorial in Fayetteville, North Carolina, then First Baptist Church in Washington, D.C. From there I went to Bay Shore Church in Tampa, Florida; Knollwood in Winston-Salem, North Carolina; then Hendricks Avenue in Jacksonville—the most moderate Baptist church in Florida.

All the rest have been in North Carolina: Henderson, Rolesville, Tabernacle, Longview, Greystone—and presently, Crabtree Valley. Being an interim has been a delight and a joy. I wouldn't have missed it for anything![13]

By the time of his 2005 launch of an interim pastorate for Rolesville Baptist Church, Randall had developed a list of "Ten Suggestions for a Congregation in Transition":

1. Celebrate your past (persons, pastors/staff, programs).
2. Re-connect with your roots (primary documents, history, covenant).
3. Assess the shape you are in (things to do, things to stop doing).
4. Agree on propelling images (visioning together, neo-traditions).
5. Communicate, communicate, communicate (there is no such thing as too much communication).
6. Structure your work teams (some in place, others not yet; all exercising patience, tolerance, faithfulness).
7. Keep the good stuff going (mission, ministries, finances).
8. Decide on interim strategies and leadership (interim/intentional interim/consultation).
9. Expect surprises. Embrace serendipities. Have some fun.
10. Remember: *Esse Quam Videri* (to be, not to seem); the Light is Alive (Epiphany).

---

13. Savage-King, *Finding Somewhere Else to Go*, 64. The reader will count eleven congregations. In a three-page biographical recapitulation titled "My Journey through the Years" and dated November 2013, Randall added Raleigh's Forest Hills Baptist Church. (In private conversation, Randall and Lou recalled that Randall had to impose a *terminus ad quem* on several of these congregations when their pastor search committees would appear to grow complacent and suspend their work.)

Randall headed his list with a further exhortation: *REMEMBER: The ending is the beginning.*

Chapter 11

A Pilgrim Personality

The idea of *pilgrimage* reverberated strongly through the mind of Randall Lolley, who seemed convinced that fruitful living was more about journeys than about destinations. In 1954, he and Lou had first journeyed from their beginnings in Lower Alabama ("L.A.") northward to "The Forest of Wake," later turning west to Greensboro and southwest to Ft. Worth, and come 1972 back to North Carolina for good.

In his final seminary "President's Message," printed in the *Southeastern Outlook* (January–February 1988), Randall described another approaching transition:

> I am writing during the days between Christmas and the New Year. We are experiencing our last special family holidays in "the big house" at 308 Durham Road. Soon we will be doing what pilgrim people have done through the ages—we will break camp and move on.

By July the Lolleys had again broken camp, putting in at nearby Raleigh for a year and three-quarters before returning to Greensboro for their capstone, six-year vocational pastorate. Come October 1996, they at last retired back to the Raleigh area, where they continued life and a ministry that grew to a dozen full-time and part-time interim church pastorates.

Meanwhile, through his five-decade journey of institutional and congregational service, an additional kind of "pilgrimage" came to form a significant parallel focus for Randall. It was the leadership of students, church members, and friends to "the lands of the Bible": Israel/Palestine, Jordan, Egypt, Greece, and Turkey.

In his meticulously compiled "My Bucket List" (see Appendix C), an entry titled "Walk where Jesus walked" appeared first among a grand total of 237 destinations.[1] Likely this was not accidental; its first position implied its relative importance. Moreover, while other destinations were listed without reference to the number of times visited, the "where Jesus walked" inclusion was qualified parenthetically: "Walk where Jesus walked (15 trips to the Holy Land)."

Beginning with leadership of Bible land tours during his 1962–1974 Winston-Salem pastorate, continuing with trips tailored for students at Southeastern Seminary, thereafter supplemented by at least two forays during his nearly eight years of subsequent pastoral service, and finally concluding with additional journeys during his retirement years, Randall (often accompanied by Lou) performed something qualitatively different from his myriad other journeys around the globe: repeatedly, he went on *pilgrimage*.[2]

Spring 2007: A Pilgrimage Sampler

Eleven years after retiring from First Baptist in Greensboro, Randall welcomed me (still a member of the church's staff) to join him in co-leading his tenth Holy Land trip. Dates for the tour were April 22 to May 6, 2007, and the foray was billed as "Israel and Jordan—a Holy Land Pilgrimage."

Forty-six travelers, including First Baptist Church members and friends from Randall's past, signed on for the pilgrimage. Indigenous tour guides were required. For the Israel portion, Randall recruited Jerusalem resident Gila Yudkin, while I invited Amman's Ruby Haddad to conduct the group in Jordan.[3]

---

1. This does not count "Camp with our family in every one of the 50 United States." An addendum to the list organized the destinations by country and continent. All seven continents (Antarctica included) and 118 countries were visited.

2. Including a "Journeys of the Apostle Paul" tour to Turkey and Greece.

3. Gila, a New England native billing herself as "A Connecticut Yankee in King David's Court," had assisted Randall on previous trips. Ruby had guided me, along with four Catholic priests, from Jerusalem's Tantur Ecumenical Institute during a 2005 ministry sabbatical.

Sometime prior to the journey, Randall had acquired a compact Sony Handycam video camera. Rather than recall the impending pilgrimage with still photos and slide presentations, as he had for earlier journeys, he decided to record extensive video footage along the way, complete with his personal narration, and then make DVD discs available to the travelers upon their return.

The eventual product was remarkable, not because of the photographer's videography (sweeps and transitions were jerky and impulsive) but because of the unmistakable voice discernible from behind the camera. It was apparent that no part of the narrative was planned or rehearsed. Randall was in all cases speaking extemporaneously, almost casually, sharing whatever musings came to mind.

New Testament scholars have noted that the Apostle Paul likely was unaware that his various epistles would eventually be enshrined canonically and subsequently shared through the centuries with a global audience. For the most part, Randall likewise seemed not to be conscious that he was placing his spoken thoughts on record for later review by others. This, however, rendered the finished product all the more valuable as a window into the mind and soul of the speaker.

What follows is a partial transcription (annotated with my explanations and comments) of the two-disc video, modestly titled *Israel and Jordan 2007*. It includes the Israel portion, the first ten days of the journey:

Sunday, April 22: Departure

We're at Raleigh-Durham airport. About thirty minutes before we leave. We got this whole crowd of people here, and they look like they're feeling pretty doggone good. We're gonna fill up this first American Airlines flight to New York. . . . Here we are, we're ready to fly. . . . They all look pretty good!

[New York City] Here we are at the Hilton Hotel, about an hour after we hit the ground in New York. They've got a nice buffet set up. Everything is A-OK. I think they're really hungry. This is good: turkey there, steak there, Maryland crab cakes there, collards there. . . .

[On the bus back to the airport] Smile up, everybody! Gol-lee, y'all look full!

[At JFK airport] Here we are, as ten o'clock approaches. These brothers *[young Orthodox Jews]* are going to Israel with us. . . . Everybody's sort of tired, tired of sitting on their behinds. We've got everybody who's going to be here—forty, forty-seven people. Ready to ride soon!

Monday, April 23: Tel Aviv, Tiberias

[Aboard the aircraft, against a backdrop of flight noise] Here's our early morning crowd, after ten hours in the air. Checking everybody out. This is the back section. Four hundred-plus passengers. Seven-forty-seven Boeing—big thing. That's my seat right there. Slept a while. We're strung out here, all through this section. We got one sick lady. She's taking *[medication]*, so she's doin' all right. We're on here with a bunch of Hasidic Jews, who are going to Israel for a holiday.[4]

[On board the tour bus at Ben Gurion Airport, Tel Aviv] Here we are, folks, upon arrival, Tel Aviv, April 23, seven o'clock. That's P.M.! *[crowd laughter]* Good-looking crowd.

[Tiberius, Sea of Galilee] Here we are at the Nof Ginosar Hotel. As I look at my watch, it is now ten P.M. We're about to lean into a third buffet. We're the only people here; we kinda like the quiet. Here is a part *[of the dining room]* that is not, at the moment, occu-pewed. My soul! This thing is huge. *[Now viewing a sign, "In memory"]* Here at the Kibbutz Ginosar it's a day of remembrance. The Day of Independence, that was yesterday. This is the day that established the nation of Israel fifty-nine years ago. Yesterday was mourning, today they're crackin' firecrackers all over the country. "In memoriam"—all who gave their lives, so that Israel could exist.

Tuesday, April 24: Galilee Region

[Whispering] It's six, approaching six o'clock in the morning. Here is the north shore of the Sea of Galilee. Over there is the museum where the Jesus Boat is located.[5] *[Sweeping camera angle to the left]* Going over there, you can sit on that peninsula and watch the sun rise in about thirty minutes. This is our Lord's lake; this is our

4. Randall usually pronounced the country's name *Iss'-rul.*

5. Known also as "The Ancient Boat," the exhibit features the skeletal remains of a vessel discovered in the muddy bottom of the lake, believed by archaeologists to have plied the Sea of Galilee in the time of Jesus.

Lord's city. Over there is the Golan. Up there, Capernaum. Listen to the birds. Forty percent of the birds of Israel are in the Galilee. Incredible place. Thank ya, Lord, for giving me the chance once more to come to this holy place, this special place, that means so much to me and to those who are traveling with me. Always and in all ways, this is the sea where He said, "Peace, be still!" Whatever the future holds, I know who holds the future. In the turbulence, in the storm, in the calm—in His hand! *[Begins singing "He's got the whole world in his hands."]*

[Sun rises] Yep, there she be. It is now 6:15 almost, and Sol is up. Over the Sea of Galilee. Here's a couple from Germany. There's a person doing his devotional—singing his devotional. Beautiful world.

[At breakfast in the kibbutz dining room] Buffet here. Six-thirty in the morning. Looking out the window at the Sea. I see the sun. Beautiful tree. I can hear the doves singing from here. "I could sit here for an age and beyond, or two," and remember the Sea! Peace, be still. Amen.

[The Mount of the Beatitudes] The Sermon on the Mount. The Mount of the Beatitudes. Nature's amphitheatre. The Sea and all those who heard. Here's our people: thinking, reading, pondering, reflecting.

[Disembarking from a tour boat on the lake] There's our boat. It's a beautiful day, but we got spat upon with a little rain in that boat. Because these little black clouds came, and they don't hang around. They just drop their water, as that one right there has been out to do. . . . And here is the Golan out there—disputed territory between Israel and Syria since the Seven-Day War . . . Six-Day War.

[Yardenit—Jordan River baptism site] There's where we baptized twenty or twenty-two people, right down there. Sprinkled about four, immersed about sixteen or seventeen. River's cleaner and clearer than it was when I was here before. . . . There she goes toward the Dead Sea. Next time we see you, we'll be at the Dead Sea, old river!

Wednesday, April 25, Galilee Region—Nazareth

[As the bus passed by the traditional village of Cana in Galilee, Randall spoke of "the first of [Jesus'] miraculous signs" (John 2:11,

NIV), employing the theological language of "mystery" rather than the familiar terminology of "miracle." He then proffered the microphone (as if to invite debate), but I declined. The group proceeded to the first stop in Nazareth.]

[Mary's Well] Here's Mary's Well's water source. Everybody's come down, and one way or another, by cup or hand, took a sip of the water. Here in Nazareth. Wonderful memory, Lord, thank you! Wow, beautiful church. What a beautiful memory, Lord. Nobody in here but us, Lord. Thank ya, Lord, for that! I praise you for it. I'm grateful. Amen and amen.

[The Church of the Annunciation] This is the pilgrim church, the Church of the Annunciation. Built for pilgrims; I'm guessin' pilgrims would come and worship. This is the upper church. Murals from Spain; Portugal; the U.S.—a steel, metallic medium; Patagonia; Venezuela; Australia; Our Lady of Guadalupe—Mexico. This is the Japanese mural—pure pearl; the Canadian mural; France. Down in there *[pointing toward a cave]* is where it's said Mary's family lived. So be it.

[From an attraction called Nazareth Village, looking toward the Hill of the Precipice, a traditional site where Luke recorded that enraged members of the synagogue attempted unsuccessfully to dispatch Jesus. Someone asked if Jesus ever returned to Nazareth.] No! There's not any evidence at all that he ever came back here. *[to tour guide Gila]* It's not an absolute site, is it? Probably nearest. Yeah, it's a good site.

[Atop Mt. Carmel] Traditional site. What a panorama! Galilee in the distance, Jezreel Valley to Jezreel, Naboth's Vineyard and all that. Then a panorama toward the Mediterranean Sea. Almost clear enough to see it. Steve has introduced us to chapter 18 and 19 of 1 Kings, the story of the battle between the gods, the battle between the representatives of the gods, Baal and Ahab, Elijah and Yahweh. In time, the battle between Elijah and Jezebel. That the Lord God be the Lord God in truth. Thank you, Lord, for the most beautiful day in Carmel. *[facing the statue]* Elijah on Carmel, the prophet of fire!

Thursday, April 26: Galilee Region—North

[At Tel Dan] Thank you, Lord, for letting us stand here on the bridge, on the River Dan, one of the three sources of the River

Jordan. . . . Look around at the excavation of Dan. Very authentic. Ruins—how thick the walls! Down there's the altar. The oldest, most authentic city gate ever found in Israel, it's this city gate, in Dan. . . . But that's where kings or dignitaries would sit, and embrace and hold their decision-making, and decide the destiny of their citizenry. Ancient Dan. . . . We're gonna be leaving Dan, but it's been a good stop.

[At Banias/Caesarea Philippi] Our little group at Caesarea Philippi, and behind is a lot of school children, making a foray up this way. And here *[looking toward the Cave of Pan]* is my favorite place in the Holy Land. . . . Caesarea Philippi. Its water—they've made diversion channels since I was here. See that water tumbling off, going south to die in the Dead Sea. Sort of says it all. One of the three sources of the Jordan River. That tree up there, standing stately and alone above the Cave of Pan. They say human sacrifices were possible in that day; no way to know.

Friday, April 27: Jezreel to Jerusalem

[Atop Mt. Tabor/Mount of the Transfiguration, from within the Basilica of St. Francis] Come August 6, Transfiguration Day, the sun sets on that picture of Jesus. That translucent sun rises on August 6 and illuminates Jesus' face.

[At Tel Megiddo, atop the tel, overlooking the Valley of Jezreel] Here it is, Armageddon! As far as you can get, up against Nazareth, and looping in this direction. This is Armageddon . . .

[Following an introduction from tour guide Gila, Randall assembled the pilgrims and acknowledged the view by some interpreters, based on Revelation 16:14-16, that on the occasion of the Second Coming of Jesus a final and decisive battle will pit the forces of evil against the forces of good. "Armageddon" (Heb., mountain of Megiddo*) and the adjacent Plain of Esdraelon would, according to this view, be the site of the battle. Based on his amillennial interpretive posture, Randall discounted the view, suggesting that the scriptural forecast was largely symbolic and not meant to be taken literally.*

Again, and without prior notice (as when earlier he had spoken of the "mystery" of Jesus transforming water into wine), Randall turned to me and asked for comment. Citing 2 Peter 3:10, I suggested that a final, literal, apocalyptic battle, where the day of the Lord would "come like a thief, and then the heavens [would] pass away with a loud noise, and the elements [would] be dissolved with fire," was not an impossible scenario for a battleground as broad and flat as the valley of Armageddon. Randall, invariably content to engage in good-natured controversy, smiled, said thank you, and directed the tour to continue.]

[Emerging from the subterranean Megiddo water tunnel following a 200-step climb] Lord, I'll not forget this. Thank you, thank you, thank you. *[Seeing fellow climbers standing alongside the bus]* These are the veterans of the Megiddo tunnel! You're not supposed to look very good when you do this . . . that's why we don't do anything else today. We go home and go to bed!

["Home" turned out to be Jerusalem, as the tour bus continued southward.]

And there it is! The Holy City, the Temple Mount, the Dome of the Rock, the walls—the panorama. There *[below]* is David's city. And the excavations that kicked up a furor a few weeks ago—Al Aksa Mosque, the third-holiest spot in all Islam, behind Mecca and Medina. . . .[6] Thank you, Lord. I appreciate it!

Saturday, April 28: Jerusalem

[The Garden of Gethsemane and the Church of All Nations, viewing a mural above the church altar, depicting Jesus at prayer in the garden] The Gethsemane stone. *[Lowering the camera to view a stone beneath the altar]* That rock is supposed to be a picture of **that** rock. "Not my will but thine be done."[7]

[Inside the Old City walls, beginning to walk the Via Dolorosa] I have told them *[fellow pilgrims]* they're tough! Focus, vigilance, and discipline. Focus, vigilance, and discipline are the rules of this game!

[The Church of the Holy Sepulchre] And here we are at the Church of the Holy Sepulchre. Already filled with the feet of pilgrims. There's the entrance area. We're goin' in . . . *[Upstairs]*

6. The "furor" related to the opposition by Israeli archaeologists to the decision by the Waqf—the Muslim religious trust controlling the Temple Mount—to excavate an additional mosque below the level of the Temple Mount platform.

7. Without doubt, Randall reflected here on his 1974 receipt, while touring Jerusalem with pilgrims from Winston-Salem's First Baptist Church, of the invitation of Southeastern Seminary to become its third president.

And here is the stone of the crucifixion. Incredibly ornate, gaudy. Dozens of people all in line, trying to put their hand on the stone that held the cross. Jesus was crucified here. This was the pinnacle of a hill. Here is where they think he was crucified. *[Viewing a mural]* And they took his body down, and they say this is where it was laid, right here. . . . The tomb is on the other side. *[Approaching the Edicule, which houses the tomb]* This is holy. Holy. Here people wait to go into the tomb. People going in . . .

Sunday, April 29: Jerusalem and Bethlehem

[At the Grand Court Hotel. Randall, illustrating his attention to the minutest details of his experience, described his sleeping quarters] Here is my room. No. 653 at the Grand Court. I have this sitting area. Sofa, two chairs, nice desk, where I do my work. Then my bed, where I sleep well—it's a good bed. My TV, my dinette, bed lamp, place where my bag is, a safe, and a place to hang my clothes. Then a bathroom with a nice ledge to put my stuff on, a shelf where I can put my gear. This is one of the better rooms I've ever had as a guide—a tour director. I've been sitting there, doing my devotional, looking at the bright sun. We're off to the Old City today, then Bethlehem this afternoon. Thank you, Lord, for this journey. Thank you.

[Atop the Temple Mount, viewing the golden Dome of the Rock, and offering a politically incendiary suggestion] That's gold! That's pure gold! [Tour guide suggests it cost $10 million] Oh, no! Ten million would hardly buy one piece of that stuff. King Hussein put that on top of that, the Dome of the Rock. Beautiful place. There it is, right there! Over it is a mosque; one day, maybe a cross, or a Star of David? Who knows?

[At the Western Wall] It's five minutes till two, and we're at the Western Wall. Part of the wall left from the ancient, Herodian temple. Very, very serious and special place. I'll leave the names of the most significant others in my life, all of those who are on my daily devotional list. Thank you, Lord, for giving me the chance once more to stand in the open plaza before the Wailing Wall. Amen. *[Scanning wall with videocam]* Orthodox Jews, mostly. There's my buddy Steve, my partner Steve, my friend Steve, who's worked so hard for this tour. And his prayers are real. He loves Jerusalem. He loves you, Lord. . . .

[South wall, Temple Mount, near the Huldah Gates] These are new parts of the archaeological dig—right underneath the Al Aksa Mosque. Steps of Jesus. . . . The entrance and exit steps are from the first century. And there, in that old *[unrestored]* place are steps where Jesus actually walked!

[In Bethlehem, at Manger Square] Church of the Nativity, in Bethlehem. *[As pilgrims entered through the low door]* Don't bump your heads! Now inside the church. Gonna get to go into that cave next. We're next—things are comin' out fine and dandy. *[Below the altar, inside the birth grotto]* This the cave where our Lord Jesus, they say, was born. Steve's just lit up a candle; Charlotte and Ruth just added theirs. Thank you, Lord, for letting me add to our candles today.

Monday, April 30: Jerusalem

[Outside the Israel Museum] This is the Hebrew museum. Here's the model of Jesus' Jerusalem. *[Fellow pilgrim says "Gosh!"]* That's a pretty good word—"gosh"! It was no mean city. This is the reconstructed, newly located, credible model of Jesus' Jerusalem. A gorgeous depiction: the Praetorium, Temple Antonia (named for Mark Anthony of the Roman heyday), Kidron Valley, old City of David, Tomb of David, house of John Mark, Golgotha, Calvary—right there! Thank ya, Lord.

["Gordon's Calvary" and the Garden Tomb] Here we are. I still like this, even though I know that it might not be here that you *[God]* gave the Lord. But wherever you did it, you did it just for me, and for all the world. Thank you for that. *[Viewing a rock cliff called "The Skull," behind the Arab bus station]* Now it's a little eroded, but you can still see that face. Down below, Jerusalem bus station, up above, graves to this day. Mt. Moriah? Palestinian buses going in all directions through this disputed, holy, bloody land. *[At the Garden Tomb]* Empty tomb! Remember Easter! Amen, and amen!

[Anglican docent Ken argued for the authenticity of the site, as over against the Holy Sepulchre church. Tour member Jim objected that the shelf inside the Garden Tomb did not appear long enough for a human body. Noting Jim's six-foot-two height, Ken replied, "Well, it's good you weren't the one who was crucified!"] He's got you nailed, Jim! Thanks for being a good prop!

Tuesday, May 1: Dead Sea Area

[Qumran: Here Randall stood beside the excavated scriptorium—where the Dead Sea Scrolls were thought to have been laboriously copied—and offered his single allusion of the pilgrimage to his seminary presidency and the Baptist battle over the nature of Scripture. Variations in separate copies of the same biblical books—insignificant though they might be—demonstrated that the adjective "inerrant" was technically inappropriate.]

[Entering his suite at the Meridian Hotel] Look at this bathroom! Lou, I'd like to see you here, in your "spa"! *[Wife Lou did not accompany Randall on this trip. Randall scanned the amenities of his room.]* This is the perk of a tour leader. I don't deserve it, but I sure enjoy it! *[Later, after darkness fell]* Here's a picture from the balcony of my Dead Sea room. That's a big old, beautiful, full moon. That full moon is the first full moon after Passover, 2007. It has risen over the Dead Sea and is making its trek across the sky. Hello, moon, hello!

Wednesday, May 2: Wilderness of Zin

Sunrise over the Dead Sea. Six-fifteen, May 2. Old Sol, so predictable, so every day. Thank you, Lord, for me and the pilgrims on this journey, and all our loved ones, far and near. Amen.

[A remote oasis in the Negev, the biblical Wilderness of Zin. At the suggestion of tour guide Gila, Randall and other pilgrims dispersed to sit alone, beneath parched trees and bushes, and meditate on 1 Kings 19:1-5ff. In the passage, Elijah flees from Jezebel to Mt. Horeb (Sinai), stopping over in the wilderness to rest beneath a broom tree. In verse 7, an angel touches the forlorn prophet, shows him food and water, and bids him, "Get up and eat; otherwise the journey will be too much for you."]

[Whispering] Below Sinai. Wilderness altar. Place of silence. My Wilderness of Zin altar. Place of the Lord's meeting. Elijah story. You don't trust in "I've got the blues." Learn to trust "in," and move "out." *[Takes small stones and forms a cross on the ground]* A cross I left in the Wilderness of Zin. In thee, O God, I trust!

[Following a group luncheon of "quail and manna"—kosher wieners and pita bread—the group boarded their rugged safari vehicles for the return trip to their motorcoach. Amid the roar of the diesel engines and the lively conversation of fellow pilgrims, Randall focused

his videocam back on the oasis, as it faded from view. His narration was difficult to distinguish above the noise, but the following is an approximation.]

Lord, there's my not-to-worry oasis, in the middle of the Wilderness of Zin. I sat on a log, right down there. I made a decision. I won't ever be blue. I'll get out of it. I'll go right back to work and minister to people. Amen.

Randall's plethora of pilgrimages invariably took him afield but then returned him to those starting places where he lived most of his life and performed most of his work.

The year 2007—when the above Holy Land excursion took place—was two-thirds of the way through the dozen interim pastorates that Randall undertook, post-retirement. Much ministry lay ahead for a man resolved to "go right back to work and minister to people."

In many ways, "Israel and Jordan: a Holy Land Pilgrimage" induced me and the forty-six others—mostly senior adults—who accompanied Randall to do likewise. Much in the way of "breaking camp and moving on" lay ahead for everyone. The twin examples of a Lord who had illuminated the way and a faithful minister who had followed would continue to inspire.

Chapter 12

Everybody Dies a Hero

"Marrying and burying: there's no two things a pastor does that matter more." Randall Lolley's open-handed application of himself and his giftedness to Christianity's solemn rites of passage lent credence to this declaration.[1] The end of a person's life and the consequent funeral, in particular, were invested with deepest significance and prioritized over virtually every other ministerial consideration.

Late on a Saturday evening in March 1996, Randall's church member and longtime bird-hunting companion Paul died at his Greensboro home, suddenly and unexpectedly. Though distraught, Paul's wife waited until the following morning to notify her pastor, who was already in his office at church, preparing to lead worship.

"My buddy Paul has died," Randall announced, as he placed the telephone receiver back in its cradle. His tone was familiar for such a circumstance, at once sorrowful and matter-of-fact. "I need to be with Ruth. Tell the others to go on with the service, and I'll get back in time to preach."

In days following, the pastor would sit with the widow and her children at least one more time, sharing their grief and encouraging them to talk. Were he not already familiar with the life story of their loved one, he would have elicited the information in the course of his visit. The act of generously eulogizing the deceased was central to his practice of the art of the funeral.

---

1. I recall the statement. Randall's administrative assistant Jo Covert held a similar memory: "He once told me that the two most significant times of lasting importance between a pastor and his congregation were weddings and funerals. I never forgot that statement, and thought of it many times when he was officiating. . . ."

Randall once advised ministry associate Charles Qualls, "*everybody dies a hero.* But our job is not to manufacture the hero. We have to *find* the hero—and he's there in everybody's life."

Having undertaken his first pastorate while a college student in the early 1950s, Randall had through forty-five years of ministry doubtless witnessed the changes in funeral practice that were outlined in 2009 by author and preaching professor Thomas G. Long: "With surprising swiftness and dramatic results, a significant segment of American Christians has over the last 50 years abandoned previously established funeral customs in favor of an entirely new pattern of memorializing the dead."[2]

Long expressed caution about several aspects of the "new pattern," including preference for "memorial services" (where the body is not present); observances that are "brief, simple, highly personalized and customized"; a focus on the life story of the deceased; a "celebration of life" that emphasizes joy over sadness; and a private burial or inurnment.

Because Randall himself had always focused on life stories, it could be said that he was, for good or ill, ahead of his time. Nevertheless, just as he had supported other traditional practices—including the reading of familiar Scripture and the performance of quality sacred music—his recalled and recorded funeral meditations display the dual emphases of historically Christian observances: (1) recognizing the reality of death while (2) pointing to the believer's hope of resurrection unto the life hereafter.

During the funeral service for his friend, Randall unquestionably "celebrated" the man's life. He recalled the good times, the challenges, the hardships, and the victories that accompany most of human experience. But from Gospel and Epistle he also recalled words of confidence and faithful expectation, pointing a grieving widow and her family to their reason for hope and consolation.

Tracing the history of funeral observance, Thomas Long noted that Christians in prior centuries would carefully prepare the bodies of their dead and then carry them in procession to the cemetery, "the

---

2. *Accompany Them with Singing—The Christian Funeral* (Louisville: Westminster John Knox, 2009), 58.

place of farewell." Along the way, they would stop over at the church for a time of Scripture reading and prayer, conducted by a priest or clergyman. But the main focal point of the observance, Long noted, would be the graveside rite. "The burial phase took place at graveside and included the commendation of the deceased to God and the actual burial of the body."[3]

For Randall Lolley, a typical graveside committal would include words indicative of the climactic nature of that aspect of the funeral rite:

> This is a miracle moment.
>
> We come in reverence and humility to offer [this loved one's] life to the Lord, who gave it to us in the first place.
>
> *Let the winds that blow, the seasons that come and go,*
> *The sunshine and shade from the skies that God made,*
> *Sanctify this place.*
> *Let the trees that arch above, and the far view from this slope*
> *Draw our thoughts to the beauty of a life that lives on.*
> *And let God's amazing grace transform us, and this moment for us,*
> *Making us conscious of the spirit of this one we love, ever with us,*
> *Through all the days to come.*[4]

Following such introductory expressions, Randall would open his Bible and read familiar words of hope and comfort from the Gospels and from the Epistles of Paul. *Blessed are the pure in heart . . . I am the resurrection and the life . . . Peace I leave with you . . . O death, where is your sting? . . . We know that all things work together for good to them who love God . . . For me to live is Christ, and to die is gain.*

On the way from the large sanctuary in Greensboro, en route to the grave of his hunting buddy, Randall Lolley did an uncharacteristic thing: he paused at the front door and quietly wept. "I guess I've been at this too long," he whispered. "Now I've gone to burying my friends."

Burying friends would not become easier in the years to follow. On a yellow sticky note affixed to a sheaf of printed papers in his

---

3. *Accompany Them with Singing*, 71.
4. Author unknown.

office files in Raleigh appeared this note, in Randall's familiar handwriting and signed with his initials "WRL": "These are 2 of the toughest funerals I ever tried to conduct!"

Both services had occurred at Randall's and Lou's home congregation in retirement, Raleigh's First Baptist Church. The first of these, titled "In Memoriam," had been delivered for the February 2011 funeral of Randall's colleague and closest associate during his Southeastern Seminary days, Dr. Morris Ashcraft. The second, titled "My Tribute," was preached one year later during a service for Randall's close friend and confidant Edwin Vick Jr., a lay leader at First Baptist.

Between the two "tough" services were clear similarities. One parallel was a succinct statement of the essential character—from Randall's perspective—of the person remembered. Family context informed his opinion. In Morris Ashcraft's case, Randall recalled what he doubtless had learned during their years of close association: Morris arose from a mid-twentieth century Arkansas family, who were "Free-church Baptists to the core."

He would use this observation to explain the difficult choices Dr. Ashcraft had made in the course of his long career as a Baptist educator—including his decision to join a dozen other dissenters as they departed the faculty of Louisville's Southern Seminary in 1958 and his choice to stand with Randall as they resigned their posts as dean and president, respectively, at Southeastern in late 1987.

As important as their free-church Baptistness was the Ashcraft clan's status as unforeseen high achievers. Randall observed that, born into a carpenter's home, Morris and his seven siblings were "original thinkers, serious students, quick learners who became theologians, ethicists, archaeologists, philosophers, public servants, mayors, housewives, and, most of all, model Christians."

When months later Randall experienced the loss of another close friend, Ed Vick, he turned from the challenge of describing a scholar to that of characterizing a technocrat. Ed was a North Carolina State-trained civil engineer and founder of an elite consulting firm. Randall grew close to him when in summer 1988 he undertook the pastoral leadership of Ed's church. In the course of his brief, year-and-a-half Raleigh pastorate, Randall preached funerals for both of Ed's parents. "These two experiences," he acknowledged during the funeral service, "as much as anything else, bonded the two of us together as friends over the long haul."

His departed comrade, Randall asserted, was more than a friend: he was "my mentor, my parishioner, and one of the most inspiring and challenging pieces of God's creation I ever met." In naming Ed as his "mentor," Randall engaged in what was, for him, typical: he characteristically subordinated himself, in some ways, to the person whose memory he recalled.

> Ed saw farther than most of us see. He focused on the big pictures. His sight never clouded his vision. He looked around corners and pushed hard to catch dreams. . . . Ed was values-contagious. We caught his values from him like we catch mumps or chicken pox. He passed them on—to his children and grandchildren, his colleagues and business associates, his church friends and community leaders.

While his funeral sermons tended to weave generalized expressions of appreciation and admiration into lengthy paeans, Randall almost always supported his assertions with concrete illustrations. In Ed Vick's case, his "greatness" lay first of all in his humility (he "did not know he had any greatness") and second in his accomplishments. Not only had Ed performed admirably in his profession, but he had also applied his extracurricular energies to denominational involvement, principally to upholding the moderate cause in "the Baptist wars."[5]

Earlier, and in a different way, Randall had similarly piled compliment upon commendation in his description of the character of Morris Ashcraft, who "never thinned when things around him thickened. He rose to occasions. He grew into situations. He matched wits with circumstances."

While mentioning Dr. Ashcraft's prior history as a Navy fighter pilot and subsequent academic odyssey as professor and administrator

---

5. Ed Vick was credited with having first suggested the name for a new organization of theologically moderate Baptists: the "Cooperative Baptist Fellowship."

in five Baptist institutions, Randall permitted his departed colleague to intimate the measure of his own character through his appreciation of people he [Ashcraft] adjudged greater than himself.

"He said he had never been much for fan mail," Randall recalled. "He said that he had, however, written three fan letters in his life." One was to Bob Bratcher, who "gave his defense for the nature of the Biblical revelation by loving [the Bible], translating it, and passing it on."

Other fan letters had gone to Heber Peacock, an Episcopal scholar and Bible translator who had concluded his career among the native American Cherokee in Western North Carolina; and to Jack Flanders, the Furman University dean who in 1958 had made a place for Morris Ashcraft following his termination from Southern Seminary.

Perhaps the highest compliment Randall attached to Morris Ashcraft was unwitting, for it was an unconscious comparison with himself:

> He was the friend of scholars right, left, and in the middle. I once asked Dr. Clifton J. Allen how he chose Ash to write the commentary on The Revelation for *Broadman Bible Commentary* in the 1970s. He said, "Ashcraft knew enough about it to know how much he didn't know about it, so I asked him to write the commentary . . . ."

In both funerals—Morris Ashcraft's and Ed Vick's—Randall combined refreshing pathos with a measure of homespun humor. "Having Morris Ashcraft as a friend was like having a perpetual cover for your backside." (In the typed and printed copy of his manuscript, Randall noted, "At this point, the speaker unapologetically had to stop, gain composure, and then go on.")

Of Ed Vick he insisted, "He chased ideas like a dog chases cats. He was never afraid of a new idea whose time had come. He had a bulldog's don't-let-*goishness* (or a Wolfpack's!)."

In March 2014, Randall returned to the pulpit of First Baptist Church, Winston-Salem, to assist in the funeral of his onetime staff colleague Mitzi Roddick Moore. Recalling what his wife Lou would later qualify as his most satisfying accomplishment during his

1962–1974 pastorate, Randall noted, "Shortly after I became pastor of this fine church . . . it became apparent that one of our exciting challenges was to build a staff fitting for the church and the beautiful campus it had just completed."

The capstone addition to the Winston-Salem staff, he suggested, was Mitzi Moore, who came to fulfill the church's dream of "a world-class child development program." Having "hit the ground running, she blew past excellent to marvelous, raising the bar for a church desiring to minister to children and their families. First Baptist's child care ministry became second to none, flourishing on Sundays and during weekdays. Mitzi lived by a simple formula: to live a life and do a work well, one must love life and enjoy work. Mitzi did both!" As such, Randall applied to his onetime colleague his highest commendation: she was "my mentor."

Pointing to Mitzi's underlying ministerial uniqueness, Randall referred to a theme that appeared to predominate his thinking during the second half of his career:

> In 1962 she joined a staff full of men. . . . Mitzi bumped her head against a "glass ceiling" lots of times, but it never disheartened her. . . . Without making too much of a fuss over it, she became a pioneer in her calling to be a full-fledged minister of the Good News of God in Jesus Christ.
>
> Thanks to her and countless others like her, that "glass ceiling" is being shattered across the country and around the world. Ministers can wear skirts just as sure as they can wear trousers. Nowadays, when we see a door open to Christian ministry for a female, we owe it to Mitzi and dozens like her who blazed a trail, weathered the storms, and achieved the goal of ordination in spite of gender.

Randall's last-preached funeral sermon was delivered in winter 2015 to the first congregation he had served as a seminary graduate, Greensboro's First Baptist. The wife of a high-profile lay leader and prominent local businessman had died, and his onetime pastor was honoring an earlier promise he had made to return for her service.

In fanciful but undeniably boilerplate fashion, Randall took the name *Hazel* to the encyclopedia and discovered characteristics of the

Hazelnut that comported with her personality: e.g., versatile, earthy (down to earth), flavorful, a savory contrast to the cloying sweetness sometimes associated with Southern womanhood.

Best remembered among Randall's funeral meditations were those he prepared and preached for such high-profile church members and friends as Hazel. Important, however, is that he invariably invested the same degree of preparation and the same quality of delivery for humbler and lesser-known people. "You gotta do it," he explained, recalling Jesus' parable of the lost sheep.[6]

Southeastern Seminary history professor Fred Grissom recalled a 1987 dinner meeting with Randall and Morris Ashcraft, where the small talk turned to the events of that particular day:

> Randall said that he had conducted a home funeral ceremony for an elderly black man, who was on Randall and Lou's Meals on Wheels route. . . . Since he did not know much about the man, Randall said he decided to talk generally about life and death. He knew that the man had had a long life and told the family that they should celebrate that instead of mourning his passing.
>
> He then said that [the man] did not fear death, and [quoted], "I don't want a long life, I just want to live long enough to see Ronald Reagan out of the White House." And the family applauded.

When Randall returned from seminary to church leadership, his procedure was unvarying. Once the pastor's office received notification of a church member's death, he prioritized his response over other matters, regardless of their urgency. Wherever possible, he departed his study immediately and went straight to the side of the nearest of kin. Within two days Randall would make a point of contacting and extending ministry to anyone among that group of survivors he termed "the circle of eight"—wife, husband, son, daughter, father, mother, sister, brother.

Occasionally the passing of a church member would occur—as in the case of his hunting friend—without warning. Otherwise, relatively few deaths caught Randall by surprise. Closely involved as

6. Luke 15:4-6.

pastor with the entirety of the senior adult membership, he was typically up to date with their personal circumstances. He often amazed Wednesday evening prayer meeting attenders with his comprehensive knowledge of individuals' health circumstances.

In a lower desk drawer in his study in Greensboro, Randall maintained a confidential file he labeled "Special Diagnosis." Recorded within the file were names of individuals who had made him aware of potentially life-limiting health circumstances, along with his notes regarding their current health status. Whenever these individuals should die, their departure dates would be recorded. Pages would be added as additional people with "special diagnoses" came to their pastor's attention.

Randall's hospital visitation routine in Greensboro saw him make "rounds" at up to three local hospitals on two or three days of each week, plus weekends as needed. On rare occasions he would enter an unusual pact with a dying church member to visit that person more often.

Madeline (not her real name) was a younger, middle-aged woman, hospitalized with terminal cancer. During her pastor's biweekly visits, she disclosed that she was always buoyed by his presence and found herself depressed until he appeared at her bedside again. Randall summarily promised that he would begin at once to see Madeline and pray with her every day. It was a pledge that he fulfilled, day by day, week after week, up to the time of her death. His close attention and ministry of careful listening enabled Randall to stand at Madeline's funeral and speak authoritatively of her inner struggles and eventual spiritual victory, information that served to strengthen her grieving husband and school-age daughter.

During retirement, and living near the capital city of Raleigh, the terminal illness of a former seminary student and current employee of the Baptist State Convention of North Carolina came to Randall's attention. While sitting at Ken's (not his real name) hospital bedside, Randall made a similar pledge to begin visiting daily. The subsequent steady contact and intense personal involvement transported him to the patient's inner psyche. Randall later marveled that Ken, a beneficiary of theological education and a deep thinker, nevertheless appeared near the end of his life to "revert to the simpler faith of his youth."

Happier rites of passage, of course, were the hundreds of weddings that Randall Lolley performed through the years. Most occurred at the three First Baptist churches he served (Winston-Salem, Raleigh, Greensboro), but a few—including the nuptials of daughters Charlotte and Pam—took place in Binkley Chapel, on the campus of Southeastern Baptist Theological Seminary.

Having established lasting relationships in the various venues of his decades-long ministerial career, Randall continued to receive invitations to "tie the knot" during his retirement years. This circumstance was further accelerated by his twelve post-retirement interim pastorates, which occurred over the course of the ensuing fifteen years.

If, through the years of his various ministries, Randall observed that funeral practices were changing, the same was true of weddings. An early alteration, observable during his concluding vocational pastorate in Greensboro, was the transition of the traditional wedding reception from the church fellowship hall to another location. (This was precipitated largely by the desire of many couples to include dance bands and popular music, and to make alcoholic beverages available to their guests.)

By the time of Randall's 1996 pastoral retirement, the "venue wedding" was coming into vogue. Eschewing the significance of traditional church observances, many couples began to locate their weddings in hotels, banquet halls, country clubs, or outdoor settings. Randall adapted himself as necessary, sometimes traveling appreciable distances to officiate at a "destination wedding."

Ceremonies also began to change, as couples—following the fashion of the times—would seek input sufficient to personalize their occasions. Again, Randall cooperated in the production and performance of fresh, if not altogether novel, promises and expressions of love and fealty.

An example would be the wedding of Brittany and Peter (not their real names), performed in Raleigh during the latter years of Randall's retirement.

The pastor began with a characteristically warm welcome to wedding guests, a welcome that he offered in the name of the soon-to-be-married couple themselves. Acknowledging the "high and holy" nature of the marriage ceremony—regardless of the venue—he lent his own voice to the couple's desire to thank their families, honor the contributions that their parents had made in their lives, and acknowledge all who "could not be with us here today."

In Randall's categories of theological thought, the idea of "miracle" merged with "mystery." Thus, "We are here to celebrate a mystery, actually a miracle, the discovery of Peter and Brittany that of all others, they have come to love each other so much as to become husband and wife. Theirs has been a journey, and will be a journey still."

Next came words that consecrated, to the best of the pastor's ability, the venue in which he and his wedding couple were met: "Here at this beautiful place, in God's great outdoors, they come to make promises and to seize the challenge of taking care of each other for the rest of their lives."

As an aside, Randall entered a cautionary word to the guests: "It is daring, even dangerous, to attend a wedding. It means that you have become involved in Brittany's and Peter's lives. So welcome! Let us rejoice! Let us celebrate!"

Substituting vows written by the engaged couple themselves in place of the traditional promises of the "Protestant-Episcopal" ceremony was not a novelty, for Randall had encountered that desire from the midpoint of his ministry career. Inwardly, however, he may have scratched his head over the pledges he administered that day:

I (Peter/Brittany) take you (Brittany/Peter) to be my (wife/husband) /
I promise to be kind and unselfish /
And to support you in moments of joy and sadness /
I promise to laugh and cry with you /
And to love you faithfully through good times and bad /
I promise never to take you for granted /
Nor the little things that make our love special and everlasting /
With these vows I pledge my life and love to you.

Following more familiar language during the exchange of rings ("In token and pledge of my constant faith and abiding love, with this ring I *you* wed"), Randall concluded the ceremony with an unambiguously Christian pronouncement and ministerial blessing:

> For as much as Peter and Brittany have consented together in holy wedlock, and have witnessed the same before God, their family and friends, and thereto have pledged their faith to each other and to their Lord Jesus Christ, and have declared the same by the giving and receiving of rings, I pronounce that they are husband and wife together. Those whom God has joined let no one ever put asunder!

A few years earlier, my onetime pastor and boss joined me at our former church in Greensboro to add his blessing to the wedding of my younger daughter. The prayer he spoke was "vintage Randall Lolley":

> Almighty God, we are here surrounded by a great cloud of witnesses, and also by strange arithmetic. Normally one plus one equals two; but here, now mysteriously, one plus one equals many more than two.
>
> You are here, and thanks be to your grace-filled presence, that makes three. Lauren's and Scotty's families are here, and thanks be to your love and theirs, that makes a great circle. Time-tested and true acquaintances and friends old and new are here. Thanks be to your Spirit-made koinonia, that makes a mighty assembly.
>
> Bless all of us, empower all of us to celebrate together this incredible creation of a new home. This afternoon will pass, and apace will come the night. The night will pass, and apace will come the day. The days pass, and apace come the weeks. The weeks pass, and apace come the months. The months pass, and apace come the years.
>
> Almighty God, we invoke your blessing upon every day, week, month, and year, that Scotty and Lauren and their families and all of us together may help build their home from the timbers of this marriage.
>
> We invoke your blessing upon every word spoken, promise made, liturgy voiced, prayer prayed, scripture read, meditation

brought, praises sung, words of greeting extended. And we give you our thanksgiving for this wonder-filled, cheerful, and solemn afternoon of worship and praise.

Now bless us together, as we pray the petition you've taught us to pray, when you were here with us, when you were here like us . . . [Everyone joined in praying the Lord's Prayer.]

Chapter 13

Dearest Lou

It was autumn 1951 when twenty-year-old Randall Lolley took his seat in the bleachers at Alabama's Troy State Teacher's College to witness the annual homecoming football game. Baseball was his preferred sport, and Birmingham's Howard College was his team. But it was more than an athletic competition that drew Randall 200 miles south that day.

As halftime arrived, he sensed an emotion unfamiliar to a "lead dog": jealousy. When Geneva's Clara Lou Jacobs was introduced among the ladies of the court, the man who by then was her presumptive fiancé could scarcely ignore her escort—a "big, handsome football player."[1]

Even had this football player been a threat, Randall had come out on the long end of romantic rivalries before. A few weeks earlier he had honored an invitation to preach at a revival service at New Prospect Baptist Church, which lay between Geneva and his own hometown of Samson. It was then and there that he first laid eyes on Clara Lou, who sat at the piano accompanying a duet sung by the daughters of Jacobs family friends.

From his seat on the dais, Randall had taken note of the pianist. Following the service he asked his boyhood friend John French who she was. "Oh, that's Clara Lou Jacobs," answered John. "But she'll never date you—she won't even date me!"

Not easily deterred, Randall drove to Geneva the following week and stopped by the Jacobs Grocery Store to ask about the owners' comely daughter. As it happened, Clara Lou was home at that moment. But her mother telephoned her and said, "There's a

---

1. Unless otherwise noted, words and expressions in this chapter that are in quotation marks represent actual quotations and recollections from Randall's family members, friends, and associates through the years.

preacher here at the store, and he's asking about you. Can I send him to the house?"

She consented, checked her hair and makeup, greeted her visitor at her door, and engaged him in conversation. "They spoke for a good while" before Randall departed with the feeling that his friend John had been wrong. Dating Clara Lou was in the realm of possibility. One week later he phoned her, she agreed to his invitation, and the two were an "item" from that time forward.

Let me not to the marriage of true minds Admit impediments.

Well known among William Shakespeare's love poems is "Sonnet 116." There the poet spoke not so much to the subject of marriage as to the just reason for such a relationship to take place. When a union did occur as the "marriage of true minds," the poet—recalling the cautionary word within the traditional Protestant Episcopal wedding ceremony—insisted that no one should object.[2]

Apparently, nobody (apart, perhaps, from his friend John) objected when Randall, on August 28, 1952, met Clara Lou at the altar of her home congregation in Geneva, Alabama.[3] For she was, in ways that would be demonstrated in all years to come, his perfect "match."

Lou had found him to be "sincere, inspiring, confident," and "comfortable to be around." Moreover, "she trusted him," in no small part because "he appreciated me."

Meanwhile, Randall's appreciation for Lou extended to "her smile" and "her independence," even as he found her to be "good-natured, caring, a woman of faith"—and beyond all else, "gorgeous."

While Randall had graduated earlier that year from Howard College, Clara Lou lacked one more year of study for her education degree from Troy State. This became no impediment, however, as Randall deeply respected her desire for a college education. Even

---

2. "If either of you know any inward impediment why you should not be conjoined, speak now . . . ."

3. The ceremony was on a Thursday, since the family's store was normally closed on that day.

though he nurtured a sense of pastoral calling and a desire for seminary training, he committed himself to bide his time by teaching English and science at Montgomery's Starke University Military School.

Neither did Clara Lou's Methodism constitute an impediment. Later, when completing an online biographical profile that asked for a statement on religion, Randall would write, "Any individual, child, or otherwise cannot be baptized until they come to a saving knowledge of Jesus Christ—then, and only then, would a person be baptized."[4] While Clara Lou may have questioned that rationale, she at length yielded to her new husband's conviction and underwent—at his administration—baptism by immersion at the Lolley family's church, Samson Baptist.

Regarding their respective personalities and personal will, however, neither Lou nor Randall would later be observed by daughters Charlotte and Pam to be stronger than the other. Even with "Dad in the spotlight, with Mom supporting, theirs was a true partnership. At home, Mom was the handyman while Dad was the supervisor. If something needed fixing, you went to Mom. If something needed 'wording,' you went to Dad."

At home, "Mom wore the pants, since Dad wasn't home all the time." The two were of one mind on most subjects, but "she always had the freedom to do things her way." Should they disagree, they never argued in the presence of their children.

Randall never forgot that, as a male, he was a minority member of the Lolley household. His daughters and their mother were always welcome to interrupt him in his home study office. And when they did, he would greet them with good humor: "Here comes the War Department!"

And while Lou Lolley routinely respected her husband's opinions in his own areas of expertise, church members and fellow staff ministers recall that he "deferred to her in matters of style and design." She was his co-equal, his "match: God called her as surely as he called him."

---

4. World Biographical Encyclopedia, *Prabook Profile*, undated.

Love is not love
Which alters when it alteration finds,
Or bends with the remover to remove.

The familiar Bard of Avon supplanted his initial poetic couplet's positive image of love—as the rightful foundation of marriage—with a second couplet that projected a negative image of vacillation in response to the changing circumstances of life. The bridge between the disparate couplets is a firm declaration: such vacillating, altering love is not real love.

"For better or for worse, for richer, for poorer, in sickness and in health, to love and to cherish; from this day forward until death do us part" are words that Randall Lolley and Clara Lou Jacobs undoubtedly repeated to each other, as did most marrying couples in 1952. Their traditional wedding vows reinforced Shakespeare's declaration about love's constancy in the face of life's inevitable transitions.

"Love, honor, and obey" would likewise have been a part of the promises made. But given the philosophical commitments that issued from both parties in years to follow, the scriptural admonition, "Submit to one another out of reverence for Christ" (Eph 5:21, NIV), may have been more applicable.

As their "marriage of true minds" got underway, Clara Lou's gift for teaching became manifest. First entering her fifth grade classroom in Montgomery while Randall completed his assignment at the military academy, and the next year relocating to a school in Knightdale, North Carolina, as he undertook his studies at the new Southeastern Baptist Seminary, "Mrs. Lolley" demonstrated her teaching gift.

Yet at no point—neither at Southeastern nor during the three staff and pastoral callings between Randall's time at Southeastern as student and his later years as president—did he seek to exploit his spouse for church lay leadership. She was "not pressured by Dad to lead," their daughters said. Again, "she always had the freedom to do things her way."

Still, Lou managed her life in such a manner as to correspond with her husband's calling, their churches' needs, and her own desire to deploy her natural and spiritual gifts. Surrendering her public school teaching career in order to bring forth and nurture their two daughters (born 1957 and 1958), she thereafter gradually reapplied her energies toward youth ministry.

With the family's arrival in Winston-Salem in autumn 1962, Lou co-led First Baptist's high school department in Sunday school. When she and Randall built their first new home at 1939 Greenbrier Road, Lou designated the spacious basement area as a meeting hall and discussion room for youth. Daughters remember group-building exercises devised by their mother, with a particular emphasis on ensuring that no individual youngster felt excluded.

With children who were rapidly rising to "youth department age," Lou found it easy to be present with them for group activities, missions gatherings, midweek fellowship and studies, Sunday worship gatherings, and youth choir. Meanwhile, as their father's spouse, she never seemed to experience frustration over how to apportion her time between him and their children. "She was definitely [the one who was] raising us. Dad was away a lot, and worked long hours. [But] it always seemed like a true partnership; [she] never felt divided."

The dozen years in Winston-Salem witnessed numerical growth in the church, Randall's growing visibility and popularity in the community and in state and national denominational life, and his family's happiness with life in their adopted hometown. Lou would later refer to that chapter of their lives as "our Camelot." She said, "We would never have left if Southeastern hadn't called."

But in 1974, Southeastern did call Dr. Randall Lolley as its third president, and wife Lou respected and responded to the appropriateness of the call. Again displaying her gift for balancing the necessities of a life transition, Lou remained in Winston-Salem for a year to see older daughter Charlotte finish high school and begin college. Then she arranged for a church couple to serve as live-in companions to younger daughter Pam, as she also completed school.

Joining Randall in the president's home at Southeastern, and with her "nest" suddenly empty, Lou again demonstrated a love that would not "alter when it alteration finds." Departing the "big house at 308 Durham Road" each day and plunging headlong into the life of the seminary and of its small town of Old Wake Forest, she became a beloved public personality in both venues.

"Mom loved spending time with students and staff, entertaining [them] at the house—Mom was a great cook. Mom and Dad loved being in the community together. They knew the restaurant owners, the service station attendants . . . . Mom would eat in the student cafeteria and talk to students. One man was visiting the seminary and asked if he could speak with Mrs. Lolley. He was told, 'Just head over to the cafeteria—she's probably there having lunch with the students.'"

As a former Methodist, Lou's "Wesleyan spirituality" seemed to mesh well with her husband's Arminian/Calvinist Baptist synthesis. She and Randall blended convictional Christianity with open-handed activism. While he labored at building his learning community, she discovered small, simple ways to improve its environment. One newly arriving professor recalled how she "showed up" at his rented house, needle and thread in hand, to hem a sagging living room curtain.

"She was as different from other seminary presidents' wives we had known as Randall was different from other presidents."

O no! it is an ever-fixed mark
That looks on tempests and is never shaken . . .

The "ever-fixed mark" in Shakespeare's poem was a lighthouse, an immovable object in an undulating sea of threatening waves and obstructions unobserved beneath the dark surface of the water, yet an object that illuminated the horizon and suggested a pathway to peace and stillness.

A former student recalled of Lou Lolley, "She stood beside [Randall], with him and behind him. She was quiet when necessary and a voice when called upon. Her smile, warmth, and laughter helped him shine that much brighter as a pastor, leader, and president."

Said one SEBTS professor, "I cannot imagine Randall without Lou."

What Randall repeatedly called the "firestorm," which engulfed the seminary as denominational conflict overtook its parent denomination during the mid-1980s, left Lou Lolley "very upset and angry."

Doctrinally, she was in complete agreement with the man under whose preaching she had sat in congregations they had served and in churches they visited as he performed weekend supply preaching while at Southeastern.

"She was totally integrated with Randall and the mission of the school," recalled one of his professors. "There was genuine affection between them, [even as they remained] distinct people in their own right."

During occasions of hosting faculty and staff at the Durham Road president's home, Lou had listened to their growing anxiety over what they considered encroachment upon the academically free teaching environment that Randall had carefully cultivated during his first ten years of leadership. Then day by day in the school cafeteria, lunching with students whose ministry preparation was being impacted and overshadowed by gathering clouds of dissension, she had heard them out and sought to commiserate.

She confessed that she was frustrated. The couple's daughters, by then college-educated, engaged in their new professions, and involved with their own families, sympathized from a distance. "She gave [Dad] encouragement that he was doing the right thing—especially in his defense of women who were called to ministry," they recalled. (In years following the seminary's transition to conservative leadership, Lou and the daughters would continue to take some satisfaction in the presence on campus of Lolley Hall, a dormitory for women.)

Through it all, "There was enough fire in her that she stoked the fire in Randall," observed one student. "She was proud of a husband willing to be on the front lines of denominational battle."

At the same time, added one former professor, "She was an inspiration to all of us as to what it means to love your enemies. She was an amazing combination of grace and strength."

It is the star to every wand'ring bark,
Whose worth's unknown, although his height
be taken.

Literary critics note that the "star" in Shakespeare's sonnet likely is to be identified with *Polaris*, also called the North Star. The sense of the fourth couplet is that authentic love—the foundation of "the marriage of true minds"—functions as a visible north star to ships wandering at sea. While the star's altitude might in some sense be measurable, its ultimate value is incalculable.

There was always a quality to the relationship of Lou and Randall Lolley that onlookers could see but not fully comprehend. "They have a pure, soul-deep love. He ached for her anytime she was ever away."

"Dad would have been a success, no matter what. But Mom was the support, the love, the grounding that made him able to soar."

Associate pastors and other employees in church staff meetings with their boss noted that "he'd drop everything when she called." While such interruptions were uncommon, Randall clearly remembered his vows and prioritized his marital counterpart, trusting her enough to know that she would never try to reach him with a matter less than urgent.

Although she never appeared to seek the limelight, Randall's "north star" routinely became a "star" in the various settings in which they performed their joint ministry. "Church members loved Mom." While exercising her freedom to choose her path and utilize gifts that were uniquely her own, "she was a true gift to the church."

"She'd walk right up and hug you," reflected one of her husband's pastoral staff members.

During their concluding vocational ministry in Greensboro, Lou normally confined her actual church participation to attendance at Sunday school, worship, Woman's Missionary Union (WMU) meetings, and senior adult arts and crafts (principally ceramics). But at one WMU meeting she reprised a signature dramatic routine, wherein she impersonated a homeless woman she called "Ludie

Mae"—inspired by an actual person encountered when Lou was growing up in Alabama.

Ludie Mae, a "bag lady" who pushed a rickety grocery cart piled high with her meager belongings, was presented as a challenge to have mercy on the poor, whom Jesus predicted "you will always have with you" (Matt 26:11, NIV).

"Star" or not, Lou "struck a careful balance between being her own person while not overshadowing her husband, which was difficult to do in the '70s and '80s," observed a former seminary student.

Aiding Lou's familiar adeptness at balancing the demands, requirements, and expectations of life and ministry was a husband who—far from being threatened by her popularity—enjoyed and even extolled it. At every opportunity, Randall displayed his wife as his partner and co-equal, welcoming and encouraging her support and her leadership in her own areas of expertise.

At yearly, warm-weather reunions of the "Yellow Ribbon" group of people who had served alongside Randall at Southeastern Seminary, Lou joined Randall in presiding over the reminiscing, fellowship, worship and hymn-singing, and supper. Particularly memorable were the barbecued ribs she prepared and served at "The Lolliday Inn," the cabin she and he owned and maintained near Valle Crucis, outside Boone, North Carolina.

"Randall, we're wasting our time!" Lou once protested as her husband proudly led a newly employed church staff member on a car tour of homes too expensive for him to afford. Scarcely answering to the description of a "submissive wife," she nevertheless yielded to certain passions and commitments that were primarily her husband's.

One example was Randall Lolley's dogged determination to complete his "bucket list" of travels to destinations both domestic and worldwide.[5] The very first "Lolliday Inn" was a "Scamper"—a fold-out, towable camper that Randall purchased when the family lived in Winston-Salem. Each August was set aside for family vacation, which Randall applied year after year to satisfying his ambition to have his family "camp out" in every state of the union.

---

5. See Appendix C: Randall Lolley's Bucket List.

The rear bumper of the camper was dotted with stickers denoting the various states and attractions the Lolleys had visited, as Randall methodically populated his bucket list. "We'd wake in the morning and he'd say, 'It's Tuesday, and here we are at the Grand Tetons!'"

Arriving at particular attractions or campsites became its own event for "Lightnin' Lolley," as he would take out his stopwatch and challenge the family to break their most recent record for folding out and setting up their Scamper accommodation. Meanwhile, Lou joined the excursions with unfeigned enthusiasm, happily preparing suppers for four over the campfire or the Coleman stove.

On some occasions, she and her many-hatted husband would co-labor as chef and *sous-chef*, preparing a meal to share with young staff members at campgrounds where they would spend the night. It was yet another example of the servant spirit that impelled the Lolleys, in later years at the seminary, to lead faculty and staff in serving a traditional New Year's Day meal of hog jowl and black-eyed peas to the entire town of Old Wake Forest.

Love's not Time's fool, though rosy lips and cheeks Within his bending sickle's compass come . . .

Already having asserted in the second of his poetic couplets that genuine love is not threatened by life's changing circumstances, the bard next turned to "the ravages of time" itself, maintaining that they are no match for the durability and constancy of a "marriage of true minds."

As revealed by a cursory examination of his collected sermons stored within his home office, Randall rarely used a typewriter. His handwritten "manuscripts"—from which he preached—were turned over to his administrative assistant on Monday mornings and subsequently converted to a typed format for printing and distribution to people who requested copies.

Even when the age of the personal computer and word processor dawned during the late 1980s, Randall's habits did not change. As late as the final sermon he produced for a September 1996 Sunday evening service in Greensboro, his message (titled "Finally" and based on Paul's farewell message to the Ephesian church in Acts

20:16-36) was laboriously handwritten in his typical, one-sentence-per-paragraph style.

However, as retirement came about in October, the Lolleys at last relented and equipped themselves with a desktop computer. The primary purpose was email, since Randall planned to spend several of his beginning weeks of retirement in CBF-sponsored missions involvement, teaching English at a Bible college in Irkutsk, Siberia.

Lou would not accompany her husband on that trip, so they would require email accounts for use in their mutual correspondence. The part of the email address they had to choose (one that is maintained as of this writing) indicated their sense of togetherness in their relationship, as well as his desire to prioritize her in every setting: louran@ . . . .

Lou and Randall were, more than most couples in public life, nearly always identified together. Because "Mom was the love of his life—she was always at his side."

This reality was apparent also in various pieces of Randall's personal correspondence. In his stinging rebuke to Dr. Paige Patterson's 1996 invitation to attend an SBC gathering of former seminary presidents and wives, Randall had written "Lou and I have made our choice. We do not intend to be window dressing for you . . . ." In a 1976 letter of condolence to Southern Seminary president Dr. Duke K. McCall on the death of McCall's father, Randall wrote, "I just want you to know that Clara Lou and I are thinking of you . . . ."

"He would tell you she was the best thing that ever happened to him: beautiful, charming, witty, and bright, she was his confidant and encourager," summarized a former student.

As life changed and events unfolded in unanticipated ways during their years of retirement, the positive dynamics of Lou and Randall's relationship would not alter.

Love alters not with his brief hours and weeks, But bears it out even to the edge of doom.

Shakespeare's use of the word "doom" was not an allusion to hopeless demise but rather a reference to the simple end of earthly life—which Christians approach in a spirit of expectation of better things to come. Meanwhile, authentic, changeless love maintains its purity throughout the twists and turns of an all-too-brief life, all the way to life's conclusion.

Randall Lolley spent the initial fifteen years of his retirement energetically serving a total of a dozen interim pastorates, ranging from the District of Columbia to the Sunshine State of Florida. As he approached the beginning of his ninth decade of living, however, he began to experience the deterioration of certain physical and mental faculties, a decline often associated with the aging process.

First noted was a slight loss of hearing. "When hearing began to go, Mom helped him with conversations." Next was short-term memory: "When memory began to fail, she was at his side helping him remember."

The first indication of the onset of dementia came when Randall, at that time comfortably situated in his and Lou's retirement community in north Raleigh, inquired about his longtime friend and former editor of the *Biblical Recorder*, R. G. "Gene" Puckett. He had forgotten that Gene had died a short time earlier.

Many times, Randall would depart his home at The Cypress of Raleigh and drive a short distance away to get his lunch from his favorite Chick-fil-A. After he became confused and lost his way on two occasions, he and Lou consulted his doctor. Randall seemed aware that something was amiss. "I'm having trouble remembering some things," he admitted. Subsequent memory tests confirmed an impairment, and the doctor recommended that Randall thereafter leave the driving to his wife.

"That's good," he replied. "She's always been a better driver than me, anyway!"

For the following half-dozen years, Lou established a satisfactory "new normal" for herself and her husband. Happy to manage the driving, she transported him to his doctor appointments and to gatherings with friends. She enrolled him in a special program for the memory impaired, offered by their retirement community. He responded by continuing to relate so well that many friends were unable to detect that anything had changed.

"Love alters not." That being the case, Lou was predictably philosophical about the surprising turn her life had taken. "He has taken care of me," she reminded her daughters. "And now it's time for me to take care of him."

Until summer 2017, Lou attempted to manage Randall and his gradually declining circumstances at home. Only when the daughters worried that their mother—who was dealing with back problems and a series of corrective surgical procedures—might experience a fall was the decision made to relocate their father to The Rosewood, the memory care unit of their retirement community.

Lou at first resisted the move. She relented when The Cypress staff reassured her, "Let us become his caregivers so that you can remain his loving wife."

From the beginning of his residence at The Rosewood to the onset of the 2020 coronavirus pandemic, Lou visited Randall every day. Once both of them were quarantined in their separate living spaces, her visits were relegated to FaceTime video calls, made possible by Rosewood staff. Randall, who continued to be well physically, nevertheless appeared confused by the unusual method of contact.

"Now he is quarantined, and she hasn't [been with] him since March—more than three months," the daughters reported in summer 2020. "We've never seen her quite so blue. She seems lost at times—like a part of her is missing."

All the same, "Their current love is as deep and as strong as ever. [Prior to the quarantine] Mom would sit in a chair beside him, and . . . they would just hold hands. No words are needed when your hearts are one."

And so Shakespeare concluded,

If this be error and upon me prov'd,
I never writ, nor no man ever lov'd.

Chapter 14

Mirrors on the Man

Just as some interpreters view the four New Testament Gospels as a means to look at the same person (Jesus) from "different corners of a single room," so those who encountered Randall Lolley through the years viewed the same man but from their own individual perspectives.

The following tributes arise from people observing the man from different corners of the vast "room" that Randall occupied during the course of his life: a pastor who once served as a fellow church staff minister; a high-profile Baptist leader in the state Randall called home and where he served most of his ministry; a medical professional and lay leader in one of his three First Baptist churches; and a Lolley family member.

Dr. Charles L. Qualls, Pastor, Franklin Baptist Church, Franklin, Virginia

Someone has said that a friendship begins when one person says to the other, "Hey, me too." Randall Lolley specializes in "Hey, me too." From his leadership to his preaching and relationships, his brilliant gifts have always been wrapped in an inviting layer of Southern approachability.

I suppose I met Randall in the most "Randall" way I possibly could have. We were to have a rather clandestine meeting up in Atlanta because a search committee from Greensboro was looking at me for a staff position—one he would soon persuade me to accept. He flew in, and I met him at the gate. Back then, you could do that. Also, there was no searchable Internet just yet. So my brother, who had gone to Southeastern, sent me a packet of newspaper and magazine clippings so that I could see photos and recognize who I was watching for.

We headed to a nearby hotel and claimed a lobby corner where we spent a few hours talking. Because I had been aware of him as a Baptist leader, I was intimidated at first. Randall quickly disarmed that, and we struck up what would turn out to be a surprising friendship. One of the most indicative memories I have of him happened in my very first week. He had asked about it in that initial meeting, so I had confided that in my first church I was not great about taking my days off. He made it mandatory that I would do so at Greensboro.

On about my third day in the office, he asked what I was doing that Friday. I told him I didn't have any plans except not to be in the office. "Good. I have to run over to the cabin and I want you to go with me. We need to have a meeting." The rest of the week, I wondered what I had already done—or not done—that we needed to have a meeting. Randall, Lou, and I arrived at the cabin, and they had told me on the way that they were going there to meet a delivery truck. So we sat down in rocking chairs on the front porch and began to talk as we waited. Eventually, the gentle sound of a brook that babbled right up underneath the left corner of the porch had almost put us to sleep. Drowsily I said, "Randall, you told me we needed to have a meeting. What did we need to have a meeting about?" He said, "This." I smiled and rocked on. Later, the sound of a heavy truck crunching on the gravel driveway woke us all up.

The time I worked with him was instructive. Obviously, some of Randall's innate giftedness could not be taught. But plenty of what I learned from him has stayed with me to this day. He was an empathetic, active listener. He was a quick study who would take a briefing on a situation and then immediately help you to think through options and future scenarios. I deepened my love for the Bible listening to him preach all the way through it, from Genesis to Revelation, in a sermon series that lasted a year and a half. It was evident that he held the Scripture in the highest regard, yet of course he also brought deep scholarship to his work.

There wasn't a lot of what we did in a local church that was beneath him. If we went on a mission trip, he worked. If we hosted a July Fourth concert and cookout, he was in the middle of the crowd and a gracious presence. Randall's love for the local church is captured in the reality that shortly after retiring, he began a prodigious string of interim pastorates that lasted more than a decade.

Since my time there, I have conducted hundreds of funerals—each of them with the imprint of Randall's instruction to me about how to approach that important life event. Some of my pastoral care and hospital visitation practices came directly from his mentorship. He shared fine details that make working one's way through a hospital more efficient, but also big-picture values that keep us focused on our task.

Two vignettes remain perhaps most vivid of all. In two travel groups, we took the largest contingent of volunteers over to Prague during the massive European Baptist Theological Seminary move. Our groups from FBC Greensboro overlapped by one week. During that time, Randall and I worked most days side by side. Some days we painted. Some days we scraped plaster on walls of a 1700s building that had once housed Nazi interrogation headquarters. I'll never forget the time spent working with him. We discussed pastoral challenges, including one marital infidelity we had both been made aware of. He said, "I have my theories on why people do that. Why they cheat on their spouses. But I can tell you in two words why I never have: 'Lou Lolley!'"

The other instance is something that happened after he had officially retired. Randall and Lou had bought a personal computer. He wanted to learn how to send and receive emails, and by then home use of the Internet was also in its infancy. "Would you and Elizabeth come show us how to run the doggone thing?" In a handful of evenings at their invitation, we would dine with the Lolleys and then work at the computer for a while. No longer coworkers, we were now delightfully friends. Over especially the earlier years of retirement, Randall and Lou traveled to some parts of the world they were curious about. He even did a stint evaluating a theological seminary in Siberia. Elizabeth and I probably gained more of our love for travel from their adventures than anything else.

What a gift Randall is. What a legacy of life and ministry he has left. What an impression on generations of younger ministers he has made. Celebrating a life this well lived is one of the world's profound pleasures.

Dr. Michael C. Blackwell, President, Baptist Children's Homes of North Carolina

"That ain't no ordinary preacher."

My Methodist minister friend, Doug Jesse, was as right as he was ungrammatical. He had just heard Randall Lolley for the first time. Doug accompanied me from our church pastorates in Carthage, North Carolina, to the fall convocation at Southeastern Baptist Theological Seminary in Wake Forest.

Fact is, there isn't anything ordinary about Randall Lolley. He is *Brilliant* with a capital B. To this day, his influence is writ large in my life and ministry, and his mirror on my life is still a reflection that shines brightly.

When Olin T. Binkley announced plans to retire as Southeastern Seminary president, the ink had barely dried on the news release when the name of Randall Lolley was bandied around by everyone as the logical choice to assume the big office in Stealey Hall.

For Randall, the SEBTS presidency was his dream job—a nudging he had felt deep in his bones for several years. The dream became reality, and he assumed the presidency at the ripe age of forty-three, after a dramatic and dynamic twelve-year pastorate at First Baptist Church, Winston-Salem, North Carolina.

Randall Lolley had me hooked years before he became Southeastern Seminary president. When I graduated Southeastern in 1970 (Master of Divinity), he was the graduation speaker. Twelve years later, in 1982, I received the Master of Theology degree, and President Lolley presented me my diploma.

For decades he remained Coach, Colleague, Teacher, Encourager, Role Model, and Stalwart Friend.

Three times—during my seven-year pastorate at First Baptist, Carthage—he spent a weekend with my wife and me. Clara Lou Lolley, a true blessing herself, accompanied him all three times.

They shared with deacons and spouses on Saturday night, and Randall preached on Sunday. The first Sunday he was with us (1975),

I specifically asked that he preach the sermon he delivered at my 1970 seminary graduation.

I questioned him about his methodology of sermon preparation. He preached from a handwritten manuscript but seldom referred to it. He went to bed early, often by 9:45 p.m., was up early to walk or jog, and then had a full day of appointments, often including lunch visits and a possible morning visit to a Wake Forest eatery where he would meet with students.

I visited him many times during his presidency—at least once a quarter—until I moved to Richmond, Virginia, to assume the pastorate of the Monument Heights Baptist Church. I would have it no other way but for Randall Lolley to be the *Preacher* at my installation service.

The next day he met with my church leadership and led us through a strategic planning session. . . . [W]e laid out membership and stewardship plans for 1981–1982.

In February 1983, I received a phone call from Olin Binkley (Randall's predecessor at Southeastern), informing me that he (Dr. Binkley) was the chairman of the search committee for a new president of the Baptist Children's Homes of North Carolina. The committee wanted to interview me for the job. I agreed, and three interviews later I assumed the presidency on July 1, 1983.

Formal announcement of my election had barely been made when I got a congratulatory call from Randall and Lou. In early 1984, I visited with him in his office. He was still jovial and affirming but obviously concerned about those who wanted to make Southeastern Seminary fit a pattern that was incongruent with his established vision for the school. What eventually happened with Dr. Lolley's departure in 1988 is detailed elsewhere in this book, but the stress took a toll on the entire Lolley family.

Randall Lolley had a backbone of steel. He would neither compromise his integrity in light of the Southeastern "takeover" nor bend to pressure to conform to theological exclusivity. His days at Southeastern were numbered, and his dream job went up in flames.

But Randall Lolley "ain't no ordinary preacher." He was called as pastor of First Baptist, Raleigh, the downtown church across from the state capitol. He was then called to First Baptist, Greensboro, where he, as usual, served with distinction.

During his Greensboro years, we were close because of a long-standing tradition of the BCH president speaking at what was then a traditional Thanksgiving eve dinner. Sitting with Lou and Randall, it was still obvious that they both continued to bear scars from their Southeastern exit.

In 1998, I observed my fifteenth anniversary as BCH president. Randall was one of the main speakers. He said many nice things about me, but one thing he said is something that I consistently strive to live up to—that I was an *inclusive* leader and not an *exclusive* one.

Randall's charismatic personality opened many doors—especially with donors, faculty, students, church members, and others who willingly followed his leadership. He was "King of Relationships," with an abundance of emotional intelligence, combining empathy and understanding with self-awareness and organizational ability.

What did Randall Lolley teach me?

1. People are more important than programs, but it does take people to make programs work.
2. Say a good word to anyone you meet, especially those who are struggling, less fortunate, or in obvious distress.
3. Cast a vision of challenge, compassion, and hope.
4. Seek wise counsel when having to make a difficult decision.
5. Respect your various constituencies and they will come to trust you.
6. Leadership is valid when others willingly follow your direction.
7. Stand in your own truth.
8. Never stop learning.
9. Have (and maintain) a good sense of humor.
10. Pray without ceasing.
11. Live, love, laugh, and be happy.

Randall's influence lives on in women and men who are open to follow *New Light*, wherever that Light may lead. Fearless and humble, courageous and curious, the life of W. Randall Lolley will bless many others for generations to come.

I count myself fortunate to be among those he touched and blessed along the way.

Dr. Laura Lomax, Greensboro Dermatologist and First Baptist Church Deacon

There are very few people on earth whom I hold in as high esteem as Randall Lolley. And there are many reasons why—let me share a few.

My husband and I had grown up at First Baptist Greensboro, on the cradle roll together, high school and college sweethearts, and had been in Chapel Hill for twelve years for school, work, and medical training. When I joined a practice back in Greensboro and he found a job at a local hospital, our parents were overjoyed. We were returning with an infant son, and we were eager to establish ourselves in our home church again. The minister who had married us had departed, and First Baptist had wisely called Dr. Lolley as his successor. Randall was a healing spirit during a tumultuous time in our church, a calming and restorative bridge over troubled water.

I had heard so many good things about Dr. Lolley from my mom and from my husband's parents. Randall had been much loved on pastoral staff in the 1950s, during the early years of my mother's marriage. I knew he had been president of the revered Southeastern Baptist Seminary but had left when the conservative faction had forced many changes that he had opposed. I admired him for holding fast to his convictions. One would have expected a certain bitterness or cynicism to be etched on a person from that contentious episode, but I found just the opposite in Dr. Lolley—a warm open-heartedness, a guilelessness, and a youthful energy that belied his former struggles, a strength and optimism that surely had to be rooted in the supernatural leading of the Holy Spirit. My mom always loved Randall because he was the same with the widows who only had a mite to give as he was with those who were the big donors. She had sometimes felt unseen with other ministers, but never with Dr. Lolley.

His sermons were inspired and inspiring. After years of training in science and medicine, I had some revising of my faith to do, and many doubts and questions. Dr. Lolley's sermons provoked deep thinking as well as deeper faith. There was no unwelcome oversimplification of the hard questions. There was truth, rooted in biblical text and also in real life. I was pleased to know that the Baptist church of my youth still welcomed women as deacons and pastors. The doctrines of soul competency and the priesthood of the believer became real to me as an adult. Our Sunday school class was an eager group of young marrieds who became lifelong friends. Our son enrolled in preschool at FBC. We had a second child, this time a daughter. We were spiritually home.

Then came an event that rocked my world. My husband declared that he felt our marriage could not go on. The first person in the church we went to talk to was our pastor, Randall Lolley. My husband had so much respect for Randall and had worked closely with him as a very young chair of deacons just the year before. I couldn't imagine a life apart from the person I had grown up with! But Randall was so adept at listening to us, mourning with us, understanding us. I later talked to him alone, about my fears and my questions. He gave sympathy without platitudes, solace without false reassurances. He continued to check in on me, and on my husband, as we went through the pain of separation that year. And as a further encouragement, the year I was going through divorce, he and a friend from the church came to see me at my office to ask if I'd consider becoming a deacon. He didn't consider "the big D" to be a stain. I can't overstate my appreciation for that, even looking back twenty-five years later. Even as we know that our Lord and Savior is accepting of all people, many times those in the world of the church are not. Dr. Randall Lolley had my back. My dad had passed away when I was twelve, and I had not really known another father figure in my youth and young adulthood. But if I had to name one I could consider to be that in my thirties, it would be Randall.

Over the ensuing years, I navigated the new world of functioning as a single mom with a busy medical practice. Life was topsy-turvy, a busy hamster wheel, but I began to date some, hoping for someone to share life with me and my children. I had some criteria that had to be met. When in doubt, guess whom I consulted? Randall, or sometimes Randall and his wife, Lou. Even after they had retired and moved away, they were willing to meet me for a serious talk about a man with whom I was becoming serious. Randall always had good counsel without being too directive or acting like he had all the answers. He always promised to pray for me. (And I know he did. I did not end up marrying the man I consulted Dr. Lolley about, but much later the perfect mate came along, a sure answer to prayer.)

Dr. Lolley, please know how much you mean to me. Part of God's provision in my life was providing me with a spiritual mentor and friend in you. One like Jesus—wise, loving, willing to counsel and guide with encouragement and optimism. Real, with a smile and energy that always lifted me up. God bless you and keep you.

Rev. Tim Lolley, Pastor, Hazelwood Baptist Church, Waynesville, North Carolina, and Nephew of Randall and Lou Lolley

Growing up as the son of a father who was a Baptist minister and a mother who was a public school teacher, I learned early in my life that people would often form their opinions and keep a watchful eye on me because of my family lineage.

I can still remember people saying to me, "Lolley. Are you related to Tom and Sydney Lolley?" And with that question, I would always experience a proud moment because of who they were, their example from the lives that they were living, and the legacy that they were passing down to me and my sister.

I also remember being out with my family when someone would pose the same question to my father. "Lolley. Are you related to *Randall Lolley*?" My father would sometimes only add to the inquiry through his candid response, "We had the same father and mother!"

Those formative years of growing up were some of the best days of my life. The love and legacy of a family have always been important to me, as I learned at an early age the special bond that exists within those relationships. Throughout my life, there have been heroes that

I have admired and respected far beyond the ordinary accolades. My father and my uncle have been my heroes.

Dad and Randall were the best of brothers. Dad being six years younger than Randall, they shared so much throughout life. Their ministries took them in slightly different directions, but they formed an amazing story of grace and purpose. I saw firsthand how these two brothers from south Alabama shared a bond that was strong and loyal. To be blessed and nurtured by these two—especially as I, too, entered into the gospel ministry—proved to be a gift that continues to influence and guide me even today.

While a student at Mars Hill College, I was called to my first church—Victory Baptist in Asheville, to be minister of music and youth. Shortly after beginning, I received a congratulatory note from my uncle letting me know that he "was proud" of me and that "Lou and I will be praying for you as you embark on the journey that God has marked out for your life and ministry."

In July 1984, I was ordained into the gospel ministry by the Victory Baptist Church. My father Tom brought the Charge to the Congregation, admonishing them with regard to their responsibilities as a church in "sending one into ministry." My uncle Randall brought the Charge to the Candidate. It was a message that resonated with me then and continues to speak to me nearly thirty-six years later. I recently reread the words that he shared with me:

> In the Pastoral epistles, Paul charged young Timothy, Titus, and Philemon three basic things. It all boils down to three loves. Third [was] love—love *Tim.* Paul loved a Timothy too. He wrote him a lot. It's the most personal thing that he ever wrote in the New Testament. He said it lots of ways, but my favorite way that he said it is that verse, "Timothy, stir up the gift of God that is in you." Paul said, Timothy, God's got a lot invested in your young life. You will either stir it up or you'll bottle it up.
>
> It would be easy—it *is* easy—for ministers to get down on themselves because they fail a lot. Whenever you become tempted to get down on yourself, remember Paul told Timothy—in the 3rd love—love yourself, because God loves you so much. He has invested so much in you. He has seen in you, God has, gifts that

He is calling into His ministry in a special way. If you and folks no better than you—no worse than you—do not do God's work in this world, it won't get done. [So] third love—love Tim.

Paul says that there is a second love. And he charged Timothy, Titus, and Philemon to that in 1 Timothy 2:1-6 of that charge, and that is to love *people.* Paul did. He had a lot of trouble with people. He got lied about and beaten up by them. But Paul went to his death—when a person lifted a big blade to cut off his head and make him a martyr.

I believe that I heard Paul saying, "Sticks and stones can break my bones, but you cannot stop me from loving you." He was a people person. Folks are all God made in which He invested into them the breath of Life. And then He invested in them His own image. Tim, if God's got that much going in every human being that He has ever made, you and all of us who try to minister in His name have a lot of homework in loving the people.

There is so much that could be said about that. You seem to have been given a gift somewhere back in your life and through your family that makes it somewhat easy for you to love the people.

Some of them will disappoint you—what's new?

Some of them will abuse you—what's new?

But most of them will follow you, and that is the good news!

I trust that God has given you, and I think He has, the kind of inner will that makes you know how important His folks are.

[But] first love—love *God.* Paul traced his own ministry to his first love. That was his love for Jesus. Tim, love the people. Love God. Now you know as well as I do, what that means. You will follow Him though the votes don't always go the way you feel they should.

In many perilous times, you have to search the closet in the dead of night and on your knees and in the struggle—like our Lord did in Gethsemane—to find out what His purpose is. Then—because you love Him, because you belong to Him—you follow Him.

Three loves. Love Tim. Love the people. Love God.

Little did I know in July 1984 how those words would become bedrock to me.

Graduating from Mars Hill College in 1985, I knew that I wanted to pursue my theological education . . . and I knew that I wanted to attend Southeastern Baptist Theological Seminary. Both my dad and Randall had walked the "Forest of Wake" and graduated from there. I prayed and was drawn there to walk and learn from dedicated scholars that were at Southeastern.

It didn't take long for the question to once again be asked. "Lolley. Are you related to Dr. Lolley?" And with admiration I would answer as my father would, "Yes, he and my dad had the same parents!" I was always so proud to be his nephew and wanted to be a part of continuing the journey that both he and my father had started years earlier. The move to Wake Forest was a tremendous happening in my life.

I entered Southeastern in fall 1985. I was thrilled. The Scriptures came alive in a new and powerful manner. The professors all shared a common goal in equipping men and women for ministry within the local church and around the world. It soon became my spiritual home.

Yet it soon became apparent that my theological education would include not only knowledge gained through books and lectures but also what came to be known as "practical theology." My years at Southeastern were turbulent ones. So much unrest and division. The dream of Southeastern was now evolving into something that I, and many of my fellow students, would not recognize in the years of our education. With a broken heart I watched men and women that I respected and admired as they were attacked and ridiculed at the core of their being. I watched a power play strip an institution of its calling and its founding dream.

Yet, in the midst of the fundamentalist coup, I was inspired by people who were not only teaching and lecturing but who were demonstrating this call on their lives that my uncle had described in my "setting apart." I watched them stand in solidarity, and I remember being tremendously impacted by their example. It was a painful time for many, and I felt the anger and vicious attacks directed at many. But for me, it was even more personal. It was an assault on my family—my uncle—and the Lolley name.

My years at Southeastern scarred and hurt me. They were filled with so much pain and wandering. Yet even in those days I witnessed firsthand those things that my uncle had shared in my ordination. I loved me. And I loved God. It was loving certain people that I found myself struggling with.

In 1988, Uncle Randall returned to present the degrees to the graduating class. I have often reflected on what I learned, not just at Southeastern but also from these two heroes of my faith.

I saw firsthand my uncle and my father stand on principles that marked their lives. Truth. Honesty. Integrity. They always did. From a father who served Baptist folk through the local congregation and the Baptist State Convention of North Carolina and who persevered courageously through a debilitating stroke and his ultimate home-going to Heaven; to an uncle who pastored Baptist folk and pioneered on the denominational level—I rejoice that they left for me a good name, a good example, and the conviction to "love the Lord with all of your heart, mind and soul, and your neighbor as yourself."

Inevitably, there are still occasions when I am approached by people as they ask me the proverbial question: "Lolley. Are you related to Tom and Randall?"

And my response: "Yes. We had the same Father." And that is perfectly fine with me.

"A good name is rather to be chosen than great riches, and loving favour rather than silver and gold."[1]

---

1. Proverbs 22:1, KJV.

The Oblong Blur

In spring 2016, Lou and Randall Lolley paid yet one more visit to their friends at First Baptist Church, Greensboro. It was a bright Sunday morning, with sunlight filtering warmly through the shutters of the seven tall east windows of the massive sanctuary.

Their visit was informal, and the two occupied pews alongside other worshipers, near the left front of what Randall always called "the big room." Invited to come to the pulpit and offer the benediction as the service concluded, Randall responded and prayed in characteristic fashion. He challenged the congregation to carry its witness beyond the church and into the world, and he conferred his and his Lord's blessings upon them as they went.

And then, perhaps recalling the last published words of his old friend and colleague Morris Ashcraft, Randall exclaimed, as his own closing amen, "I'll see you in the morning!"[1]

By winter 2016, Randall and Lou were three years along their slow journey into memory loss. In the beginning, "little things" were noticed, such as an uncharacteristic withdrawal from social interaction, which family at first attributed to slightly impaired hearing. Twice Randall had become disoriented while driving.

"Dad realized it was happening," his daughters said, and he had readily agreed to a neurological evaluation. Successive tests indicated the situation was gradually deteriorating.

---

1. "I'll see you on the other side!" *The Will of God* (Nashville: Broadman, 1980), 143.

As the months passed, there came also a noticeable lack of curiosity about matters that Randall previously had found intriguing.[2] A thing not overlooked, however, was an upcoming wedding anniversary. August 28, 2016, would mark sixty-four years of rewarding marriage. As the date approached, Randall noticed it on his calendar and sat down to pen—in large letters and clearly legible script, filling an entire page—the following:

> My dearest Lou—the Love of My Life,
>
> As August 28 approaches I know that you are feeling growing pressure from my obvious mingled experiences with my memory. I am becoming ever more aware that some things I can remember well; other things I can recall scarcely at all.
>
> That is **new** for me and for you. I suppose it is the worst fear of my life—that all my years will slowly end with everything becoming an oblong blur. All I can do is hope and pray.
>
> Thank you for loving me and for putting up with me.
>
> Ran

The "oblong blur" (recalled perhaps from a so-named 1949 publication) is an image that compares life's accelerating progression to a passing train, viewed at close range and moving too quickly to focus on.[3] In any case, it was, according to his children, a scenario that as early as 2010 their dad had called "the one thing I fear most."

In an earlier, undated Communion meditation titled "Memory Loss," Randall turned to Luke's description of Jesus gathered with his disciples in the upper room.[4] He recalled that, taking first the bread and then the cup, Jesus had given thanks and offered the elements to

---

2. E.g., Randall had been inquisitive about my plan for an autumn 2014 church sabbatical in Jerusalem. At dinner the following January, however, he appeared scarcely to recall the event and asked no questions about it.

3. Philip Hamburger, *The Oblong Blur and Other Odysseys* (New York: Farrar, Straus, 1949).

4. An attached sticky note indicated that the reflection was delivered in early 1993 in Greensboro and again in early 1998 at Knollwood Baptist Church in Winston-Salem.

his followers with the admonition, "This do in remembrance of me" (Luke 22:19).

There followed a lengthy and possibly telling introduction to a sermon otherwise devoted to the importance of spiritual contemplation. "We hear a lot these days about memory loss," Randall began. "The medical community is all abuzz."

Noting that several million Americans had, at that time, been diagnosed with Alzheimer's disease, Randall defined the condition as "a disease that gradually destroys the brain cells that enable us to reason, concentrate, and perform the simplest tasks of daily living. There is no known cure." Hope, however, could lie in the development of a pill that would "clear the brain of lesions leading to memory loss."

Randall painstakingly guided his hearers through a description of "good genes," "housekeeper genes," and "high-risk genes," the inherited combination of which would forecast probabilities of contracting dementia. Then he suggested, "In essence . . . our odds at getting Alzheimer's may boil down to a biological game of Russian roulette."

Characteristically resolved to accentuate the positive, however, he noted, "A pill to supplement [the good gene] would be a Godsend. [Doctors are] optimistic that in a matter of years we will have one."

By 2015, such a pill had not become available. Aware that his own memory was beginning to fade, Randall came to June 2, the anniversary of his birth, and sat down at his computer. In oversized, twenty-point font, he typed "Thoughts Following My 84th Birthday." The thoughts were itemized:

> 1. My interims are finished; my supply work is sparse.
> 2. My days are now available for Lou, for family, for friends, and for fellowship with the vast supply of memories stored in my heart.
> 3. I am committed to a robust devotional life and a constant reflection on things past, present, and future.
> 4. I commit to keeping up with the news of the day and happenings in the world. I may be OLD, but I am not a FOSSIL—at least not yet!

About a "robust devotional life" Randall was serious. In similarly large type, he had sometime earlier assembled an undated, two-part, five-page document titled "WRL's Practice of Prayer." In the way of disclaimer, he prefaced the document: "My devotional life is personal and mostly private. I do not prefer to parade it or to overemphasize it to make impressions."

The first and longer part of the document was labeled "miscellaneous petitions," the offering of which Randall suggested required thirty minutes to one hour of prayer each morning:

> [These begin] with prayers for the most Significant Others in my life: Lou, Daughters, their husbands, relatives, friends, and the memories of dear ones who have died, but their memories still impact my thinking and my living.
>
> This leads me to think of and to pray for persons, living and dead, who have met my needs in a variety of ways: physicians, dentists, nurses, pharmacists, lab technicians, etc. These trigger my thoughts to pray for MY HEALTH and overall well-being, including my own financial security.
>
> Furthermore, I then pray prayers of thanksgiving for five simple rules that have marked my life over time: (1) Get well, stay well; (2) Celebrate life by staying yoked to the "biggies"—people, places, things, events; (3) Accentuate the positive; (4) Diversify; (5) Give thanks for personnel, resources, and properties which bless me and contribute to my well-being.
>
> This leads me to say prayers regarding the WORLD God has made for us to live in: Time, Space, Matter, Motion, Energy, and Spirit, along with the prayer that I will always be a Man in the Spirit like the Apostle Paul.
>
> There follow prayers that God will empower me to thwart the FLAWS in a moral universe, such as Pride, Prejudice, Presumption, Cocksureness, Carelessness, Distraction, Poverty, Hunger, Disease, Crime, Calamity, and all sorts of Terrorism.
>
> This leads into my prayers for what I call "My Paradigm of Engagement." By that I mean throughout the day, as I encounter hard-to-love and hard-to-appreciate people, before I lose my temper or my focus, I will remember: that those people are created

in God's image, they bear God's image now, and they have a right to be here.

Next come prayers for PEACE on the Earth, an end to wars and to the forces which lead to wars, [and] guarding and guidance for our Military and Service Personnel.

My morning prayers climax with reflection on the Gigantic Condescension and the Gigantic Sacrifice our God in Jesus Christ made at Bethlehem and at Gethsemane, Golgotha, and Joseph's Garden. Jesus' miracle Birth, Death, and Resurrection split time in two: BC and AD, making these events the hinges of history.

[As an aside, Randall reminisced about the multiple occasions he had conducted tours to the Holy Lands and about the spiritual significance he attached to the excursions.]

I thank God that I have been privileged to make so many trips to the lands where these events transpired (no fewer than a dozen trips); and have watched the people there attempt to come to God through Judaism, Islam, and a score of other faith systems. This makes me all the more eager to be credible in my efforts to come to God through Christianity (and Baptist at that), and be a faithful witness to the Presence of Christ in my life each day.[5]

[Then resumed the description of his daily petitions.]

My morning prayers conclude usually by a final look at the four words which changed everything: Jesus' own prayer in Gethsemane the night before he died: THY WILL BE DONE. I pray that my life that day becomes saturated with those four words for myself, and that they will be the scaffolding for my living of the day.

Just before my Amen, I pray that as I live and particularly as I conclude the day, I can adopt at day's end the prayer the children sing: "Now I lay me down to sleep, I pray the Lord my soul to keep. If I should die before I wake, I pray the Lord my soul to take."

Amen.[6]

---

5. As evidenced by his preaching on the subject of salvation, Randall was not a *pluralist*—i.e., he did not hold that all religions are pathways to God. He could, however, be termed a *soft inclusivist*, maintaining hope for devout monotheists (viz. Jews and Muslims) he had encountered and befriended during his Holy Land travels.

6. A second, single-paragraph section stated, "My evening prayers are more brief and are COMPLETELY PRAYERS OF THANKSGIVING."

Notable among the written expressions above are the references to *memory*—"memories stored in my heart," "memories of dear ones who have died," "memories [which] still impact my thinking and my living."

Regarding the progression of the condition known colloquially as *memory loss*, there has been the suggestion that anything once learned is permanently stored in the human brain. In a concluding, poignant chapter of his autobiography, Cecil Sherman reviewed his and his wife Dot's experience with her failing memory:

> I tried to learn as much as I could about Alzheimer's Disease. People who know say the things learned as a child are the things most likely to be remembered when the mind begins to fail. . . . Everything Dot has ever known is still stored in her mind. Alzheimer's had damaged the retriever; she can't pull that information up when she wants to.[7]

Assuming Dr. Sherman and the experts he consulted were correct, then "the memories stored in [Randall's] heart" remained in place with the passing of months and years. Some semblance of the "robust devotional life" he had committed to at age eighty-four may likewise have continued, even if interior and unobservable.

Significant value has been attached to what is commonly labeled "quality of life." People not in a position to relate to Randall in later years often asked if he continued to experience quality of life. In his book *Rest Awhile*, the late evangelist Vance Havner—a Greensboro resident and member of First Baptist Church—wrote of his own sense of quality living as he entered his twilight years: "I know that, as for myself, God has been good to me and given me the desires of my heart. I have salvation and health and work and guidance and friends and companionship and every need supplied."[8]

The same could be said for Randall Lolley. While his *work* was limited to what he termed "fellowship with the vast supply of memories stored in my heart," his physical health remained good. Likewise,

---

7. *By My Own Reckoning*, 270–71.

8. Reprinted by CreateSpace Independent Publishing Platform, June 2014.

his closest friendships, his companionship with Lou, the supply of his every need, and above all his salvation remained intact.

And regarding the importance of *quality of life*, Randall did not equivocate. From his Apostles' Creed sermon "I Believe in the Life Everlasting":

> So, you see, it is not just how long life lasts, it is the quality of the life which lasts that counts. And in this matter the Apostle Paul speaks at his highest, not as a theologian, but as a poet. He says, "Now we see through a glass darkly, a mirror, dim; we cannot see clearly. Then face to face. Now we know in part, but then we will understand fully."[9]

As of the conclusion of this biography, and owing to the necessity of quarantine that dominated much of life during 2020, it had been a year since I had been face to face with Randall Lolley. Not to be forgotten, however, was the greeting he shared on an earlier occasion.

Guided by personnel along the hallway of his comfortable memory care facility in north Raleigh, Randall looked up, focused his eyes on my wife and me, extended his arms widely, and exclaimed, "Hello, friends!"

Cognition in memory-challenged individuals is difficult to assess, but most observers have concluded that interpersonal connection is an in-the-moment phenomenon. While later perhaps unrecalled, a familiar person can nevertheless be experienced while that person is present and visible.

The day of that encounter was reassuring. I was real and present, and the same was true of Randall. Moreover, as subsequent conversation revealed, he was manifesting himself as the individual this biography set out to describe: "Pastor and friend. . . . A pastor unlike, perhaps, any that any of us ever knew."[10]

---

9. 1 Corinthians 13:12.
10. From the introduction above.

Appendix A

Lolleyisms: A Glossary

• *Out in the weather together.* This phrase described the commonality of the human condition, the universality of sin, the omnipresence of hardship, the inevitability of death, and the essential unity of an otherwise divided humanity. It would have worked well during the 2020 coronovirus pandemic as a less hackneyed version of "We're in this together."
• *Outta whack.* A colloquialism normally employed to describe a malfunction, Randall used it to characterize times and occasions when he would be away from the office or otherwise unavailable. "I'll be outta whack most of next week."
• *On every leaning side.* Arising possibly from African American church tradition, the phrase found its way into many of Randall's pastoral prayers. As a petition, it spoke to the faults, frailties, and fallibilities of otherwise faithful people: "But Lord, continue to bear us up, on every leaning side."
• *If you don't mind . . . .* Because he believed deeply in administrative principles of "shared governance," Randall was loath to *order* anything done. When issuing a directive, he nearly always prefaced it, "If you don't mind." (Chains of command being what they were, directives were invariably followed, even if the recipient *did* mind.)
• *If it's fair to ask . . . .* Randall employed this conditional prefix anytime he was curious about something but suspected it might *not* be appropriate to ask. (It was a completely disarming strategy, for who could maintain that it was "unfair" simply to ask?)
• *Sand in the soup.* A less-lethal version of "death in the pot" (2 Kings 4:40), this sermonic metaphor was the rough equivalent of "fly in the ointment."
• *Mark it down.* Randall used this phrase sermonically, almost as a warning, to establish any claim or affirmation of which he was most

sure. It was sometimes rendered, in the way of reassurance, as *count on it.*

• *Come to taw.* This "Southernism" referred to the game of marbles and the common line from which players "shoot." It could mean returning to a mutual starting place or point of view, finding agreement. Randall lamented that opposing sides in the Baptist wars never *came to taw.*

• *I'm a-guessin'.* This phrase introduced a confident supposition. "I'm a-guessin' if you ran out of Spam, you could pop open a can of Treet."

• *The light of the world? I'm a-guessin' we're the taillights.* Randall was referring to the tendency of the church to reflect (rather than inform) its host culture.

• *Though the heavens fall.* The most positive and encouraging of Randall's assurances, this one was normally reserved for the fulfillment of scriptural promises.

• *Facts are . . . .* This was always plural—employed even when a single fact was in view. It meant "in fact" or "as a matter of fact" and was shorthand for "Verily, verily, I say unto thee."

• *Flat-out.* This expression was colloquial for "thoroughgoing." "That choir anthem was flat-out good!"

• *My soul!* This phrase was a declaration of surprise, astonishment, or disgust. Randall Lolley never "took the name of the Lord in vain" and only rarely (and under duress) used "colorful language." (A familiar caution to church staff colleagues: "Keep your thoughts pure, because when you're old, they're liable to come out of your mouth.")

• *We'll treat you so many ways, you'll have to like some of 'em.* Randall used this as a recruiting slogan for people considering enrollment at Southeastern Seminary. At his initial 1954 visit to the campus as a prospective student, Randall heard the expression from Dr. Stewart Newman.[1]

• *Hectorsville.* This word was an amelioration of the expletive "heck," as in "What in Hectorsville is going on?"

• *God has no grandchildren.* This quote originated with Pentecostal evangelist Reinhard Bonnke. An affirmation of the necessity of personal, individual decision in the matter of Christian conversion,

---

1. *Servant Songs,* 32.

this reminder was evidence that Randall Lolley was a Baptist evangelical and not a mainline Protestant.

• *I can celebrate that.* This was Randall's hyperbolic declaration of acceptance of anything he entitled another person to believe or to live out, despite his own reservations. "While personally I am an amillennialist, I can celebrate a premillennial approach to the book of Revelation."

• *The flip-side.* He used this phrase to refer to an alternative—but legitimate—way of viewing a matter.

• *A keeper.* Randall would call a memorable and greatly appreciated note, letter, or greeting card "a keeper."

• *Grief's slow wisdom.* Likely borrowed from author Cort R. Flint's statement, "While grief's slow wisdom teaches the great lessons," this was a familiar word of comfort offered in sympathy notes as a written guarantee of Randall's prayers. He was communicating the greatest lesson: "Blessed are those who mourn, for they will be comforted" (Matt 5:4).

• *I have good news for you!* Randall spoke this as a reminder to a sleepy or indifferent congregation—upon a person's public profession of faith in Christ (or other decision to join the church)—that "the angels of God rejoice over one sinner who repents" (Luke 15:10, TEV).

• *Fresh from God.* Randall's familiar description of a recently born baby was offered as words of introduction prior to the public dedication of a child.

• *With a lick and a promise, and a rushed-up prayer.* Randall offered this cautionary but critical observation of the casual manner in which Christian duty is typically addressed.

• *Not bad to come.* He described church members whose attendance was infrequent or irregular by saying, "They're not awful bad to come."

• *Ensmallment campaigns.* Randall coined this term to describe what congregations in their insularity and complacency may inadvertently be waging. It was an inversion of the "enlargement campaigns" that dramatically grew Southern churches during the 1950s.

• *Hacked his initials on a failure tree.* Randall used this phrase sermonically to describe the sorry but ineradicable legacy of familiar villains from Scripture, e.g., King Saul and Judas Iscariot.
• *Lock, stock, and barrel, ramrod and greasy rag.* He was showing that the theoretically absolute value of a familiar expression of fulfillment could nevertheless be raised to a higher power.
• *Unless you're the lead dog, the scenery never changes.* That is, unless you occupy first position, you're consigned to view the hindquarters of whoever does.
• *Peckerwood.* Randall used this affectionate nickname for those (primarily church staff members) for whom the scenery never changed. (*Pistol* might substitute in rare instances when a name slipped Randall's memory.)
• *Pop-Pop.* This was Randall's affectionate nickname for Lou Lolley, curiously reassigned to her after granddaughters Kelly and Kaitlin first applied it to their grandfather.
• *Thanks for your partnership in the task.* He used this line at the close of a memo or other written directive to staff, reminding them that the "lead dog" appreciated the importance of those who faithfully drew up the rear.
• *Tired as a beaver with a sore tail.* Used (but rarely) by an otherwise indefatigable and boundlessly energetic individual, this phrase might refer to the challenge of working under the limitation of insult or injury.
• *Like a dime in the presence of a nickel.* Randall Lolley "walked tall" but topped out at five feet, nine inches. He used this phrase occasionally in the presence of anyone taller.
• *Set-to.* Randall used this antiquated British term for *argument* indiscriminately for church committee meetings or small discussion groups.
• *Bird-dog.* Defying the traditional sense of the term, bird hunter Randall used it to refer to a desired tenacity in the accomplishment of an objective. "If you don't mind, would you bird-dog that deacon recommendation?"

• *Let's put a comma there.* Randall said this in a committee setting to refer to an important but unfinished discussion that he intended to take up next time.
• *Engine room.* A term connoting power, dynamism, and driving forces, "engine room" paradoxically was associated with a gently transformative *agape* love. Speaking of God's forgiveness, Randall wrote, "If the New Testament has an engine room, this is it."
• *Job One.* From a familiar automobile advertisement ("Quality is Job No. 1"), the phrase was applied to the primary task suggested by a congregation's mission statement.
• *Before you can preach to them, you have to be their pastor.* Randall was suggesting that preaching to a congregation is an intimate task, requiring knowledge of the deepest needs and feelings, sins, and struggles of the hearers.
• *The Go-Gos, the Slow-Gos, and the No-Gos.* This was Randall's three-part subdivision of the senior adult population of a church.
• *N'est-ce pas?* From the French expression "is it not," this "tag question" requested a yes-or-no answer, and Randall frequently placed it at the ends of notes to himself or memos to others. "Hopefully, we can remedy the situation in years ahead, *n'est-ce pas?*"
• *Warts and all.* This was an expression of the breadth of God's love and grace, extending to imperfections both visible and invisible. Often as not, Randall used it self-referentially.
• *God can draw a straight line with a crooked stick.* Recalling instances drawn from divine Scripture and human history, Randall was saying that flawed personalities could nevertheless serve godly purposes.
• *All the best.* Employed as the formal "closing" of a letter to a member of a congregation, this was shorthand for "All God's best." It reminded readers that "every good and perfect gift is from above" (Jas 1:17, NIV).
• *As ever.* Randall (and also Lou) rarely closed letters with "Sincerely" or "Sincerely yours." An informal alternative to "All the best," "As ever" (even if otherwise indecipherable) communicated constant and consistent friendship.

• *Devotedly.* Employed in correspondence during his later years of pastoral ministry, this was an approximate equivalent of "Sincerely" (which Randall once used to close a terse letter to Paige Patterson).
• *Young Turks.* This is a historic term for a popular, progressive movement that set out to reform the leadership of the Ottoman Empire in the early twentieth century. Randall used it to refer to groups of ambitious young ministers-in-training.
• *They'll cloud right up and rain all over you.* This metaphor described chronic, humorless complainers whose visits to the pastor's office invariably produced feelings of emptiness and futility.
• *More questions than a cat has fleas.* Randall meant that everything had a comparison, no matter how odd or incongruous.
• *Bright as a briar.* This was Randall Lolley's most familiar mixed metaphor. Briars are sharp. Sharp people are bright. Hence, "That girl is bright as a briar."
• *Doubts are the ants-in-the-pants of faith.* A casual internet search finds this expression attributed to Presbyterian minister and author Frederick Buechner, appearing initially in his 1973 book *Wishful Thinking: A Seeker's ABC.* Randall used it frequently and without attribution to encourage fearless and faithful inquiry into divine truth. (In reality, the expression may fit Randall's rhetorical style better than Buechner's.)
• *The expulsive power of a new affection.* Borrowing from Scottish pastor Thomas Chalmers (1780–1847), Randall used this expression to describe the power behind Paul's declaration, "One thing *I do,* forgetting those things which are behind and reaching forward to those things which are ahead, I press toward the goal for the prize of the upward call of God in Christ Jesus" (Phil 3:13-14, NKJV). Randall's "new affection" (the "prize of the upward call of God") drove him relentlessly beyond the pain of loss and toward a fulfilling finish to his earthly ministry.
• *Stay[ed] by the stuff.* This indicated the surest way to get anything done and was used either as a compliment or an admonition.
• *Down to the short rows.* This phrase recalled Randall's upbringing in the Wiregrass Region of Lower Alabama; moving diagonally to plow

or to mow a field, arriving at the "short rows" meant the task was nearly complete, and rest, refreshment, and reward awaited.

• *Packing for the Big Trip.* This expression indicated making ready, in the pattern of Joshua, to "cross over Jordan." Randall acknowledged that he borrowed the expression from his father Roscoe, who used it all of his adult life, but more frequently as he came "down to the short rows."

• *Thanks for the memories!* This was a (usually) written expression of appreciation from a man who never failed to acknowledge people who "partnered in the task." It was likely borrowed from the familiar theme song of Lolley-era comedian Bob Hope.

(The following paragraphs are excerpted from Randall's concluding "President's Message," printed in the January–February 1988 edition of his seminary's bimonthly newsletter, *Southeastern Outlook.* The reader is invited to note the "Lolleyisms" appearing in the piece, titled "Prayers and Thanks.")

> TO THE FACULTY AND STAFF:
> Time and again you have inspired me over these years. Thanks for the memories! You have stayed by the stuff and I am grateful . . .
>
> TO THE ALUMNI:
> You are all so different—and for that I am grateful. God has no cookie cutter at our alma mater. God loves you just as you are, warts and all. God speed to you.
>
> TO THE TOWNSPEOPLE OF WAKE FOREST:
> Never forget that "your seminary" has delighted in being also your good neighbor and that all of us have profited profoundly from being "out in the weather together" here in our very special forest. Happy days to all of you.

Rolesville Retrospective

In a document titled "The Lament of Dr. Randall Lolley," a member of the Rolesville Baptist Church compiled a transcript of a presentation Randall gave, apparently at the church's request.[1] It is Randall's last-known public account of what he frequently described as the denominational "firestorm" that overtook Southeastern Seminary during the 1980s. Rolesville was the seventh of a total twelve interim pastorates that Randall undertook following his 1996 retirement. The "preface" below (in italics) was attached by the transcriber; the transcription itself has been lightly edited for clarity.

On February 16, 2005, Dr. Randall Lolley gave a presentation to the Rolesville Baptist Church describing the takeover of the Southeastern Baptist Theological Seminary (SEBTS) by the fundamentalist movement of the Southern Baptist Convention. Dr. Lolley was serving as SEBTS president during this period, and this wise and gentle man suffered greatly as his beloved institution came under the province of the inerrantists. The following is a transcription of a presentation that he gave at the Rolesville Baptist Church, describing his ordeal.

What Happened among Baptists?

I don't want to change anybody's mind or make anybody angry. But I do want to give you information—or try to do that—and number two, to tell you the truth as objectively as I can, with a minimum of spin.

Now, I can't be objective about some of the things I will be talking to you about tonight at Southeastern Seminary, because I was too involved in it. It has been seventeen years since I resigned

1. Rolesville is located northeast of Raleigh, near the campus of Southeastern Seminary.

as president of the school, and I thought that I had put it all away. I thought that I had very little emotion, and I could just talk about it like anything else.

But as I was presenting this (or as I was preparing it, along with these documents that I handed out) I began to find myself getting a little more emotion. Because you revisit stuff, and you dredge stuff up that you had put away in your mind, in your heart. So forgive me, I am going to try my best not in any way to be subjective, but to be objective—to tell you the truth.

I am going to be talking to you for a while, presenting these details; and then let's stop and talk among ourselves and ask questions and try to get answers. That is the goal. As we go through this, there is a place on your handouts for you to jot down questions while we are going through my part of talking to you, so that you won't forget them.

What I am about to talk to you about is basically covered in this book [shows book]. I don't know if any of you have seen this book, published in 1994, called *Servant Songs*. It contains twelve essays, chapters, written by twelve of us who worked at Southeastern when I was there as the president.

All twelve of us put together our stories—our slant—on what we had witnessed about the Southeastern we knew. I wrote the second essay. So I am not telling you something spanking brand new; it has been published for over eleven years, and I have not had anybody come to me to tell me that it is not right, this is not what happened.

So what we are going to go through is pretty much what happened at the seminary that you own, because that school is your school. You are a card-carrying member of a church that has supported SEBTS, I suspect for as long as you have been a member of it, and I am grateful for that very much.

I need to talk to you a little bit about some language I am going to use, and to make sure you don't mishear me. "Fundamentalism" and "conservatism" are two words that I am going to use, especially today when we hear so much about fundamentalism. We hear so much about fundamentalism: Islamic fundamentalism, Buddhist fundamentalism, Shinto fundamentalism, Christian fundamentalism, Jewish fundamentalism.

We are hearing that word all over the world. I thought that we ought to take a look at what that word meant and means, and how it compares to conservatism. I am going to make an assumption that everybody in this room would—in Christian thought, the long spectrum of Christian thought, from radically conservative and radically liberal—see yourselves somewhere in the middle, moderating conservative center. That is precisely where I see myself. I am not calling anybody a fundamentalist who is not comfortable being called a fundamentalist. They want to be called fundamentalist, they are fundamentalist and proud of it, the ones I am talking about.

Let's look at two sheets, back and front, labeled "Fundamentalism and Christian History." This is not what we are talking about, this is not the essence of our discussion, about fundamentalism in Christian history. I want to go through this real fast, for this is not what we are talking about. You should know that until World War I, there was never the word "fundamentalist" used to describe Christian. It was not a word used in any way to describe anybody who was a Christian, either in fact or in action.

All of that began to change after World War I, from 1915 to 1930. What happened was that in Europe there was a flood of scholarship that was very liberal; it was called modernism by most people. It had some basic tenets. They had looked at our Bible, the Bible you and I read every day to tell us about ourselves and about our God, and concluded this Bible was full of errors.

They concluded that Jesus was not born of a virgin and that he could have been born some other way; that Christ didn't die for our sins; that there really was not physical, actual resurrection from the dead; and that any things called miracles were impossible. That stuff began to come across the ocean (German and Swiss scholars, and some British scholars).

It came under the rubric of advanced biblical criticism, and it began to wreak havoc in America, because very few people in America believed any of that, and it certainly was not taught in the seminaries. You can imagine how that began to worry people, who could look at our faith and see how modernism—real liberalism—cut the roots out from under it.

Therefore, about 1915 a group of these men published a little book called *The Fundamentals.* In that book, they defended for all of us our faith, and fought tooth and nail against the modernist positions. They came out with five fundamentals of the faith: (1) the inerrancy of the Bible in the original manuscripts—now I am going to come back to that in a minute; (2) the virgin birth of Jesus; (3) Christ's substitutionary atonement for sin; (4) Jesus' real resurrection from the dead; (5) the reality of miracles.

And then a later group of them decided to add (6) the premillennial return of Christ. That began to show the fabric of where this movement was going. A very good movement got off the ground with a very good purpose, but then it began to turn sour. Instead of saying what we *did* believe, they began to say what we *had* to believe. So instead of leaving us free to decide for ourselves whether we believed any of this (or all of this, and I do—I believe almost all of it), they began to sort of force it on Christians.

Here is what happened. That group split into two sections. One group was called Fundamentalists, and that was a very good thing. For we needed somebody, had to have somebody, to stand up to modernists from Europe, and they did it and did it well. Those who felt that they could not accept those who did not agree with them on every detail of the fundamentals of the Christian faith, people you have heard about through the years, became separatists, they became independent. They became the John R. Rices, the Bob Joneses, the Lee Robertsons. They started schools, and they are proud of that, and their schools still exist.

Then there was another group called Open Fundamentalists, who wanted to work with Christians who didn't agree with them in every detail—but who wanted to work with them on missions and evangelism. I put myself in that group—evangelical, or conservative. I would put myself in that school. Those Open Fundamentalists evolved and metamorphosed today into what we call evangelical, or conservative.

I want to go back to inerrancy. The people who took over Southeastern began to take that one fundamental of the faith and began to use it as a political tool to frighten people, to misinform people, and to gain control of something they wanted to run very much. Now the way they did it was this: for example, I don't know how many people I talked to about the nature of the Bible. What is the nature of this Bible?

By the way, Southeastern Seminary has a logo based on a Scripture passage from 2 Timothy, chapter 3, verses 15-17: "All scripture is God-breathed [the word means "inspiration," a pretty powerful statement], and it is useful for teaching, for reproof, and for training in righteousness, so that the people of God may be thoroughly equipped for every good work."

Paul wrote that to Timothy. It turned out that Paul was writing Scripture. If you had asked him, he would have probably said he was writing a letter. Paul was talking about the only Bible he knew, the Old Testament, because the New Testament didn't exist at that time. He was writing the New Testament.

To say that the Bible is God-breathed, inspired, is the highest tribute you can pay it. When people came to me and wanted me to use the word "inerrant," I said that I am not going to use that word. You can use it—I have no problem with that. I am not going to use it, because you are beginning to make it into a club. You are beginning to force it on people. Let's decide to use the words the Bible uses to describe itself.

They couldn't abide that.

The Bible says the word of the Lord is perfect, true (can't beat that), pure, trustworthy, right, righteous, precious (can't beat that). Those are seven words that the Bible uses to describe itself, but there are others. I personally took the position that I am going to call the Bible what the Bible calls itself.

I got in real trouble, because when you set up a situation where you say it is "inerrant," this is not a biblical or Baptist word. It is actually of Presbyterian origin. It was used originally to put away those who didn't believe the Bible was authoritative—the modernists, the liberals. But when you come to talk to me as a conservative—and say you have got to say this word or you don't believe the Bible—then we are fighting a different battle.

Are you hearing me? Are you hearing what I am trying to tell you? We are not talking about Christian conservatism. We are talking about Christian fundamentalism gone awry in the hands of some people who wanted to take control of the seminaries first, and then everything else that Southern Baptists operated. They had decided that *that* was the best way to get control.

It worked, because if I were to tell you in one sentence regarding the Southeastern Seminary situation, it would be that a good group of conservative people got hijacked by people who had a political agenda, not a theological agenda.

Have you ever heard of Edward J. Carnell? Some of you probably have. Ed J. Carnell was the brightest young fundamentalist of about the 1950s and '60s in this country. He became a theologian of consequence, he became an author of consequence, he became the head of a seminary. In an article that he wrote, he has offered the best definition of Fundamentalism that I have ever read—and it is by a fundamentalist. You read it—I want you to read it tonight or tomorrow. I want you to keep it and read it, I want you to remember something about it.

He decided from his studies and from working with colleagues who were radical fundamentalists, he decided that radical fundamentalism had gone too far—that they were trying to force people, free-Baptist type people, into something that *they* believed. He wanted to get away from that, he wanted to break from that.

They turned on him, accused him of everything under God's sun. Finally, one morning in a hotel room, they found him dead, dead from an overdose of medication. Now, we will never know if he accidentally took an overdose or deliberately took an overdose. We don't know. We do know that he, from within, was looking through the bars of fundamentalism.

[Carnell] wrote the best expose that I have ever read. I want to underline some sentences:

"Fundamentalism is an extreme right element in Protestant orthodoxy."

"In due time, fundamentalism made one capital mistake."

"That is why fundamentalism is now a religious attitude rather than a real movement. It is highly ideological, inflexible, intransigent, expects conformity and fears academic liberty."

"Fundamentalism is an ironic position."

"Fundamentalism is a paradoxical position."

"Fundamentalism is a lonely position."

Now look what he says about a paradoxical position: it sees the heresy in untruth but not in unloveliness. If it has the most truth, it has the least grace, since it distrusts. Fundamentalism forgets that orthodox truth without orthodox love profits nothing.

[Carnell] says that fundamentalism is a lonely position: it has cut itself off from the general systems, stream of consciousness, philosophy, and ecclesiastic position. That accounts for its robust pride, because it dismisses non-fundamentalists as those who are empty, futilely apostate. Its test for Christian fellowship is so severe that it holds that divisions in the church are considered a sign of virtue.

Split the Southern Baptist Convention! Destroy the Southern Baptist Convention! If you can't control it, kill it. It's my way or the highway—that's fundamentalism. It has become an attitude, not a set of opinions.

Most of us have said most of the expressed opinions as fundamentalists, but where we see a conservative will come to you, and we are talking about the Bible.[2] Preston says "I use the word inerrancy, and I consider myself a conservative."[3] I say, well, [Pressler], that is all right with me. You use inerrant if you want to, but I am going to use the word inspired, or perfect, or true, to describe the Bible. You are talking about the original manuscripts, but we don't have any original manuscripts. I want to have confidence in the Bible I have got.

[Pressler] looks at me and says, "No, no, no—if you won't say my word, I don't think you believe my Bible." I say to [Pressler], I believe the Bible as much as you do, and I am not going to use your word

2. This sentence, as transcribed, appears indecipherable.

3. As transcribed, but doubtless Randall said "Pressler" (i.e., Paul Pressler, one of the original "architects of the conservative resurgence" within the SBC).

to describe it. He walks away unforgiving, and tells you that I am a liberal who does not love the Bible. That makes him a fundamentalist and me a conservative; that's the gospel truth. It is a difference in truth, a difference in spirit.

Now I want to take that and show you what happened at the school that I loved. I want to tell you quickly about Southeastern Seminary. It was founded in 1951. How many of you were in or near Rolesville or Wake Forest when it was formed in 1951? Many of you were—that was just fifty-four years ago. What happened was Wake Forest College decided to move to Winston-Salem. That meant state Baptists who had owned that property had property they didn't need.

The Southern Baptist Convention, the national body, bought it for $1,200,000, for 384 acres in downtown Wake Forest. That included the golf course on which Arnold Palmer learned to play golf. He told me that. He called it "the hatchet factory." He learned to play golf on that old, bouncy course.

Southeastern has thirty trustees. That's not a lot—thirty people. They come from almost that many states. They are elected by the Southern Baptist Convention at their annual meeting, and a trustee is elected for a five-year term. They can repeat if they are willing to, or asked to, for a second five-year term. That means that a trustee can be at Southeastern for ten years.

Trustees set policy, broad policy, and they hire a president, and the president implements this policy. The president operates the institution day by day, and trustees set the policy. That is not unusual for Southeastern—that is the way most schools work. The president serves at the will of the trustees, without a contract that has to be renewed. My contract was an indefinite contract, with tenure on the faculty as a professor of philosophy of religion, because that was my field. Also, I was to work as president under the tutelage of the trustees as long as we both agreed to do it.

The next thing is that Southeastern is accredited by two accreditors. One international accreditor, called the Association of Theological Schools, accredits all the seminaries in the U.S. and Canada that want to be accredited by it. These are a group of peers who understand what theological education is supposed to be like.

They examine each other once every ten years, after days of self-study. When you graduate from Southeastern, this means that the piece of paper you get has value.

Southeastern was also accredited regionally by the Southern Association of Colleges and Schools. This is the same regional agency that accredits N.C. State University, or Shaw, or Peace, or Meredith. Most of the colleges and universities in this region are accredited like that.

I became the third president of Southeastern on August 1, 1974. It hasn't been all that long ago, but it has been quite a while, in a way, too. I was the first alumnus who became a president. I followed Dr. Olin Binkley, who had also been the dean of faculty, and who had taught ethics. And I followed Dr. Sydnor Stealey, who had been at Southern Seminary before becoming founding president at Southeastern.

Dr. Binkley retired in 1973, and I became the third president. I had been the pastor of the First Baptist Church of Winston-Salem. The trustees told me that they thought it was time for a pastor-type and an alumnus. The school was almost twenty-five years old when I became president, and it was sort of time for an alumnus, pastor-type to become president, and I agreed with that. There I had the chance to form people in their ministry, to do exactly the ministry I wanted to do in my ministry. How could you have greater impact in your life than by doing something like that? I was glad and grateful for the chance.

The controversy with Southern Baptists erupted into the open. Now, it had been simmering, but it really blew out into the open in 1979. That means I had been president for five years. That year, at the Southern Baptist Convention in Houston, Texas, Dr. Adrian Rogers, a pastor at the Bellevue Baptist Church in Tennessee, was elected Southern Baptist Convention president. He defeated, I think, six people in all, and one of them was Duke McCall, the president of Southern Seminary. Dr. Rogers was elected over him.

As it turned out—and it really was proven—the election was rigged. People were bussed in to vote just on the presidency, and left and never stayed for another vote at the convention—many people. They had the skyboxes at the Houston Astrodome rented to go through the political process exactly the way that Democratic and Republican conventions are.

I was there. I knew something was happening, but I wasn't sure what. Dr. Rogers was elected, without anybody really knowing it, in order to begin a process that had been going on privately: to use the appointive powers of the president to hardwire the trustees of every SBC institution—especially the seminaries—to a new agenda. And that agenda was to force everybody in every seminary to say what they were willing to say about the Bible.

It became known as the Battle for the Bible. After Dr. Rogers stood that day, after he had been elected, he said that this book is infallible, and everybody who doesn't call it inerrant—and he didn't finish that sentence. I remember it. He didn't say so, but he sort of laid down the gauntlet. If I didn't say it was inerrant, then it was errant.

But I had given my life since 1951, when I was ordained as a minister, talking about a book that I think is perfect, true, pure, inspired. But I am not going to use Adrian Rogers's words just because he says I ought to. I'm not going to do that. Got me in a peck of trouble, I mean right immediately, in 1979.

Their goal was to control things, and they began to work on it. Despite my best efforts, these new trustees that were elected—after Dr. Rogers had gone through his appointment of committee after committee and brought the nominees to the convention floor, and they were elected—embraced a foreign vision, brought an alien vision to my school.

Now how do I know that? Now listen to me: I went to school at Southeastern, first in 1954, in the fourth year after it was formed in 1951, and spent four years as a student. Got two degrees. I went away a while, finished some more work and was pastor of a church, came back as president in 1974 and stayed until 1988.

If you put those two together, that is eighteen years out of thirty-seven years of the school's life. Almost half of the school's life, I had been on its campus. When I became president, I had read the forming documents, where the state had given it the right to exist. The seminary had to be chartered by the State of North Carolina.

I read the articles of faith, the bylaws, the constitution, the documents that had founded that school, and not one of them said that anyone over there had to use the word "inerrancy" to describe the Bible. Not one of them! And we who worked there, and the faculty who taught there, had signed on our first day at worship in chapel an article of faith that said we believed the Bible with all our hearts, with all our souls. And that is the way we believed it.

But anyway, I want to tell you what happened. In 1982—that's three years after Dr. Rogers was elected—a student came to me early in the fall and said they needed to start a Conservative Evangelical Fellowship, CEF. They wanted to call it CEF. I said David, why do you want to do that? He said that "a few of us feel that we need fellowship with others who are truly conservative." I said that there are a lot of conservatives here, so why not have fellowship through the existing student organizations, and stuff like that?

Well, he persisted. He was a good guy. He was from Winston-Salem; I got to know him, for I had lived there twelve years. He also was a graduate of Annapolis Military Academy, the Naval academy, so he was smart. He said "there are about a dozen of us who want to do this."

We had a lot of student organizations, but you had to go through a process to get a student organization approved. It had to be approved by the Student Council first, and then by the faculty, and then by the administration. I wanted them to have a fair representation. If they felt that they did not have a fair representation, then why not let them have an organization? I really went to bat for them. I met with the Student Council, the faculty, and some of my colleagues in administration, and finally we approved it.

I went to a meeting very soon after that with the other five seminary presidents, and I found out that the same thing had happened at the other five campuses. A small group of students had come to the presidents and said we want to organize a group. Two of the presidents agreed, and four of them refused. I probably, in retrospect, should have refused also.

They wanted a voice of legitimacy, a voice, a place, and things like that. Only later did we find out that those students were being paid to do that. They became a fundamentalist cell inside our Student Council in order to do three things. I have got them written down here: (1) harass teachers and students, (2) pay bluster, and (3) report any comments made to a half-a-man headquarters in Dallas, Texas.[4]

That started in 1982. Two years after that started, we began to realize that we were living in a totally different climate. It had never been like that at my school. By 1984, and in one three-month period, I received over one hundred phone calls and letters claiming that someone had done something that was liberal, out of touch with the conservative spirit—you name it, they charged it.

Two things typify what I am talking about. Do any of you know Dr. Malcolm Tolbert, who was a teacher at New Orleans Seminary for years, and who came to our school to teach New Testament, and who was there for ten years? A seasoned, conservative teacher in a seminary like New Orleans came to work with us. In 1984, he was teaching a class and was talking about attitudes of distrust, these people who were agitating and fomenting on campus.

He made some comment like this—that if these are either being encouraged or employed to do that, they should 'fess up, and the people behind it ought to tell us all about it. Three hours later Dr. Tolbert got a call from Paige Patterson,[5] who was working in Dallas, Texas. Patterson asked Dr. Tolbert to explain why he said that, what was his basis for saying that, and reminded him that he was employed to teach New Testament and not to make inflammatory statements.

It shows the kind of climate we were having to work under.

Dr. John Durham was one of our professors of Old Testament, and he had written a series of Sunday school lessons on Job. And those twelve or thirteen fundamental students accused him of not believing in the devil. He tried to explain to them that he was explaining the meaning of *ha-satan* in the prologue of Job, and what that meant

---

4. The second objective, presented here as transcribed, is indecipherable; the third seems to have referred to statements deemed objectionable that were recorded from classroom lectures.

5. Paige Patterson was another "architect of the conservative resurgence."

about the nature of evil, both personal and spiritual—lock, stock, and barrel, ramrod and greasy rag.[6]

It did mean the devil, but it didn't mean the devil was necessarily that picture we have of the devil with a red suit, horns, and a tail—a Medieval depiction. He said some things like that.

Boy, that really got some folks upset. I spent weeks, almost months, trying to explain what he [Durham] meant by that. He believed in the devil, in the power of the devil, the personal power of the devil—but anyway, it didn't work.

In 1984, there came into being a Southern Baptist Convention committee known as the Peace Committee. That committee was charged to find out what was going on—not just at Southeastern but on every campus—and what we can do about it, and how in the world we can improve on it and find some sort of accord. Things were getting that bad.

That committee was charged to visit every campus. We set the visit to Southeastern for February 5, 1986. Get the date in your mind. That night the people on the Peace Committee came to have dinner at our house, and Lou fixed dinner for them. We thought that we were going to talk about what would happen the next day, and so forth, but they left. We didn't think too much about it until the next day, when we were supposed to have the meeting.

But first, let me tell you something. That Peace Committee meeting was carefully crafted on every campus by the president of the seminary, the chairman of the trustees, and the chairman of the Peace Committee, who was Charles Fuller, a pastor from Roanoke, Virginia—a wonderful guy.

Charles Fuller and I had talked about the fact that we had a Student Council president who said, "I have got to talk to the Peace Committee—I have got to. I want to tell them how much this school means to me." I think that is what he was saying, but I said, no, you can't do that, it is not for that purpose. They have asked for specific information, we have got it for them, and we are going to have a meeting with the chairman of our trustees tomorrow, and we are

6. A familiar Randall Lolley expression.

going to be trying to get to the bottom of this. So don't inflame the meeting with what you would be heard to be saying to them.

But they left my home that evening for a secret meeting for four hours, to meet with the members of the Conservative Evangelical Fellowship. They met with seven students; five of those where students at the seminary, and two were graduates. Those seven students gave them, during that four-hour meeting, twenty-seven things they were concerned about, against seventeen of the teachers.

One of those students, a male—all seven were men—stole a female student's class notebook and used its content without her permission, to contrast six or seven of the concerns. She had written down some of the things that teachers had said about Christian females in church ministry.

The president met with the Peace Committee the next day, and they presented those twenty-seven findings on little sheets of paper. They were cut up in little pieces and handed to me. They didn't express a single [legitimate] concern. I went to every teacher, all seventeen, and asked them to write their response to every one of the concerns; and I would report it to the Peace Committee and report it to the trustees. They did that.

I did not hear a single word from the Peace Committee about those concerns, and I wrote them and called them asking what was the situation, what do we need to do? I didn't hear a thing in the world until June 16, 1987. The Southern Baptist Convention met, and the Peace Committee made its report.

In the middle of their report, it said that the trustees of every seminary must determine the theological position of the seminaries' administrators and faculty members. This meant that what we had signed when we went to Southeastern as an article of our faith and belief didn't have any meaning anymore. We had to deal with that on the campus, and you can imagine what happened.

Something else happened, when the Peace Committee report was adopted, that made as big a difference as anything else. Six new trustees were elected by the Southern Baptist Convention, and those six, coupled with older trustees who had not put forth their real agenda, meant that out of thirty trustees, there were sixteen selected by [fundamentalists in leadership of] the Southern Baptist Convention. This meant, for the first time, they had a 16-14 majority on the board.

I had worked like a dog for my fourteen-year presidency to try to make the trustees aware and alert to anything they needed to know about Southeastern. We didn't have any secrets. We had a wonderful, harmonious relationship. I got an award recognizing my work in trustee cultivation and orientation.

I went to see every trustee when they were elected in June, wherever they lived, and they were all over the country. I stayed with them for three or four days, and ate with them, and got to know them. We brought them to campus in September every year, to give them an orientation and get them ready for their first trustee meeting. They met twice a year, in March and in October. They could meet our students, faculty, go to chapel, whatever they wanted to do.

This new majority of trustees, when I began to set up those meetings, said, "Let's wait until after the first meeting to set an agenda." I guess I should have taken that as a kind of clue that something was amiss, but I didn't. I kind of trusted the trustees.

Anyway, we had our first meeting October 12-14, 1987. That was a Monday, Tuesday, and Wednesday, and that was the way we always had trustee meetings. The way it worked is we started on Monday night with dinner, followed by a short meeting, since many had traveled. I gave them some orientation and a pep talk, and the trustee chairman said some things. It wasn't a very substantive meeting, and no actions were taken.

Tuesday was the big day. Everything that was decided was decided on Tuesday. Wednesday was the close-out day, devoted primarily to the future.

Monday night, following our short meeting, those sixteen new trustees went to some place in Raleigh—I don't know where they went—and caucused without my knowledge, and without the knowledge of the chairman of trustees or the knowledge of the fourteen other trustees. While they were there, they arrived at an agenda for the next day. They knew what the *planned* agenda was, since I had sent it to them two weeks ahead.

Here is what they did. They took five actions, and every action was approved by a one-vote majority—every one. I will let you decide if you think that was the way to do it.

The first thing they did was to elect a Maryland pastor named Robert Crowley as chairman of the trustees. We usually had a chairman for two years, and we were at the midterm. Current chairman Dr. Jesse Chapman of Asheville, North Carolina, a surgeon who left his operating room to come down for trustee meetings, was also available and had been nominated [for a second term] by the nominating committee. He had done a wonderful job and was nominated for the next year.

But they elected by a one-vote majority Dr. Robert Crowley as the chairman. Dr. Robert Crowley was a graduate of Bob Jones University—does that tell you anything?—a fundamentalist school in Greenville, South Carolina. They don't want you to call them anything but fundamentalist.

They also elected Rev. James DeLoach, who was a classmate of mine at Southeastern, who had gone to work at a church in Texas as an associate pastor, as vice-chairman. DeLoach was likewise a graduate of Bob Jones University.

Then they elected all of the other trustee officers and every subcommittee chair from that majority of sixteen, thus completely taking over the trustees by a one-vote margin. That meant that ten of the sixteen held office for the next year, and none of the fourteen trustees held any office for the next year. (The slate by the trustees that had been originally proposed had some of both, had a mix of old and new trustees.)

Here is what they really did that was unconscionable, and I get a little emotional talking about it. We had worked so hard to try to form a method of faculty selection. At a school, the selection of faculty is the single most important thing a president does. We had developed a procedure, worked on it, and had tweaked it three, four, or five times during my fourteen-year term as president.

It was a lengthy procedure. It involved the president, the dean, the alumni, the faculty, the students, and the trustees. It was a very participatory process. I took a long time to select a faculty member, and we meant business in doing it, and we did it very carefully, deliberately.

They took that process and said that this is no longer the way we are going to select faculty. They unilaterally revised the procedure to say that faculty would be selected by the president and trustees only—thus violating the document we worked so hard on, in order to develop collegiality and shared governance.

That wasn't all. We had some temporary appointment faculty, people not on tenure but who could teach a semester specialty course for us. We had a Methodist preacher who taught Methodist students about Methodist polity; we had a Jewish rabbi who once every three years came from Durham and taught what was happening in Judaism, the root system of our Christian faith.

We had Catholic priests from Raleigh, Charlotte, Durham, and other places teach courses on Catholicism after Vatican II. Because we wanted our students to know, from inside those systems, how to get along in the world.

They didn't like that—these trustees. They wanted all adjunct faculty to be appointed by the president and the trustees only. They wanted me to elect every faculty member and every adjunct teacher without any input from the dean or the faculty. Do you see what that did to the campus? It affected the collegiality, morale, and integrity of something you had worked on for fourteen years.

But that is not all. The third thing: they declared an executive session. An executive session involves just the president and the trustees. There were over 100 people at the meeting, including faculty, students, townspeople, and reporters. Anybody could come if they wanted; it was open!

A hundred-plus people had to leave the room for an hour. We met behind closed doors, and no minutes were kept for the meeting. I remember what went on, almost as if it was yesterday. I didn't write any notes, but I wrote them down later.

Jim DeLoach, my former classmate, was designated the speaker, and he spoke for almost an hour. He told me he loved me, and really loved me and respected me. He told me that I had done a fabulous job for fourteen years. He never mentioned once asking me to resign or threatening to fire me.

He then outlined the new vision of the trustees for the school. This is what I remember. I can't guarantee there weren't other elements:

1. When we talk to faculty members, ask, "Do you believe the Bible is inerrant?" If they don't use that word, and that word only to describe the Bible, you can't hire them. There was not anything or a document at Southeastern that required the word inerrant. The articles of faith required that you love the Bible, have an authoritative view of the Bible.

2. No woman would teach men, and that no woman would be ordained. You had to tell them that on the day they arrived on campus. You can be trained here, but you will never be able to serve as pastor of a Baptist church. Now, that was silly. If a church wants to ordain a woman as pastor, they can flat-out do it. That's why churches are Baptist.

3. Male pastors are to be made aware from the get-go that they are the head of the church. A layman-led church is a violation of the New Testament. Jesus Christ appointed the power and authority of the leadership over the church [to be] the under-shepherd, pastor, a man in authority over the congregation—they told me that.

4. This campus must support in every way possible the conservative resurgence begun in 1979.

Let me tell you again—and I have it written down—that [Jim DeLoach] never suggested that I was going to be terminated. Instead, here is what he did: he made it clear that the trustees intended to use me and my office, my good will and my hard work over fourteen years, to implement their vision, no matter how much it conflicted with my own conscience and my vision for my school.

A little over a week later, on Thursday, October 22, 1987—after I had spent a week with my brother in Marion, North Carolina, in the mountains, tending to my dad, who had to have his right leg amputated—I came back to campus. I had made the decision, and didn't tell a single soul except my family, that I was going to resign. I could not implement a vision that foreign to my conscience.

Dean Morris Ashcraft and three other administrative officers resigned at the same time. That was October 22. I told them [the trustees] that I would serve until the end of the academic year, or until they got a new president. They got a new president at the next board meeting in March, Dr. Lewis Drummond, who was the fourth president and served for four or five years. After him came Dr. Paige Patterson, and after him Dr. Danny Akin.

I want to tell you one other thing, and then we're gonna talk. . . . Because of the severance package I agreed to, I said I would preside over May and July graduations—two times, before the end of the school year.

There was a school song, called "The Seminary Hymn," written in 1954 by Edwin McDowell. A friend named Robert Mullinax, an old buddy of mine, and I added a verse four lines long:

For freedom, Christ has set us free,
Breaking the chains of captivity.
Bound but to God, we go forth whole,
Free from shackles of mind and soul.

The seminary sang it well and knew what it meant. The verse is based on Galatians 5:1, because the sentence is from there. Paul said for freedom Christ has set us free. The seminary continued to sing it every year until 2002, without knowing who had written the last verse.

When they told Dr. Patterson who wrote it, he became livid and demanded that it not be sung anymore.[7]

[Randall thereupon concluded his presentation with a brief question-and-answer session.]

---

7. In 2016, Southeastern Seminary introduced a new "official hymn," "For the Cause," by Kristyn and Keith Getty.

Randall Lolley's Bucket List

Randall supplied no dates or occasions for the following, which were presented—apart from the concluding "Unfinished Business" section—as having been accomplished over the course of his adult life. Some of the destinations were reached during his Holy Land travels and others as part of special group tours for church members and friends. Occasionally he would be invited to address missions conferences at exotic locations. Other travels occurred as side excursions while he was on church or seminary business, e.g., traveling to and from annual meetings of the Baptist World Alliance.

My Bucket List

W. RANDALL LOLLEY

Walk where Jesus walked (15 trips to the Holy Land)
Visit Petra (Jordan)
Traverse the Nile River (Memphis to Luxor)
See the Eternal Cities—Rome and Athens (5 times)
Dive at the Great Barrier Reef—Australia
Climb Ayers Rock—Australian Outback[1]
Land in Tasmian Glacier—New Zealand
Visit the Taj Mahal—Agra, India
Visit Angor Wat (Cambodia)
Climb/Walk the Great Wall—China
Cruise the Lei River—Qulin, China

1. Currently known by its Aboriginal name *Uluru*.

See the Terra Cotta Army—Xian, China
See the Forbidden City—Beijing, China
Go on a 5-star safari: Lion, Leopard, Hippo, Rhino, Water Buffalo—Kenya, So. Africa
See the Snows of Kilimanjaro—Kenya
Visit above the Arctic Circle
Visit below the Antarctic Circle—Antarctica
Experience the Midnight Sun and the Northern Lights—Alaska, Canada
Feel the lava steam from a volcano—Hawaii
Visit Machu Pichu, "the lost city of the Incas"—Peru
Visit the ruins of the Mayans—Mexico, Ecuador
CAMP WITH OUR FAMILY IN EVERY ONE OF THE 50 UNITED STATES
Cruise the Amazon River—Brazil
Visit Stonehenge—England
Sense the dynamism of Christianity in Siberia
Sense Dachau (Munich); Auschwitz (Poland); and Terez (Prague)
Attend the Oberammergau Passion Play—Germany
Cruise the mighty Mississippi River—USA
Be baptized in the Jordan River—Israel
Float in the Dead Sea (Israel) and the Great Salt Lake (Utah)
See Niagara Falls (Canada), Iguazu Falls (Brazil), Victoria Falls (Zimbabwe)
Catch a Pike and a Walleye too—N. Canada
Pheasant hunt in Nebraska and Iowa
Visit Disney World (Orlando) and Disneyland (Anaheim)
Descend into the Grand Canyon—Arizona
Cruise the Greek Isles—Greece
Jet Boat through the Gorge of Shotover River—New Zealand
Experience a Balloon Safari—Kenya
Visit Mast's Store—Valle Crucis, NC
See *The Lost Colony, Horn in the West, Unto These Hills*—NC
Traverse the Freedom Trail—USA
See the foliage—New England, Western NC
Go to Branson—MO

Go to Myrtle Beach—SC
Attend the Grand Ol' Opry—TN
See the Southern Cross—Australia
Straddle the Equator—Kenya, Ecuador
Walk a beach: Atlantic, Pacific, Indian, Arctic, Antarctic Oceans
Collect the 5 sands of Hawaii—brown, white, green, red, black
Survive the trip to HANA—Maui, HI
See a Broadway play—NYC
See a London stage spectacular—England
Experience the cherry blossoms of DC
Climb the Statue of Liberty—NYC
Climb the Eiffel Tower—FR
Climb the Gateway Arch—St. Louis
See the Tidal Bore on the Bay of Fundy—Nova Scotia
Visit the ruins of Pompeii—Italy
Climb Mt. Mitchell—NC
Experience: Mt. Rushmore—SD; Mt. McKinley—AL; Sugar Loaf—Brazil; Mt. Fuji—Japan; Stone Mountain—GA; Tetons—WY
Experience: Mt. Nebo—Jordan; Mt. of Olives, Mt. Calvary—Israel
Visit Hiroshima—Japan
See St. Francis's Chapel at Assisi—Italy
See the Sistine Chapel—Rome
Visit Glacier National Park—Canada
Experience the Suez Canal—Egypt; Panama Canal—Panama; Corinthian Canal—Greece
Walk: Central Park (NYC); the Bond (China); Red Square (Moscow); Hyde Park (London); Tiananmen Square (Beijing); Brandenburg Gate (Berlin); Old Town (Prague)
Visit the 38th Parallel (Korea)
Visit the White Cliffs of Dover, Coventry, Bath (England)
See the 7 lighthouses of North Carolina
Visit: Singapore, Hong Kong
See: *David*, *Moses*, *Mona Lisa* (Michelangelo); the Hope Diamond; U.S. Constitution; the Declaration of Independence (DC)
Climb Cheops's Pyramid and visit the Sphinx—Egypt
Sail on the Grand Canal—Venice

Go "punting" on the Avon River—England
Experience the Ancients: Zulu Tribe (Africa); Masai (Kenya); Inca (Peru); Bedouins (Jordan); Fulanti (Nigeria); Aboriginals (Australia); Mauri (New Zealand)
Ply the fjords—Norway
Sail in Milford Sound—NZ
Ascend the Alps—Switzerland
Ascend the Andes—Peru
See a Caribbean sunset on St. Croix
See a Bermuda sunrise—Hamilton
See the sun set over Antarctica
Ponder the Sinai, the Sahara, the Outback, and the Mojave
Visit the world's worship centers: the Glass [Crystal] Cathedral (CA); St. Basil's (Moscow); National Cathedral (DC); St. Peter's (Rome); St. Paul's (London); Westminster (Canterbury); Coventry (England); Notre Dame (Paris); St. Mark's (Venice); Milan Cathedral; Dome of the Rock (Israel); The Citadel (SC); the Blue Mosque (Egypt)
Traverse the English Channel, Chunnel—England and France
Experience a Williamsburg Christmas—VA
Experience a Biltmore House Christmas—NC
Experience a Grove Park Inn Christmas—NC
Retrace Paul's Missionary Journeys: Antioch, Tarsus, Rome, Ephesus, Corinth, Colossae, Thessaloniki, Philippi, Galatia—Greece and Turkey
Sense the Ancients: Montagnards (Vietnam); Vikings (Norway); Pilgrims (Plymouth, MA)
Sail aboard an aircraft carrier—the USS *Eisenhower*
See the Leaning Tower of Pisa—Italy
Visit the Catacombs—Rome
Go to the circus: "The Greatest Show on Earth"—NC
Attend the NC State Fair—Raleigh
Visit America's birth sites: Jamestown, Williamsburg, Plymouth
Visit Abraham Lincoln's home sites; Kentucky, Indiana, Illinois
Stroll: Champs Elysees—France; Hollywood and Vine—CA; Wall Street—NYC

Ride: The Bullet Train—Japan; Moscow Subway; Prague Tube; Amtrak—USA; Siberian Express—Russia
Ascend: The Space Needle—Seattle
Sail the Inland Passage—Alaska
Attend *A Christmas Carol* with Ira David Wood—Raleigh

Exploring the World: North America

All 50 US states	St. Thomas	Mantenique
Canada	St. Croix	Puerto Rico
Mexico	St. John's	Jamaica
Iceland	St. Maarten	St. Lucia
The Bahamas	Barbados	Arctic Circle/Ocean

Exploring the World: South/Central America

Panama	Argentina	Chile
Costa Rica	Brazil	Peru

Exploring the World: Europe

England	France	Poland
Scotland	Germany	Czech Republic
Wales	Spain	Slovakia
Holland	Switzerland	Hungary
Belgium	Italy	Greece
Denmark	Luxembourg	Portugal
Norway	Austria	Croatia
Sweden	Liechtenstein	Bulgaria
Finland	Russia	Romania

Exploring the World: Asia, Middle East, Orient

Cyprus	India	Philippines
Turkey	Thailand	Japan
Syria	Vietnam	Korea
Lebanon	China	Singapore
Israel	Hong Kong	Malaysia
Cambodia	Macao	
Jordan	Taiwan	

Exploring the World: Oceania, etc.

Australia	New Zealand	Antarctica

Exploring the World: Africa

Egypt	Nigeria	Canary Islands
Liberia	Kenya	Zimbabwe
Ivory Coast	Morocco	South Africa
Ghana	Tanzania	Swaziland

Exploring the World: The Caribbean

St. Maarten	Tortola	Trinidad
Martinique	Half-Moon Cay	St. Lucia

Unfinished Business—Not yet, but maybe . . .

See the turtles of GALAPAGOS[2]
See the Gooney Birds of Midway Island
Traverse the base of Mt. Everest—Nepal
Visit Easter Island
Sail on Loch Ness (no desire to "see" the monster)
See HEAVEN (now this I really do want to SEE) . . .

---

2. Randall noted that he accomplished this in October 2015.